"In this perceptive and thoughtful work, Dr. Johnson shows how literary sensitivity can work with theological depth, and how these together support solid historical confidence. There is so much to like here—the methods, the fairness and thoroughness, the careful critique of positions—and we profit from seeing how to work through a challenging text to a satisfying conclusion."
—**C. John ("Jack") Collins**, Professor of Old Testament, Covenant Theological Seminary

"Raymond Johnson provides a careful and compelling treatment of this neglected passage. His careful translation work, biblical theology, and literary analysis are commendable. This volume should help scholars rethink the resurrection narratives and aid pastors in preaching the riches of believing in a risen Savior."
—**Paul R. House**, Professor of Divinity—Old Testament, Beeson Divinity School

"I worked with Raymond on the development of his dissertation for several years. He continually pursued excellence with diligence and care. The final product of his dissertation is evidence of this. Raymond's dissertation is worthy of publication because of the clarity and fairness with which he addresses the long-debated issues of Matthew 27 and because of the contributions he makes to this discussion."
—**Jonathan T. Pennington**, Associate Professor of New Testament Interpretation; Director of Research Doctoral Studies, The Southern Baptist Theological Seminary

"Why alone of the Gospels does Matthew report the resurrection of 'holy ones' [ESV "saints"] at the time of Jesus' death? And what did Matthew intend to teach his readers with this mysterious detail? To answer these questions intelligently and textually, I know no better place to point you than Raymond Johnson's fascinating monograph, *I See Dead People: The Function of the Resurrection of the Saints in Matthew 27:51–54*."
—**Robert L. Plummer**, Professor of New Testament Interpretation, The Southern Baptist Theological Seminary

"Matthew 27:51–54 has been the focus of several important debates recently. Yet no evangelical scholar has attempted a book-length discussion of the text that gives proper attention to its precise translation, relationship to Old Testament texts, role in Matthew's Gospel, and significance for Christian theology. Raymond Johnson has finally risen to that important task. His unique and outstanding contribution to the study of Matthew is a great gift to both the academy and the church."
—**Charles L. Quarles**, Professor of New Testament and Biblical Theology; Director for Ph.D. Studies, Southeastern Baptist Theological Seminary

"No historical event has been the object of more scrutiny than the death of Jesus Christ. Surely no further crime-scene investigation is possible? Not so, says Raymond Johnson, who cross-examines afresh a fragment of Saint Matthew's testimony, a text that has continued to puzzle preachers and scholars alike, about the dead coming out of their tombs at Jesus' death (Matt. 27:51–54). Johnson finds a clue to the meaning of the whole in this apparently odd episode. This work does justice to Matthew's literary as well as historical and theological intentions, and in so doing helps all readers appreciate the richness, integrity, and coherence of Matthew's Gospel and its singular identification of Jesus as the Son of God and Savior of the world."
—**Kevin J. Vanhoozer**, Research Professor of Systematic Theology, Trinity Evangelical Divinity School

I See Dead People

Reformed Academic Dissertations

A Series

Series Editor
John J. Hughes

I See Dead People

The Function of the Resurrection of the Saints in Matthew 27:51–54

Raymond M. Johnson

P U B L I S H I N G
P.O. BOX 817 • PHILLIPSBURG • NEW JERSEY 08865-0817

> Was this book helpful to you?
> Consider writing a review online.
> The author appreciates your feedback!
>
> Or write to P&R at editorial@prpbooks.com
> with your comments. We'd love to hear from you.

© 2019 by Raymond M. Johnson

All rights reserved. No part of this book may be reproduced, stored in a retrieval system, or transmitted in any form or by any means—electronic, mechanical, photocopy, recording, or otherwise—except for brief quotations for the purpose of review or comment, without the prior permission of the publisher, P&R Publishing Company, P.O. Box 817, Phillipsburg, New Jersey 08865–0817.

Unless otherwise indicated, all Scripture quotations are from the ESV® Bible (The Holy Bible, English Standard Version®), copyright © 2001 by Crossway, a publishing ministry of Good News Publishers. Used by permission. All rights reserved.

I See Dead People: The Function of the Resurrection of the Saints in Matthew 27:51–54. Raymond M. Johnson, M.Div., Th.M., Ph.D., The Southern Baptist Theological Seminary. Submitted to The Southern Baptist Theological Seminary, 2017, for the degree of Ph.D. Supervisor: Jonathan T. Pennington.

Printed in the United States of America

ISBN: 978-1-62995-557-5 (pbk)

For Meghan,
"The heart of her husband trusts in her."
Proverbs 31:11

Contents

List of Tables   ix
Series Introduction   xi
Foreword by David S. Dockery   xiii
Preface   xix
Abbreviations   xxi

1. The Resurrected Saints: The Problem with Matthew 27:51–54   1
   State of the Sondergut: *The Literary Landscape of the Matthean Special Material*
   Statement of the Problem
   Recent History of Research
   Thesis
   Conclusion

2. Translating Matthew 27:51–54   35
   J. W. Wenham
   Assessing Bible Translation and Revisiting the Translation of Matthew 27:51–54
   Syntactical and Grammatical Features
   Conclusion

3. From Rigor Mortis to Resurrection: Matthean Dependence on Ezekiel 37:1–14 in the Composition of Matthew 27:51–54   66
   The Genesis of Matthew 27:51–54

Contents

Interpreting Ezekiel 37:1–14
Ezekielian Thought Connections to Matthew 27:51–54
Narrative Strategy—Using Ezekiel
Conclusion

4. Matthean Narrative Strategy: Compositional Intentionality in Matthew's Death-Resurrection Scene—Matthew 27:45–28:20   99
   Misunderstanding Matthew
   Matthean Narrative Strategy—A Methodology
   Matthew 27:51–54 as a Hinge Text
   The Purpose of Matthew 27:51–54
   Conclusion

5. Theological Meaning: The Theological Foci of Matthew 27:51–54—Christology, Missiology, and Eschatology   133
   Theological Import
   The Theological Meaning of Matthew 27:51–54
   Velum Scissum—*Matthew 27:51a*
   A Resurrection of Holy Ones—Matthew 27:52b–53
   Conclusion

6. Conclusion   160
   Summary
   Further Study

   Bibliography   167
   Index of Scripture   187
   Index of Subjects and Names   197

Tables

1.1 Literary Parallelism in Matthew 27–28   29

1.2 Macro-Chiastic Structure of Matthew's Gospel   32

2.1 Parallel of English Bible Translations   45

3.1 A Divine Ezekielian Enthymeme   79

3.2 Structure of Ezekiel 37:1–14   82

3.3 Thought-Connection Parallelism between Matthew 27:51–54 and Ezekiel 37:1–14   88

3.4 Matthew's Conscious Use of Ezekiel   92

4.1 Literary Parallelism in Matthew 27–28   107

4.2 Uses of σείω and σεισμός in Matthew 27:45–28:15   110

4.3 Parallel Sequence of Events in Matthew 27:45–66 and 28:1–15   112

4.4 Macro-Chiastic Structure of Matthew's Gospel   115

4.5 Matthew 27:51–54 As a Hinge Text within 27:45–28:20   119

4.6 Time Adjuncts in Matthew 27:45–28:20   120

4.7 Scene, Hinge Text Structure of Matthew 27:45–28:20   122

4.8 Theological Foci Accentuated in the Death-Resurrection Scene   128

Series Introduction

P&R Publishing has a long and distinguished history of publishing carefully selected, high-value theological books in the Reformed tradition. Many theological books begin as dissertations, but many dissertations are worthy of publication in their own right. Realizing this, P&R has launched the Reformed Academic Dissertation (RAD) program to publish top-tier dissertations (Ph.D., Th.D., D.Min., and Th.M.) that advance biblical and theological scholarship by making distinctive contributions in the areas of theology, ethics, biblical studies, apologetics, and counseling.

Dissertations in the RAD series are *curated*, which means that they are carefully selected, on the basis of strong recommendations by the authors' supervisors and examiners and by our internal readers, to be part of our collection. Each selected dissertation will provide clear, fresh, and engaging insights about significant theological issues.

A number of theological institutions have partnered with us to recommend dissertations that they believe worthy of publication in the RAD series. Not only does this provide increased visibility for participating institutions, it also makes outstanding dissertations available to a broad range of readers, while helping to introduce promising authors to the publishing world.

We look forward to seeing the RAD program grow into a large collection of curated dissertations that will help to advance Reformed scholarship and learning.

John J. Hughes
Series Editor

Foreword

In the initial chapters of Matthew's Gospel, Jesus is introduced as King of the Jews, heir to David's throne, one who is acclaimed by Gentiles and anointed by God. Jesus is presented as "King of the Jews" (Matt. 27:37), even while he is introduced to Matthew's readers as Teacher in the body of the Gospel, which is the most prominent feature for Matthew.

The Structure of the Gospel of Matthew

The Gospel of Matthew became the most popular of the Gospels in the early church. Its role as the first book in the New Testament canon is unique because of the way in which its opening section and overall structure connect with the Old Testament.

Matthew includes five great discourses (Matt. 5–7; 10; 13; 18; 24–25). Three basic types of material are employed in these discourses: (1) beatitudes, (2) ethical admonitions, and (3) contrasts between Jesus' ethical teaching and prevailing traditions. An introduction (1:1–4:25) and conclusion (26:1–28:20) form bookends around the five teaching sections.

Matthew introduces us to Jesus with a genealogy (Matt. 1:1–17), an account of his miraculous conception by the Holy Spirit and later adoption by Joseph (1:18–25), and his flight to Egypt and return to Galilee (2:1–23). These things establish Jesus to be the

Messiah, the son of David (1:1). Matthew then reveals Jesus to be the obedient Son of God in the accounts of his baptism by John the Baptist (3:17) and his temptation by the devil (4:3–10). He then tells us that Jesus went about all Galilee, teaching in the synagogues and preaching the gospel of the kingdom (4:23).

Matthew 26:1–28:20, the concluding section, has no teaching situations, but it highlights the account of Jesus' passion, burial, resurrection, and commission to his followers. Throughout Matthew's narrative, the Gospel writer enables readers to begin to identify the Teacher. The bottom-line question that the hearers and contemporary readers must ask is not "What do you think of this teaching?" but "Who is this Teacher?"

The Teacher in Matthew's Gospel

God's purposes were to be accomplished through a descendant of David. The people of God in the Old Testament looked forward expectantly to the coming of the promised King, their Messiah. The plan of God had been revealed through a series of God's covenant promises (Gen. 12:2; 2 Sam. 7:9; Jer. 31). In these covenants, God's intent to establish his kingdom and redeem humankind was progressively revealed. These covenant promises found their ultimate fulfillment in Jesus Christ.

The Old Testament includes two different lines of teaching about the Messiah: He would be both King and Redeemer. Aspects of each purpose can be observed in the covenant promises and the prophetic portraits, though the details of the completion of these teachings remain somewhat unclear. The New Testament, however, beginning with the Gospel of Matthew, interprets the Old Testament and announces that the promised Messiah had come in Jesus of Nazareth. In identifying Jesus as the Messiah, Matthew affirms an essential connection with the Old Testament.

Matthew indicates that Jesus understood his mission in a way that ran counter to the assumptions and expectations of his

Foreword

contemporaries: both his followers and his opponents. One thing is sure: Jesus understood his mission as a fulfillment of the Scriptures, as indicated in his teachings and those of his followers, particularly in the Gospel of Matthew.

This Teacher is a worker of miracles (Matt. 4:23–25; 8:16; 14:35–36; 15:30; 19:2), the Son of Man (8:20; 9:6; 13:37; 19:28; 20:28), the son of David (9:27; 12:23; 15:22; 20:30–31; 21:9–15; 22:41–45), the Son of God (2:15; 4:3, 6; 14:33; 16:16; 26:63; 27:40, 43), the Christ/Messiah (Anointed One) (1:1, 16–18; 2:4; 11:2; 16:16–20; 22:42; 26:63–64, 68; 27:17, 22), and the Lord (8:2, 6; 9:28; 28:18). Within this broader context, Raymond Johnson helps us understand one of the most complex and challenging passages in Matthew's Gospel (27:51–54). Particularly, Johnson carefully and insightfully explores the meaning and theological implications of the resurrection of the saints in Matthew 27:52b–53.

The Function of Matthew 27:51–54 in the Gospel of Matthew

Matthew 27:51–54 presents five signs that accompany Jesus' death, in which the curtain of the temple is torn (51a), the earth shakes (51b), the rocks split (51c), the tombs open (52a), and lifeless saints are raised to life (52b–53). In this context Matthew presents Jesus the Messiah as not merely the sacrifice for sin, but its conqueror. Christ the Victor is the key to the future. These verses point to God's new life for his people, the very same life that was seen in the resurrected Christ. No sooner does Matthew speak of the death of Jesus Christ than he brings in the material about new life, which enables readers to understand that a new age is breaking in, similar to what was presented in Matthew 24.

Matthew wants us to understand that the death of Christ is an eschatological event, a foretaste of the end of the world. The Gospel points to the end of the old age of the tyranny of death and evil. The rocks are split. The dead are raised, pointing to the death and resurrection of Christ (1 Cor. 15:20; Col. 1:18; Rev. 1:5). Johnson, after thoroughly addressing the translation issues, the referential issues, and the placement issues related to these verses as discussed by dozens of interpreters such as Hutton, Wenham, Kingsbury, Witherup, Luz, Licona, and Anderson, provides a window for us to see the significance of the "lesser" resurrection of the saints, since it anticipates the public vindication of Jesus before his enemies (Matt. 28:6).

In order to show how this difficult passage functions in Matthew's Gospel, Johnson shows Matthew's dependence on Ezekiel 37:1–14. He then interprets the intentional placement of this text at this location in the first Gospel. Primarily, Johnson brilliantly and insightfully expounds the theological purpose of Matthew's work around the themes of Christology, missiology, and eschatology. Our author notes that the passages under consideration serve as a sign of the work of Christ, whereby Matthew incorporated the fulfillment of Old Testament prophecy at the particular point in time with future effects evidenced by a historical and bodily resurrection at the time of Jesus' finished cross work.

Readers of Raymond Johnson's book will join him in wrestling with the meaning of this confounding passage in Matthew 27. The extraordinary signs accompanying Jesus' death portray Jesus as the Son of God and prepare Matthew's readers for the infusion of eschatological resurrection on Easter morning. While this resurrection was temporal and not reflective of the final state of glorification, it was nevertheless representative of the immediate impact of Jesus' death as a reversal of the fall.

Implications of Matthew 27:51–54

God created men and women in his image. Humans chose to sin, resulting in death and alienation from God. As a result of God's grace grounded in the death and resurrection of Christ at his first coming, believers experience salvation from sin and conversion to God.

Foreword

Jesus Christ, the Son of God, has fully revealed God to men and women. Having lived a sinless life, Christ died in our place, taking our judgment and conquering sin and death by his resurrection.

The resurrection of Jesus Christ is the source of the Christian's hope. The resurrection points to the final phase of God's plan that culminates in the coming of God's kingdom, which will be transformed into the new heaven and the new earth. For all eternity, believers will worship the resurrected and exalted Christ supremely without impurity.

When the resurrected Lord declared his authority to his disciples in Matthew 28:18, they understood because they had seen his authority displayed in his life, ministry, and teaching (Matt. 7:29). The resurrected Christ commanded his followers to disciple, baptize, and teach, assuring them that he would be with them even to the ends of the earth (28:19–20).

The spectacular events described in Matthew 27:51–54, which are the focus of Raymond Johnson's project, point all of us to these wonderful truths concerning the saving significance of the death and resurrection of Jesus Christ, the Son of God. Whether or not one agrees with all the details of Johnson's impressive study, readers will find Johnson's work to be a well-researched, helpful, and thoughtful guide for the perplexing questions found in this challenging section of Matthew's Gospel.[1]

David S. Dockery, President
Trinity International University

---

[1] Portions of this material have been adopted and adapted from David S. Dockery, *Our Christian Hope: Biblical Answers to Questions about the Future* (Nashville: LifeWay, 1998), and David S. Dockery and David E. Earland, *Seeking the Kingdom: The Sermon on the Mount Made Practical for Today* (Wheaton, IL: Harold Shaw, 1992).

Preface

Interest in Matthew 27:51–54 came as I prepared to preach from this text. As I reviewed commentaries and consulted major works on the resurrection, I realized there was a vast interpretive chasm between exegetes and homileticians on how this text functioned within Matthew's Gospel-narrative. There was (and is) no scholarly consensus on the function or the theological meaning of this pericope in the death-resurrection scene because an interpretive dichotomy separated the historicity of the act itself and its placement in the Gospel from its theological meaning. This study focuses on the exegesis of Matthew 27:51–54 and its impact on the theological meaning and systematic reflections drawn from a literary reading of the text.

I want to thank my wife, Meghan, who was always very patient and understanding while I spent countless hours over several years involved in the research contained in these pages. Abigail, Charlotte, Emily, and Michael—our children—for enduring my absence. Pat Johnson, my mother, for being a constant source of encouragement. The congregation I have the privilege to pastor, The Journey Church (TJC), for graciously giving a young minister several writing sabbaticals. Mark Van Teyens, Christa Mast, Dan Mason, and Matthew Burns—my interns—for faithfully serving TJC to provide me time to write. I would like to thank Billy Wilhelm and Adam Tardosky, who painstakingly made the scripture index for this book. Their work

Preface

was surely one of supererogation! Terry and Donna Kraus, my (extra) parents, for frequently opening their home so that I could be closer to a theological library. Donna Roof at Westminster Theological seminary for providing me a library carrel at which I could write. Jonathan Pennington, my supervisor, who read my chapters numerous times, always providing helpful exegetical and structural suggestions. Douglas Baker, my dear friend, who read my manuscript with an editor's eye and saved me from many errors. I also need to thank Josh and Jessie Kilpatrick, who gave generously so that I might pursue a PhD. Charles Quarles, for carefully reading my work and encouraging me to pursue publication. John J. Hughes, for the opportunity to publish with P&R's RAD series. My prayer is that through this work one understands the death-resurrection of Jesus in the Gospel of Matthew better, and thereby sees more clearly the image of the invisible God in the face of the Crucified One—Jesus, Son of God.

Raymond M. Johnson
West Chester, Pennsylvania
May 2017

Abbreviations

ANF	The Ante-Nicene Fathers
AB	Anchor Bible
ABRL	Anchor Bible Reference Library
ACCS	Ancient Christian Commentary on Scripture
ANRW	*Aufstieg und Niedergang der römischen Welt*
Ant.	Antiquities of the Jews
ANTC	Abingdon New Testament Commentaries
ATJ	*Asbury Theological Journal*
BDB	Francis Brown, Samuel R. Driver, and Charles A. Briggs, *Hebrew and English Lexicon of the Old Testament*
BDAG	Walter Bauer, Fredrick W. Danker, William F. Arndt, and Wilber Gingrich, *A Greek-English Lexicon of the New Testament and Other Early Christian Literature*, 3rd ed.
BECNT	Baker Exegetical Commentary on the New Testament
BETL	Bibliotheca Ephemeridum Theologicarum Lovaniensium

Abbreviations

BTB	*Biblical Theology Bulletin*
CBQ	*Catholic Biblical Quarterly*
CurTM	*Currents in Theology and Mission*
ETL	Ephemerides Theological Lovanienses
ExpT	*Expository Times*
Georg.	The Georgics
HeyJ	*Heythrop Journal*
HTR	Harvard Theological Review
HTS	Harvard Theological Studies
HUCA	Hebrew Union College Annual
ICC	International Critical Commentary
IBS	Irish Biblical Studies
Ign. Magn.	Ignatius *to the Magnesians*
Institutes	*Institutes of the Christian Religion*
JBL	*Journal of Biblical Literature*
JETS	*Journal of the Evangelical Theological Society*
JNSL	*Journal of Northwest Semitic Languages*
JPT	*Journal of Pentecostal Theology*
JPTSup	Journal of Pentecostal Theology Supplement
JSNTSup	Journal for the Study of New Testament Supplement
JSOTSup	Journal for the Study of the Old Testament Supplement Series
JTS	*Journal of Theological Studies*
LBC	London Baptist Confession (1689)
L&N	Johannes P. Louw and Eugene A. Nida, *Greek-English Lexicon of the New Testament Based on Semantic Domains*
LNTS	Library of New Testament Studies

Abbreviations

LSJ	Henry G. Liddell, Robert Scott, and Henry S. Jones, *Greek-English Lexicon*
LXX	Septuagint
NAC	The New American Commentary
Nat.	*Natural History*
NCBC	New Cambridge Bible Commentary
NICNT	The New International Commentary on the New Testament
NICOT	The New International Commentary on the Old Testament
NIDNTT	New International Dictionary of New Testament Theology
NIGTC	New International Greek Testament Commentary
NovT	*Novum Testamentum*
NovTSup	Supplements to Novum Testamentum
NSBT	New Studies in Biblical Theology
NSD	New Studies in Dogmatics
NTS	*New Testament Studies*
PT	*Poetics Today*
RB	*Revue biblique*
Rep.	*De republica*
Rom.	*Romulus*
SBJT	*Southern Baptist Journal of Theology*
SBLSP	Society of Biblical Literature Seminar Papers
SNTSMS	Society for New Testament Studies Monograph Series
TC	*A Journal of Biblical Textual Criticism*
TD	*Theology Digest*

Abbreviations

TDNT	*Theological Dictionary of the New Testament*
TynBul	*Tyndale Bulletin*
WCF	Westminster Confession of Faith
WBC	Word Biblical Commentary
WTJ	*Westminster Theological Journal*

1

The Resurrected Saints: The Problem with Matthew 27:51–54

State of the *Sondergut*: The Literary Landscape of the Matthean Special Material

Matthew's passion narrative contains critical texts unique to his Gospel (Matt. 26:1–5, 52–54, 62–66; 27:3–10, 19, 24–25, 51b–53). Scholars have given attention to these pericopal hapaxes while trying to ascertain their significance and meaning in Matthew's narrative.[1] One that has been particularly perplexing is Matthew 27:51–54. At the moment of Jesus' death on the cross, after he cried out with a loud voice and yielded up the Spirit (Matt. 27:50), several cataclysmic events occurred, which Matthew recounts for his readers. His Gospel includes five signs[2] that accompany Jesus' death:

---

[1] See, for example, Donald Senior, *The Passion Narrative according to Matthew: A Redactional Study*, BETL 39 (Leuven, Belgium: Leuven University Press, 1975), 336–40. Senior suggests the Matthean special material manifests Matthew's literary craftsmanship in the composition of his gospel narrative.

[2] I use "sign" instead of "symbol" since it more clearly connotes a referent that points the reader both backward to the historical event as well as forward to a greater referent—for Matt. 27:51–54 that is the resurrection in 28:1–10. That is, "sign" connotes more than a past historical referent. Like the rainbow in the Noahic covenant, these "signs" function as proclamatory covenantal revelation (Gen. 8:20–22; Matt. 27:51–54) not only of what God has done in the past but of what he will not do in the future—he will never again crush his Son as

THE RESURRECTED SAINTS

(1) The curtain of the temple is torn (v. 51a), (2) the earth shakes (v. 51b), (3) the rocks split (v. 51c), (4) the tombs open (v. 52a), and (5) lifeless people, whom Matthew calls ἁγίων, are raised to life (v. 52b).[3] The most perplexing of these cosmic events has been the resurrection of the dead saints. Their resurrection from the dead has both confounded interpreters and led to many crucial interpretive questions: What kind of bodies did these "holy people" possess? Did they die again? How public was their appearance, and how many people saw them? Were they raised *before* or *after* Jesus' resurrection from the dead? If they were raised prior to his resurrection, what did they do after they were raised but before Jesus was resurrected (i.e., did they just wait in their tombs)? Was their resurrection like that of Lazarus in John 11 or like the resurrection described by the

---

a substitute for sinners. Further, it will be argued below that Matthew prepares his readers for the events in 28:1–10 and 28:16–20 by proleptically foreshadowing them through the "signs" in 27:51–54. Additionally, by "signs" I mean cosmic portents that manifest divine approval of Jesus' work as a penal substitute—these are divine portents that testify to the legitimacy of Jesus' claim to be the Son of God. For a recent argument on interpreting the symbolism in Matt. 27:51–54, see Daniel M. Gurtner, "Interpreting Apocalyptic Symbolism in the Gospel of Matthew," paper presented at the Evangelical Theological Society National Conference, New Orleans, November 2009, 1–38.

[3] Strauss contends that only four events accompany Jesus' death: (1) the curtain of the temple is torn, (2) an earthquake occurs, (3) the tombs are opened and the "holy ones" are resurrected, and (4) the centurion and those with him exclaim, "Surely he was the Son of God!" See Mark L. Strauss, *Four Portraits, One Jesus: An Introduction to Jesus and the Gospels* (Grand Rapids: Zondervan, 2007), 238. Others, however, include the centurion's confession as a sixth sign. However, it seems the centurion's confession is a positive result of the five signs that happen after Jesus yields up the Spirit rather than a result of Jesus' death on the cross. The cosmic signs overcome his Gentile unbelief. This is in contrast to Sim, who contends the events surrounding Jesus' death on the cross were not a sufficient basis for the centurion's profession of faith in Matt. 27:54. See David C. Sim, "The 'Confession' of the Soldiers in Matthew 27:54," *HeyJ* 34 (1993): 416. For a thorough treatment of the tearing of the temple veil, see Daniel M. Gurtner, *The Torn Veil: Matthew's Exposition of the Death of Jesus* (Cambridge: Cambridge University Press, 2007). Gurtner argues the rending of the veil is cosmological imagery signifying the rending of the heavens.

apostle Paul in 1 Corinthians 15 (i.e., glorified bodies)? Is it possible these "saints" were taken up to heaven like Enoch (Gen. 5:24)? Was Matthew speaking of a historical event or merely using phenomenological and metaphorical language in his Gospel narrative?

It is not surprising that interpreters across the span of interpretive history have labored to apply this pivotal text in their respective hermeneutical and homiletical endeavors. The interpretive confusion results from a misassumption that the resurrection of the saints is either a glorified resurrection and, therefore, displaced in the Matthean Gospel or is ahistorical and legend.[4] For this reason further study of the Matthean pericope is required. Utilizing the tools of literary analysis, this dissertation aims to assist interpreters in bridging the text's interpretive chasm. Further, this work intends to demonstrate that a literary reading of Matthew 27:51–54 should be adopted. This type of reading will deepen one's understanding of the Matthean passage in question and reveal that its meaning is about more than its canonical relationship with 1 Corinthians 15:20, Colossians 1:18, and Revelation 1:5.

Though the aforementioned questions highlight the difficulty in ascertaining the meaning of this text, it is clear that this Matthean pericope actually informs both the way one understands the conclusion of the Gospel according to Matthew, particularly the scenes surrounding these events (Matt. 27:32–50; 27:55–28:20), and the implications of Jesus' resurrection from the dead. By the way he has constructed the narrative, Matthew has set the stage in his Gospel story line by means of the "lesser" resurrection of the saints since it anticipates the public vindication of Jesus before his enemies—he is not dead; he rose just as he said he would (Matt. 28:6; cf. 16:21; 17:23; 20:19). For Matthew, the resurrection of the saints creates

---

[4] Regarding the former, see D. A. Carson, *The Expositor's Bible Commentary with the New International Version*, vol. 2, *Matthew 13–28*, ed. Frank E. Gaebelein (Grand Rapids: Zondervan, 1995), 581–82. Regarding the latter, see Michael Licona, *The Resurrection of Jesus: A New Historiographical Approach* (Downers Grove, IL: InterVarsity Press, 2010), 553.

anticipation through literary parallelism. Jesus dies and some other unidentified dead are made alive, and the vindicating resurrection of Jesus brings the plot of Matthew's Gospel to its literary resolution. The religious leaders fear Jesus' "greater"[5] resurrection because it proves that they were wrong about him. They propagate a lie and further prove themselves to be evil (Matt. 28:12–15). His "greater" resurrection proves to Jesus' doubting disciples that he is truly alive and does indeed have "all authority in heaven and on earth" (Matt. 28:18). Jesus' "greater" resurrection gives hope to all of his followers that the Lord is the resurrected Christ. He has conquered sin, death, and hell. Now he is God with his people as they go about proclaiming and offering a gospel of repentance and forgiveness of sins (Matt. 28:20; cf. 1:23), and he is God in his people, empowering them by the Holy Spirit he and the Father have sent to them (John 20:19–23; Acts 1:8; 2:4; 1 Cor. 6:19; Eph. 1:13–14).

Statement of the Problem

A perusal of commentaries on Matthew[6] as well as a consultation of noteworthy works on the resurrection[7] manifests that a

---

[5] For reasons specified below, this dissertation argues Matthew structured this section of his Gospel with a "lesser" resurrection (that of the "saints") and a "greater" resurrection (that of Jesus) in order to (1) accentuate christological, missiological, and eschatological motifs and (2) to climactically bring his Gospel plotline to resolution. Additionally, it is crucial to note that by "'lesser' resurrection" this dissertation means "not glorified" and by "'greater' resurrection" this dissertation means "glorified."

[6] See, for example, W. D. Davies and Dale C. Allison Jr., *A Critical and Exegetical Commentary on the Gospel according to Saint Matthew*, ICC, vol. 3, *Matthew 19–28* (New York: T&T Clark, 2004); Craig Evans, *Matthew*, NCBC (Cambridge: Cambridge University Press, 2012); and David Turner, *Matthew*, BECNT (Grand Rapids: Baker, 2008).

[7] See, for example, Dale Allison Jr., *Resurrecting Jesus: The Earliest Christian Tradition and Its Interpretation* (New York: T&T Clark, 2005); Dale Allison Jr., *Constructing Jesus: Memory, Imagination, and History* (Grand Rapids: Baker Academic, 2010), 452–53; R. Bieringer, V. Koperski, and B. Lataire,

vast interpretive chasm exists between exegetes and homileticians on how the text under consideration, Matthew 27:51–54, functions within Matthew's narrative and what this particular pericope means for readers of his Gospel. In the absence of scholarly consensus, interpreters must overcome three problems to exegete this Matthean pericope rightly: mistranslation, misreferent, and misplacement.

Mistranslation

The first problem that this dissertation aims to address is mistranslation. Recent Matthean interpreters have largely relied on a translation of the Matthean pericope that has argued for a full-stop punctuation in the middle of Matthew 27:52.[8] The full stop, for these interpreters, conveys a temporal lapse between the time when the tombs opened as a result of the earthquake in Matthew 27:51 and the subsequent resurrection of the sleeping saints in Matthew 27:52–53. Further, this temporal gap enables them to reconcile Matthew's pericope with the subsequent teaching in the Pauline and Johannine epistles that Jesus is the firstborn from the dead— ἀπαρχὴ τῶν κεκοιμημένων (1 Cor. 15:20; cf. Col. 1:18; Rev. 1:5). This interpretation has been helpful in dealing with a "pesky" Matthean text, but it is too convenient. This reading is more concerned with understanding the conclusion to Matthew's Gospel in light of the New Testament epistles rather than in light of the Matthean narrative. It implies that Matthew's crafting of the conclusion to his Gospel was haphazard in that he "misplaced" a resurrection account within the passion narrative. Consequently, this interpretation forces

---

eds., *Resurrection in the New Testament*, BETL 165 (Leuven, Belgium: Leuven University Press, 2002); and N. T. Wright, *The Resurrection of the Son of God*, Christian Origins and the Question of God, vol. 3 (Minneapolis: Fortress Press, 2003).

[8] Concerning this thesis, three in particular stand out: J. W. Wenham, "When Were the Saints Raised?," *JTS* 32, 1 (1981): 150–52; Carson, *Expositor's Bible Commentary*, 2:581–82; and Craig L. Blomberg, *Matthew*, NAC, vol. 22 (Nashville: Broadman Press, 1992), 421.

a reading of the pericope in Matthew 27:45–28:20 that is foreign to Matthew's literary intentions.

This dissertation, therefore, will address the issue of translation in relation to Matthew 27:51–54. Chapter 2 will argue that the most natural translation of the Matthean pericope is as follows:

> Behold, the curtain of the temple was torn in two from top to bottom, the earth quaked, and the rocks split, the tombs, also, were opened and the bodies of many saints who had died were raised to life; coming out of the tombs, they went into the holy city after his resurrection, appearing to many people. When the centurion and those guarding Jesus with him saw the earthquake and the things that took place they were terrified and said, "This really was the Son of God!"

Further, chapter 2 will argue that a comma at the end of Matthew 27:51 is more grammatically appropriate because it links the five signs that occur as a result of Jesus' death on the cross after he yields τὸ πνεῦμα (Matt. 27:50). Additionally, chapter 2 will argue that a semicolon at the end of Matthew 27:52 suggests a close relationship between the resurrection of the saints and their emergence from the graves that a period would not sufficiently indicate. This dissertation will contend that this reading tethers the signs in Matthew 27:51–54 with the events of Good Friday and accentuates the three theological foci Matthew is featuring in this pericope: Christology, missiology, and eschatology. It is because the βασιλεία has broken into the present *in* the person of Jesus (Matt. 4:17; cf. 3:2; 10:7) that Jesus dies like no other person in history.[9] The signs accompanying Jesus' death on the cross testify to his divine identity as the Son of God. They underscore the missiological and eschatological foci of

---

[9] Robertson notes that such manifestations of God's power are connected with both the birth and death of Jesus, God's Son, in Matthew's Gospel. See A. T. Robertson, *Word Pictures of the New Testament*, vol. 1, *The Gospel according to Matthew, the Gospel according to Mark* (Grand Rapids: Baker, 1930), 236.

his death—his death has meaning for the nations because there has been a rending of the veil, signifying the end of separation between God and the people (Matt. 27:51, 54; 28:16–20).

Misreferent

The second problem this dissertation aims to address is misreference, because consideration of the Matthean special material in Matthew 27 raises the issue of origin (Matt. 27:3–10, 19, 24–25, 51b–53). From where did Matthew receive the material in his arrangement of Matthew 26–28? What sources were used in the composition of the Matthean *Sondergut*? Donald Senior suggests that "Matthew's theological perspective owed much to Mark" and that "Mark was the only formal source used by Matthew in the passion narrative."[10] Further, he contends that "the most compelling explanation was Matthew's direct dependence on the Gospel of Mark *and no other as his source*" in the formation of the Matthean passion narrative.[11] Similarly, when addressing the issue of "origin" in relation to the *Sondergut*, David Hill states, "Little or nothing is gained by the hypothesis of an already existing apocalyptic fragment edited by Matthew: it is as likely, if not more so, that the evangelist himself brought together a number of well-known apocalyptic images in order to convey his own distinctive message."[12] Therefore, in Senior's and Hill's assessment, a preexisting body of material informing Matthew's composition of the *Sondergut* is unlikely. However, it is noteworthy that previously Senior had suggested that Matthew 27:51b–53 is solely dependent on Ezekiel 37, not solely

---

[10] Donald P. Senior, "Matthew's Special Material in the Passion Story: Implications for the Evangelist's Redactional Technique and Theological Perspective," *ETL* 63 (1987): 273, 274.

[11] Ibid., 273 (my emphasis). Senior states his conclusions are based on Matthew's use of Old Testament and Jewish theological traditions as well as his exploration of cues in Mark's Gospel.

[12] David Hill, "Matthew 27:51–53 in the Theology of the Evangelist," *IBS* 7 (April 1985): 77.

dependent on Mark's Gospel.[13] Further, James Dunn notes that the presence of the *Sondergut* suggests that Matthew's material was not a single collection or from a single source.[14] This supports the proposal of this dissertation: Ezekiel 37:1–14 is the primary referent for Matthew 27:51–54.[15]

Chapter 3, therefore, will advocate that there is textual and interpretive evidence that the resurrection vision in Ezekiel 37:1–14 is close in the background of Matthew 27:51–54.[16] This chapter will further argue that Matthew's pericope, laced with divine signs testifying to Jesus' divine identity as the Son of God (i.e., Matt. 27:51–54), finds its primary origins in the Ezekielian Old Testament prophetic narrative. Contra many scholars, this dissertation will argue that the Matthean pericope under consideration does not find its background in a mixture of myriad Old Testament passages. Moreover, this dissertation will reject the suggestion that Matthew's pericopal hapax finds its primary roots in an extrabiblical, pre-Matthean tradition. Rather, this dissertation will argue that an examination of Ezekiel 37:1–14 in its Septuagintal form manifests

---

[13] Senior, *Passion Narrative according to Matthew*, 207–23.

[14] Matt. 27:52–53 is one of several sections of Matthew referenced by Dunn. He is commenting on all the special material in Matthew's Gospel. See James D. G. Dunn, "How Did Matthew Go about Composing His Gospel?," in *Jesus, Matthew's Gospel and Early Christianity: Studies in Memory of Graham N. Stanton*, ed. Daniel Gurtner, Joel Willitts, and Richard A. Burridge, LNTS (New York: T&T Clark, 2011), 43–44.

[15] When reviewing Senior's dissertation in book form, Hutton notes that Senior fails to treat Matt. 26:62–66 in his study of the *Sondergut*. Analysis of Matt. 26:62–66 in his treatment of the Matthean special material would make the parallels to an independent tradition outside of Mark's Gospel more manifest. Hutton correctly notes that Senior's conclusions overlook the influence of non-Marcan material as well as oral tradition. Delvin Hutton, review of *The Passion Narrative according to Matthew: A Redactional Study*, by Donald P. Senior, *JBL* 96 (1977): 308–9.

[16] Grassi, too, makes this connection. Thus, he states, "The early Christian tradition described the death and resurrection of Jesus in terms of Ezekiel's resurrection of the dry bones." J. A. Grassi, "Ezekiel 37, 1–14 and the New Testament," *NTS* 11 (1964–65): 164.

numerous links to Matthew's Gospel. Thus, Matthew has Ezekiel 37:12–14 (LXX) as his *primary* Old Testament referent when composing this resurrection pericope in Matthew 27:51–54. Awareness of Matthean dependence on Ezekiel 37 (LXX) manifests the pericope's theological foci—Christology, missiology, and eschatology.

Misplacement

The third problem this dissertation aims to address is misplacement; interpreters have been unable to agree about whether the pericope under consideration should be understood as historical and, therefore, displaced in the Matthean Gospel or as ahistorical and legend. On the one hand, those who propose Matthew 27:51–54 is ahistorical hold this interpretation because the imagery in the pericope has apocalyptic overtones—darkness over the land (Matt. 27:45), a revelatory earthquake (Matt. 25:51), resurrection from the dead (Matt. 27:52–53), the metaphorical destruction of the temple (Matt. 27:51). Though the passage definitely has apocalyptic connotations and cosmic significance, it is not ahistorical or legend. The pericope occurs within a historical scene—the crucifixion and murder of Jesus. Therefore, these interpretations are hermeneutically and homiletically unsatisfying.

On the other hand, others contend for the historicity of the pericope while suggesting its historical resurrection is displaced within the Matthean narrative. These interpreters make this suggestion because they fail to observe Matthew's purposeful narrative strategy informing the literary parallelism of Matthew 27:51–54 alongside 28:1–10 as well as the intentional placement of Matthew 27:51–54 within the death-resurrection scene (Matt. 27:45–28:20). Therefore, these interpretations are hermeneutically and homiletically unsatisfying when one considers the compositional intentionality of Matthew throughout the entirety of his Gospel's narrative.

Interpretive misunderstanding is manifest in the absence of consensus concerning the placement of Matthew 27:51–54 within the death-resurrection scene. Therefore, in chapter 4 this dissertation will argue that reading Matthew 27:51–54 in light of the entirety of the crucifixion scene and observing Matthew's purposeful narrative strategy and intentional placement of the pericope renders a proper interpretation of the passage.

Recent History of Research

Matthew 27:51–54 in Biblical Studies

The world of biblical studies has produced massive tomes on resurrection in the New Testament as well as major exegetical works on Matthew's Gospel. As a result, the pericope under consideration has received attention in well-known scholarly works. Yet a significant gap exists in the amount of attention given especially to the literary aspects of the pericope as they relate to Matthew 28 as well as the pericope's christological, missiological, and eschatological significance when contending for a historical, Lazarus-like resurrection. Noteworthy scholars who have postulated translation issues, apocalyptic resurrection theses, narrative interpretations, and varying historical claims in their appropriation of this Matthean pericope will be examined.[17]

Delvin D. Hutton

Hutton's "The Resurrection of the Holy Ones (Matt 27:51b–53): A Study of the Theology of the Matthean Passion Narrative" is his unpublished dissertation from Harvard in 1970.[18] His work is a redaction-critical analysis of the Matthean pericope that begins by briefly summarizing three ways Matthew 27:51–54 has been appropriated hermeneutically—to advocate *descensus Christi ad infernos*,

---

[17] This survey of the Matthean literature focuses on recent contributions to this pericope rather than those spanning the history of reception. Additional analysis of reception history will be relegated to the dissertation proper.

[18] Delvin D. Hutton, "The Resurrection of the Holy Ones (Matt 27:51b–53): A Study of the Theology of the Matthean Passion Narrative" (ThD diss., Harvard University, 1970).

to advocate the death of a Hellenistic "divine man," and to advocate cosmic participation in the death of a cosmic deity.[19] He contends that these are "hermeneutically inadequate" and seeks to show that Matthew's narrative has both reshaped and replaced the pericopal scene for theological purposes.[20] Further, he clearly states, "It will be noted at no time does the writer concern himself with the question, 'Did it really happen; is it empirically verifiable?'"[21] Rather, the question he concerned himself with throughout his thesis is, "What was the meaning of the tradition expressed in Mt 27:51b-53 for the individual evangelist and for the community in which and for whom he composed his Gospel?"[22]

He concludes that the scene Matthew has crafted in his Gospel is a combination of the Markan material and oral epiphanic traditions.[23] He also contends that the placement of the redacted material belonged originally with the scene Matthew portrays in the following chapter, Matthew 28:2–4.[24] He suggests that Matthew's rearrangement of the material is to accentuate a new eschatological reality.[25] More specifically, he contends that Matthew has crafted a scene with the resurrection of τῶν κεκοιμημένων ἁγίων[26] as he relied on apocalyptic traditions in order to emphasize the eschatological nature

---

[19] Ibid., 14. His analysis of interpretive history is short. Further, the significance of the distinction between his second and third appropriations of the text is not entirely clear. I would argue the divinely caused cosmic portents testify to the "deity" of Jesus. Thus, there appears to be (1) categorical overlap and (2) other interpretive appropriations of the text to explore.

[20] Ibid., 15.

[21] Ibid. Unlike Licona (see below), Hutton is not concerned with questions of historicity in his work on the resurrection.

[22] Ibid., 16.

[23] Ibid., 109.

[24] Ibid., 108.

[25] Ibid., 117, 119, 126, 172–76.

[26] Hutton speculates on the identity of τῶν κεκοιμημένων ἁγίων in his work. He suggests they are "the patriarchs, prophets, and martyrs, who, having joined their brethren in the sleep of death were set apart for vindication and blessing in the resurrection." Ibid., 142, 137–43.

of Jesus' death on the cross.²⁷ The portents surrounding Jesus' death connote that something decisive in salvation history has occurred in the death of Jesus.

Assessment. Hutton's work rightly notes that the pericope under consideration is eschatologically oriented and is marked with apocalyptic imagery. Further, his work rightly notes that Matthew's work is "theologically arranged."²⁸ Yet his redaction-critical work ultimately, and wrongly, places the resurrection of τῶν κεκοιμημένων ἁγίων after Jesus' resurrection from the dead and misreads the literary intentionality manifest in the scene.

J. W. Wenham

In 1981 J. W. Wenham published his article "When Were the Saints Raised? A Note on the Punctuation of Matthew xxvii. 51–53," arguing for a full-stop punctuation in the middle of Matthew 27:52.²⁹ He suggested that it was inappropriate for translators to translate ἀνεῴχθησαν without punctuation because it wrongly ties the resurrection of τῶν ... ἁγίων to events that occurred on Good Friday after Jesus yielded up his spirit on the cross (Matt. 27:50). To substantiate his thesis, he argues that καὶ ἐξελθόντες ... πολλοῖς forms a partial parenthesis. That is, the words καὶ ἐξελθόντες ... πολλοῖς are parenthetical, but they lack a subject within the versification in which they are currently found. Rather, Wenham argues that the subject is found in the previous verse (πολλὰ σώματα; Matt. 27:52). Consequently, he contends that this places the resurrection of the saints with the events that follow instead of the events that precede—namely, he claims that the saints are both resurrected

---

²⁷ Ibid., 145.
²⁸ Ibid., 115.
²⁹ Wenham, "When Were the Saints Raised?," 150–52. Though Wenham's article is short, his contribution is significant because his thesis persuades well-known modern commentator D. A. Carson. See Carson, *Expositor's Bible Commentary*, 2:581–82. See also Blomberg, *Matthew*, 421. Carson and Blomberg are two of many Wenham has persuaded.

and come out of the tombs *after* Jesus' resurrection from the dead.[30] According to Wenham, then, the translation of Matthew 27:51–53 would read as follows: "And the earth quaked, and the rocks split, and the tombs were opened. And, many bodies of the saints who had fallen asleep were raised and came out of the tombs after [Jesus'] resurrection and they went into the holy city and appeared to many."

Wenham's concerns are twofold. First, the temporal lapse between the opening of the tombs caused by the earthquake in Matthew 27:51 and the subsequent resurrection of the many sleeping saints neatly places the events *after* Jesus' resurrection and maintains his title as the firstborn from the dead—ἀπαρχὴ τῶν κεκοιμημένων (1 Cor. 15:20; cf. Col. 1:18; Rev. 1:5). Second, he wants to tie the resurrection of the saints with Jesus' vindicating resurrection from the dead in Matthew 28:1–10. For Wenham, their resurrection is caused by Jesus' resurrection. This causal relationship accentuates the power of Jesus' resurrection from the dead, a resurrecting power accessible to "all who fall asleep in Jesus."[31] Therefore, he connects the resurrection of the saints with the resurrection of Jesus to emphasize his "defeating the powers of evil."[32]

Assessment. Wenham's interpretive instinct to connect the resurrection of τῶν κεκοιμημένων ἁγίων (Matt. 27:52–53) with Jesus' resurrection (Matt. 28:6) is correct. Close examination of the narrative manifests that Matthew has placed the pericopes parallel to each other in order to emphasize the theological foci of the passage: Christology, missiology, and eschatology. Wenham, however, incorrectly assumes the raising of τῶν κεκοιμημένων ἁγίων

---

[30] Wenham is concerned with alleviating Matthew of the erroneous assumption that the saints were resurrected for three days while remaining around the tombs until Jesus is raised from the dead in Matt. 28:1–10: "Then the succession of events on Good Friday is clearly delineated, and the whole episode of the resurrected saints is placed after the resurrection of Jesus, thus absolving the evangelist from the charge of depicting living saints cooped up for days in tombs around the city" (ibid., 151).

[31] Wenham, "When Were the Saints Raised?," 152.

[32] Ibid., 151.

threatens Jesus' right as ἀπαρχὴ τῶν κεκοιμημένων (1 Cor. 15:20). Rather, Matthew intends for his readers to interpret the raising of the sleeping saints as Lazarus-like and testimonial. As Jesus' power was demonstrated and naysayers' mocking comments were overturned when he restored the life of the sleeping-dead girl (Matt. 9:24–25), so now through the cosmic portents once again his divine power is on display as the dead are raised to life as a testimony (Matt. 27:52–53). As Jesus' fame was heralded for overturning death previously (Matt. 9:26), so now Matthew recounts that his fame is heralded in τὴν ἁγίαν πόλιν and, ultimately, to the ends of the earth (Matt. 28:16–20).

Jack Dean Kingsbury

Kingsbury has been a proponent of reading the Bible literally by means of the tools of narrative criticism. In his work *Matthew as Story*, he describes his interpretive method as a literary-critical approach to reading the Gospel narrative. His project consciously moves away from "the historical-biographical, the form-critical, and the redaction-critical" approaches to the interpretation of Matthew's Gospel.[33] Following Seymour Chatman, he analyzes the final form of Matthew as a unified narrative by arguing that the Gospel, like all other narratives, has two parts—the Gospel's story and the Gospel's discourse.[34] The story, according to Kingsbury, is the events that

---

[33] Jack D. Kingsbury, *Matthew as Story*, 2nd ed. (Philadelphia: Fortress Press, 1988), 2.

[34] Ibid., 3. Chatman's work is a structural analysis of narratology. He defines "story" as "the what of narrative" and "discourse" as "the way of narrative" (Seymour Chatman, *Story and Discourse: Narrative Structure in Fiction and Film* [Ithaca, NY: Cornell University Press, 1978], 9–42). Further, he seeks to explicate the elements of storytelling and their connection with the structure of narrative. That is, he seeks to provide a comprehensive approach to the general theory of interpreting narrative. His work *Story and Discourse*, though not a theological work, can aid the interpreter who rightly understands the care with which Matthew as an *author* has crafted his Gospel so that the elements of the story, which are historical, are theologically arranged in this discourse to

make up Jesus' life from his birth to his death-defying resurrection. The discourse, then, is the medium by which this story is told to Matthew's readers.[35] Throughout this work, he accentuates literary elements—arrangement and development of theological themes in the narrative, irony, contrast, and character development—in his reading of the divine story that Matthew recounts.[36] Kingsbury's narrative-critical reading is further developed in his work *Gospel Interpretation*, in which he contends that discernment of the narrative's arrangement is central to interpretation. The author intends for the "arrangement" of the narrative to solicit a desired response from the readers; discernment of the "arrangement" of events or time or place or topic gives meaning to the plot of the story. Discerning the plot, for Kingsbury, enables the exegete to interpret the "positioning of each episode within the story and the literary role this episode plays within the story as a whole."[37] In relation to Matthew 27:51–54, Kingsbury contends that Matthew recounted the supernatural portents in his narrative to (1) substantiate Jesus' claim to be the Son of God by "the counter-assertion, elicited by God himself" through the cosmic events surrounding Jesus' death[38] and

---

convey truth. Jonathan Pennington has recently advocated a literary analysis akin to Chatman's for Gospel interpretation. See Jonathan Pennington, *Reading the Gospels Wisely: A Narrative and Theological Introduction* (Grand Rapids: Baker, 2012), 169–82.

[35] Thus, "story-time" reflects the chronological order in which all the events cited in the Gospel's narrative occur. "Discourse-time," however, is the order in which the readers of the Gospel are told about the events that constitute the story. Kingsbury, *Matthew as Story*, 40–41.

[36] Jack D. Kingsbury, ed., *Gospel Interpretation: Narrative-Critical & Social Scientific Approaches* (Harrisburg, PA: Trinity Press International, 1997), 1–5.

[37] Kingsbury, *Gospel Interpretation*, 3.

[38] Kingsbury, *Matthew as Story*, 89. Earlier in his academic career, in *Matthew: Structure, Christology, Kingdom*, Kingsbury contended the climax of Matthew's Gospel is intended primarily to convey Jesus as the Son of God. As Jesus' resisting of Satan's temptations proved he was the Son of God (Matt. 4:3, 6), so now staying on the cross and resisting the temptation of the Pharisaic naysayers to come down from it proves he is indeed the Son of God. See

(2) to bring the third part of his Gospel story to its initial narrative climax.³⁹

Additionally, another of Kingsbury's contributions in *Matthew as Story* is utilizing his literary-critical approach to interpret the actions of the antagonists in Matthew's narrative. For Kingsbury, next to the Gospel's protagonist, Jesus, no group represented in the story influences the events narrated in Matthew's Gospel more than the antagonists, the religious leaders.⁴⁰ By means of their hostile actions to Jesus, they assume that they are protecting the Jewish people from a pseudo-messiah. The narrative, however, describes their actions as positively moving the Gospel's story toward its resolution. Further, their actions not only repeatedly fulfill Jesus' mission and positively move the narrative forward but also fulfill Scriptures that prophesied his redeeming mission.⁴¹ Kingsbury's analysis enables one to see more clearly how the actions of Jesus' antagonists achieve salvation for the world (Matt. 28:16–20; cf. 27:54). Their God-rejecting actions that precede the scene of Matthew 27:51–54 accentuate the tension created by the narrative when the Gentile

---

Jack D. Kingsbury, *Matthew: Structure, Christology, Kingdom* (Philadelphia: Fortress Press, 1975), 74–77.

³⁹ Kingsbury adds a third (for him it is the second of the three) significance of the portents surrounding Jesus' death. He contends the centurion's confession calls attention to this fact: the cross signifies the end of Jesus' earthly ministry and the end of the temple cult as the "place" of salvation. See Kingsbury, *Matthew as Story*, 89–90. Though Jesus' death on the cross does indicate the end of his earthly life, it seems more accurate to argue the tearing of the veil, not the confession of the centurion, marks the end of the temple as the mediator of salvation's blessings. Thus, the centurion's confession is a result of the portents and a proleptic narratival indicator that the gospel will be taken to the Gentiles (Matt. 28:16–20; cf. 27:54).

⁴⁰ Kingsbury, *Matthew as Story*, 115, 126. From the beginning of his Gospel, Matthew has indicated that "evil" characterizes the religious γεννήματα ἐχιδνῶν (Matt. 3:7). Thus, Kingsbury argues that conflict is a central motif throughout the plot of Matthew's story.

⁴¹ Some of the more explicit fulfillment texts scattered throughout the Gospel narrative include Matt. 1:23; 2:6, 18; 3:1; 4:14; 12:18–21; 13:14–15, 35; 15:8–9; 21:5, 16, 42; 26:56.

centurion confesses Jesus to be θεοῦ υἱὸς ἦν οὗτος (Matt. 27:54). His confession manifests that the cosmic portents are not only christological, in that they demonstrate Jesus' death on the cross is a life-giving death, but are also missiological as both resurrected Jewish saints and a Roman Gentile testify to his identity as God the Father's Son.[42]

Assessment. Kingsbury's narratological emphasis enables readers to more keenly discern theologically arranged literary structure, through which the Gospel writers obviously intended to communicate truth. In relation to Matthew 27:51–54, Kingsbury's analysis fails to note the intentional literary parallelism as well as the connection between Jesus' divine identity and gospel mission, both of which are conveyed in Matthew 27:51–54 and 28:1–10.

Ronald D. Witherup

Under the tutelage of Kingsbury, Ronald D. Witherup wrote his dissertation on the Gospel of Matthew, specifically on Matthew 27—"The Cross of Jesus: A Literary-Critical Study of Matthew 27."[43] His thesis argues, "Matthew 27 is the central and most important section in the passion/resurrection complex which concludes Matthew's Gospel (26–28)."[44] Further, he contends that the events surrounding Jesus' death in Matthew 27 bring together four central themes that are prominent in Matthew's Gospel: "salvation-history, prophecy and fulfillment, discipleship, and most importantly, the theme of Jesus' identity as the royal, obedient and faithful Son of God."[45] When commenting on the pericope that this study focuses

---

[42] Kingsbury contends the presence of these two groups together in the narrative is a prefigurement of the post-Easter church. See Jack D. Kingsbury, *Matthew*, Proclamation Commentaries, 2nd ed. (Philadelphia: Fortress Press, 1986), 57.

[43] Ronald D. Witherup, "The Cross of Jesus: A Literary-Critical Study of Matthew 27" (PhD diss., Union Theological Seminary, 1985).

[44] Ibid., xi.

[45] Ibid.

on, he notes that it "is the climax of the entire chapter" since it should be read as "portraying the consequences of Jesus' death."[46] According to Witherup, the silence of the historical scene is broken by means of the divine portents through which God speaks.[47] His final conclusion is that the pericope is "displaced" in the Matthean narrative. That is, Matthew has a literary tendency of completing a story line that he interjects into the main thought.[48] For Witherup, this solves the interpretive conundrum created by the phrase μετὰ τὴν ἔγερσιν αὐτοῦ (Matt. 27:53). Their resurrection further accentuates Jesus' resurrection as a climactic event. Matthew's intention in recording it in Matthew 27:52–53 is to proleptically prepare the reader for the events of Matthew 28:1–10.

Assessment. Though his literary interpretation of Matthew 27 accentuates the care with which Matthew crafted the passion narrative concluding his Gospel, Witherup's reading falls short by displacing a historical event from the historical scene in which it occurs. If Matthew intended for the resurrection of the saints to be read as a result of Jesus' resurrection, it seems odd that his placement of it is interjected into the midst of other cosmic portents that narrate events occurring as a result of his death, not his resurrection.

Ulrich Luz

In his Matthean commentary, after a redaction-critical analysis of the structure of Matthew 27:51–54 along with the sources utilized by Matthew to compose the passage, Luz offers an overview of the pericope's reception history and notes that interpretations of the passage are divided into five broad categories—the redemptive history interpretation, the christological interpretation, Christ's descent into hell, the allegorical interpretation, and the eschatological

---

[46] Witherup is inconsistent in this argumentation, though. He later contends the resurrection of the sleeping saints was caused by the resurrection of Jesus. Ibid., 277, 285.

[47] Ibid., 280.

[48] Ibid., 284.

interpretation.[49] This is, for Luz, the prolegomena for his own interpretation, which accentuates God's intervention in the narrative scene.[50] Repeatedly, he notes that Matthew is laboring to convey that the events surrounding Jesus' death are "acts of God" or "supernatural interventions" intended for self-revelatory purposes.[51] When it comes to the resurrection of the saints, he contends that though their resurrection does not belong to the general eschatological resurrection, the "saints" could have been any of the "righteous" throughout redemptive history.[52] Their presence in the narrative is a sign of God's coming judgment on the people of Israel and the city of Jerusalem.[53]

Ultimately, though, Luz admits the interpretive difficulty of the passage and suggests that it has "multiple levels of meaning."[54] He accentuates two levels of meaning in particular—the christological and the redemptive history dimensions of the text. Concerning the former, Luz suggests that the events recorded in Matthew 27:51–53 are "victory signs."[55] The self-revelation of God reaches its climax through these victory signs in the resurrection of the saints. Regarding the latter category, Luz accentuates God's revelation of the impending judgment on Jerusalem. The temple is rendered obsolete and the future faith of the redeemed will no longer be geographically or ethnically confined; rather, it will go with Jesus and those who place their faith in him.[56]

Assessment. Luz rightly notes that Matthew is communicating

---

[49] Ulrich Luz, *Matthew 21–28*, trans. James E. Crouch, ed. Helmut Koester, Hermeneia (Minneapolis: Fortress Press, 2005), 560–65.

[50] Ibid., 566–70.

[51] Ibid., 566. Later, he connects the self-revelatory events with the centurion's profession. Based on God's revelation of Jesus' identity, the centurion confesses Jesus to be the Son of God as the disciples had done previously.

[52] Ibid., 567.

[53] Ibid., 568.

[54] Ibid., 570.

[55] Ibid., 571.

[56] Ibid.

multiple truths simultaneously in his Gospel by means of the pericope under discussion. Yet he fails to note literarily how Matthew has employed the passage broadly in Matthew 27:45–28:15. Further, he admits that he has no satisfactory explanation for the phrase μετὰ τὴν ἔγερσιν αὐτοῦ.[57]

R. T. France

In his commentary, France notes that Matthew's material in Matthew 27:52–53 is "special material"[58] in that it has no parallel in the other Gospel accounts.[59] Further, he contends that Matthew's lack of concern with "explaining" the meaning of the resurrection of the saints in his Gospel is due to the fact that he is concerned primarily with its symbolic significance.[60] Matthew's placement of the scene within the narrative connects Jesus' death with his resurrection as the "key to new life which is now made available to God's people."[61] Thus, he contends, contrary to J. W. Wenham, that Matthew's series of paratactic clauses with aorist verbs should not be broken up in order to interpret the resurrection of the saints as happening after Jesus' resurrection. Rather, like Wenham, he argues that they did not come out of their tombs until after Jesus' resurrection, because their resurrection was the "consequence" of his resurrection from the dead."[62]

Assessment. Though France rightly contends that Wenham's reading of the Matthean pericope unnaturally breaks up the paratactic clauses with aorist verbs, he fails to note that Matthew's placement of the pericope in his Gospel is not "out of order." Rather,

---

[57] Ibid., 568–69.

[58] France is one among many scholars who refer to Matt. 27:51b–53 as Matthew's "special material" since several of these portents are unique to his Gospel. See also Gurtner, *Torn Veil*, 144–52.

[59] R. T. France, *The Gospel of Matthew*, NICNT (Grand Rapids: Eerdmans, 2007), 1081.

[60] Ibid.

[61] Ibid., 1082.

[62] Ibid.

having already been "resurrected" on the day of Jesus' death, the saints leave the area of the tombs to enter the holy city after his resurrection.

Michael Licona

Licona's *The Resurrection of Jesus: A New Historiographical Approach* is a defense of the historicity of Jesus' bodily resurrection from the dead. He challenges the presuppositional claims of post-Enlightenment biblical interpreters who contend that historical evidence of Jesus' resurrection is inaccessible to the modern historian.[63] He contends that the best evaluation of the evidence, for those who do not engage the evidence with a priori commitments to the impossibility of the resurrection, commends belief in Jesus' bodily, historical resurrection from the dead. In fact, he asserts, "There is no indication that the early Christians interpreted Jesus' resurrection in a metaphorical or poetic sense to the exclusion of it being a literal event that had occurred to his corpse. Indeed, that a bodily resurrection was the primary intended interpretation seems clear."[64]

Licona does not merely assert the historicity of the resurrection of Jesus; he also states that "the canonical Evangelists and Paul intended their statements regarding Jesus' *death* by crucifixion to be interpreted literally."[65] It is unexpected, therefore, when Licona writes that "the data surrounding what happened to Jesus is fragmentary and could possibly be mixed with legend" in reference to the scene of the resurrected saints in Matthew 27:51–54.[66] Further, considering his adamancy that Jesus' death and resurrection are historical, it is inconsistent when Licona suggests that the narrative scene surrounding Jesus' death is "theologically adorned" with conceivably ahistorical

---

[63] He responds to two leading well-known advocates who deny Jesus' resurrection from the dead: Bart Ehrman and John Dominic Crossan.

[64] Michael Licona, *The Resurrection of Jesus: A New Historiographical Approach* (Downers Grove, IL: InterVarsity Press, 2010), 553.

[65] Ibid., 545, emphasis original.

[66] Ibid., 185.

events—such as the darkness (Matt. 27:45), the tearing of the veil (Matt. 27:51), and the resurrection of the saints (Matt. 27:52–53). The latter, he suggests, is metaphorical[67] and connotes eschatological imagery.[68] After surveying both Jewish and Roman literature in relation to resurrection as well as to the death of an emperor/king, in his final assessment of the pericope he suggests the following:

> Given the presence of phenomenological language in a symbolic manner in both Jewish and Roman literature related to a major event such as the death of an emperor or the end of a reigning king or even a kingdom, the presence of ambiguity in the relevant text of Ignatius, and that so very little can be known about Thallus' comment on the darkness (including whether he was even referring to the darkness at the time of Jesus' crucifixion or, if so, if he was merely speculating pertaining to a natural cause of the darkness claimed by early Christians), it seems to me that an understanding of the language in Matthew 27:52–53 as "special effects" with eschatological Jewish texts and thought in mind is most plausible. There is further support for this interpretation. If the tombs opened and the saints being raised upon Jesus' death was not strange enough, Matthew adds that they did not come out of their tombs until after Jesus' resurrection.[69]

Thus, Licona contends that the phenomena surrounding Jesus' death should be interpreted as "poetic device" and eschatologically

---

[67] Licona refers to Matt. 27:52–53 as "that strange little text in Matthew 27:52–53, where upon Jesus' death the dead saints are raised and walk into the city of Jerusalem," ibid., 545–46. Further, he notes Mark and Luke record some of the phenomena surrounding Jesus' death—the darkness covering the land and the rending of the temple's inner veil—but it is Matthew alone who records the earthquake, the rocks splitting, the tombs opening, the raising of the dead saints, and their subsequent entrance into Jerusalem.
[68] Ibid., 550.
[69] Ibid., 552.

flavored "special effects" used by Matthew to communicate to his readers that Jesus died as the Son of God and that an impending judgment awaits Israel.[70] Licona adopts this position as a rebuttal to Crossan's metaphorical interpretation of Jesus' resurrection from the dead. Licona argues that it is the idea of "the harrowing of hell" that "most strongly persuades Crossan to go with a metaphorical understanding of Jesus' resurrection."[71] It is because he rejects the way this text has been appropriated to argue for the harrowing of hell and against Jesus' bodily, historical resurrection that Licona finds himself denying the historicity of these cosmic portents.[72]

Assessment. Licona's work is magisterial in the breadth of its analysis. Unfortunately, in relation to Matthew 27:51–54, he is unable to reconcile how Matthew's work is both historical *and* eschatologically flavored. The events surrounding Jesus' death have an apocalyptic "feel" as they accentuate the cosmic impact of the occasion and manifest the end of the temple as the mediator of God's soteriological blessings to the Jewish people and the foreign nations.[73] Yet Matthew records historical events.

---

[70] Ibid., 553. Though he understands some of the events surrounding Jesus' death to be poetic device, he contends that "interpreting the phenomena at Jesus' death as poetry does not lend support to interpreting Jesus' bodily resurrection as nothing more than a poetic or symbolic device."

[71] Ibid., 546.

[72] Ibid., 546–48, 552.

[73] Though his work is highly acclaimed, Licona's interpretation of this Matthean pericope resulted in interpretive-evangelical tumult from two leading figures in particular—Norman L. Geisler and R. Albert Mohler, Jr. Mohler's assessment of Licona's work can be found here: R. Albert Mohler, Jr., "The Devil Is in the Details: Biblical Inerrancy and the Licona Controversy," *AlbertMohler.com*, September 14, 2011, accessed September 14, 2011, http://www.albertmohler.com/2011/09/14/the-devil-is-in-the-details-biblical-inerrancy-and-the-licona-controversy/. Geisler's numerous interactions with Licona and his work can be accessed here: Norman L. Geisler, "'Licona Controversy' Articles," *NormanGeisler.net*, accessed February 11, 2014, http://normangeisler.com/licona-articles/. Even though Licona adamantly affirms the historicity of both Jesus' death on the cross as well as his bodily resurrection from the dead, Mohler's and Geisler's concern is with the implication(s) of denying the

Douglas W. Anderson

With the guidance of Paul Trebilco and Ivor Davidson, Douglas W. Anderson wrote his dissertation on the Gospel of Matthew, specifically on Matthew 27:51–53—"The Origin and Purpose of Matthew 27:51b–53."[74] His thesis "argues that Matt 27:51b-53 is not a Matthean literary creation but rather is a fragment of a very early Jewish Christian passion tradition, a tradition closely related to some Jewish expectations of what the Messiah's coming would achieve."[75] Further, Anderson argues that Matthew 27:51b–53 is an attempt to "reconcile two contradictory positions: (i) a Jewish belief that the Messiah's coming would initiate the final End, and (ii) the Christian belief that Jesus the Messiah's advent initiated the age of salvation but not the final End."[76] The whole Gospel narrative, according to Anderson, "reflects the thought of Israel as the covenant people of God."[77] Therefore, Anderson suggests the following:

> Matthew has used Matt 27:51b-53 to express, and highlight, the basic message of his narrative: that as the loyal

---

historicity of events occurring within a scene that is historical—namely, Matt. 27:45–54. Since the aftermath of this interpretive argument was so public, Southeastern Baptist Theological Seminary devoted an entire journal to the assessment of the theme of resurrection, Licona's work, and the implications of Licona's arguments. That assessment can be found here: Heath Thomas, ed., *Southeastern Theological Review* 3, 1 (Summer 2012): 55–98. Since the thesis of this paper affirms the historicity of these portents and is not an analysis of the relationship between interpretation and inerrancy, I do not explicate these arguments here.

[74] Douglas William Anderson, "The Origin and Purpose of Matthew 27:51b–53" (PhD diss., University of Otago Seminary, 2014). Anderson's work can be accessed digitally here: https://ourarchive.otago.ac.nz/bitstream/handle/10523/4962/AndersonDouglasW2014PhD.pdf?sequence=1&isAllowed=y.

[75] Ibid., i.

[76] Anderson, "Origin and Purpose of Matthew 27:51b–53," 330.

[77] Ibid.

and obedient vassal of the Lord God, Jesus, the Messiah, has through his death defeated Satan, initiated the final Eschaton, and created a whole new people of God—the Church. This new people consists of saints from both OT times as well as from the NT era. Further, and significantly, it includes Gentiles as well as Jews (Matt 27:54).[78]

Anderson contends that Matthew 27:51–53 is to be interpreted in the context of covenant—that is, "Matthew's Gospel is a document reflecting the establishing in OT times of the covenant people, Israel."[79]

Assessment. Anderson's work must be applauded for its breadth and scope. With thoroughness appropriate only to doctoral dissertations, he carefully navigates the works of major interpreters weighing in on one's understanding of Matthew 27:51–53. However, Anderson's covenantal reading has some interpretive problems. He writes,

> Thus, according to Matthew, not just the nation of Israel, *but Jesus himself was in a covenantal relationship with God*, his heavenly Father. Being in this covenantal relationship Jesus was at all times obedient to his Father's will (contrast the disobedient Israel). According to Matthew, Jesus' obedience eventually resulted in his death on the cross. From Matthew's point of view Jesus' death was not only a miscarriage of justice—it was also the supreme moment of his life of obedience. Accordingly, this thesis suggests that to express the significance and accomplishments of Jesus' supreme act of covenantal obedience, Matthew made use of Matt 27:51b–53.[80]

---

[78] Ibid.

[79] The concept of "covenant" is central to Anderson's understanding of Matt. 27:51–53. See especially ibid., 312–23.

[80] Ibid., 313–14 (emphasis added).

The Resurrected Saints

Matthew may have used this pericope to accentuate Jesus' initiation of the final eschaton through his death on the cross; he may have intended for his readers to see that Jesus' death and resurrection created the new servant people of God—the church.[81] But Anderson's covenantal reading of Matthew 27:51–53 wrongly asserts that Jesus himself is in covenantal relationship with God.[82] Jesus is the mediator of the new covenant, not a participant in it (Heb. 8:6). He inaugurated the new covenant and is its executor. But he is in no way in "covenant relationship" with the Father (Heb. 7:22–28; 8:1–13; 9:11–28; 10:1–18). Anderson's reading falls short by focusing primarily on the (debatable) covenantal aspects of this Matthean pericope to the neglect of the christological, missiological, and eschatological foci overflowing from Matthew 27:51–54.[83]

Further, though Anderson acknowledges the existence of textual correspondences between Matthew 27:51b–53 and Matthew 28:1–6, he wrongly excludes Matthew 27:51a from consideration in his thesis.[84] This exclusion contributes to the placement of excessive interpretive stress on each of the individual portents in Matthew 27:51–54. Thus, Anderson's thesis inadvertently focuses on one portent in particular, to the exclusion of the others contained within the pericope.[85] But Matthew 27:52b–53 is not the central portent

---

[81] Ibid., 330.

[82] When speaking of Jesus' covenantal relationship with God, Anderson suggests, "Matthew presents Jesus as being under *divine obligation* to lay his life as a ransom for others" (ibid., 69 [emphasis added]). However, the Gospel of John explicitly presents Jesus as having absolute control of his destiny in relation to the salvation of sinners; he is under no obligation (see John 10:11, 17–18). Rather, without compulsion, Jesus willingly offers his life for the elect.

[83] Though he may not affirm my critique, Anderson acknowledges the limitations of his thesis when he writes, "I also readily acknowledge that this contention reflects my own background and subjective presuppositions. While using various aspects of the historical-critical method to study Matt 27:51b-53, I do not claim to be completely disinterested, or to have achieved anything like objective truth" (ibid., 325).

[84] Ibid., 159–62.

[85] Ibid., 313, 320, 324. This dissertation will suggest that focus on the

in the pericope. Rather, it is merely one of five portents within the death-resurrection conclusion of Matthew's Gospel. This dissertation's suggestion of a literary reading of the death-resurrection scene mitigates this interpretive stress.

Thesis

In light of the interpretive problems surrounding Matthew 27:51–54 as well as its recent history of research, this dissertation's thesis propounds that both Matthean resurrection pericopes (Matt. 27:51–54 and 28:1–10) must be fused and read together in order to understand the theological significance of Matthew 27:51–54. Over time, an interpretive dichotomy evolved that separated the historicity of the act itself and its placement in the Gospel from its theological meaning. A literary reading of Matthew 27:51–54 incorporates the entire scope of the death-resurrection narrative so that it is properly interpreted in light of the entire death-resurrection scene rather than isolated as a singular phenomenological occurrence. By failing to observe Matthew's purposeful narrative strategy that informs the literary parallelism of Matthew 27:51–54 alongside 28:1–10, as well as the intentional placement of Matthew 27:51–54 within the death-resurrection scene (Matt. 27:45–28:20), the interpretation of Matthew 27:51–54 has been obscured. By properly understanding the pericope's translation, its primary Old Testament referent, and its compositional structure and placement, interpreters will be able to ascertain (1) how Matthew 27:51–54 is functioning in the death-resurrection scene and (2) the three theological foci of the pericope—Christology, missiology, and eschatology. Failure to observe the intentional structure of Matthew 27:51–54 as a strategic pericope in the death-resurrection

---

function of the portents in Matt. 27:51b–53 rather than the function of the entire pericope within the death-resurrection scene (Matt. 27:45–28:20) places hermeneutical pressure on the Matthean passage.

scene of Matthew's Gospel places inordinate interpretive stress on the five divine portents, particularly the resurrection of the sleeping saints (Matt. 27:52b–53).

Regarding the theological significance of Matthew 27:51–54, some of the missiological implications are manifested in how the pharisaic naysayers challenged Jesus' divine sonship (Matt. 27:40, 43), and it is precisely the signs surrounding his horrific death that testify so loudly that even the Gentiles believe (Matt. 27:54). Thus, the "lesser" resurrection of the saints proleptically anticipates the "greater" resurrection of Jesus in the Matthean narrative and visibly manifests Jesus' identity as the Son of God. The "lesser" resurrection of the saints proleptically anticipates the gospel mission to the ends of the earth (Matt. 28:16–20).

Further, a thorough perusal of the Matthean passion narrative manifests the intentional literary parallelism used by the Gospel author to accentuate three theological foci—namely, the christological impact of the scene, a missiological agenda for the world, and eschatological implications as the temple cultus is rendered obsolete. This can be seen in table 1.1 below.

While many interpreters may be able to recall a plethora of proposed literary readings that have, in many ways, overextended themselves hermeneutically, Matthew's literary intentionality in the conclusion of his narrative is manifest. As he has at other points within his Gospel, Matthew utilizes literary parallelism to emphasize theological truth as well as Jesus' identity. Two character examples from the narrative's introduction, along with an example from the scenes surrounding Jesus' birth and death and one macro-structural example of the Gospel, will suffice to manifest his intentionality in the use of this literary device.[86]

---

[86] For more on narrative design as well as literary intentionality in the Gospels, see Timothy Wiarda, *Interpreting Gospel Narratives: Scenes, People, and Theology* (Nashville: B&H Publishing, 2010).

Table 1.1. Literary Parallelism in Matthew 27–28

Matthew 27:45–66	Matthew 27:62–28:15
darkness (27:45) σκότος	dawn (28:1) τῇ ἐπιφωσκούσῃ
earth shook (27:51) ἡ γῆ ἐσείσθη	earthquake (28:2) σεισμὸς
raised (27:52) ἠγέρθησαν	risen (28:6) ἠγέρθη
tomb (27:52–53) τὰ μνημεῖα … τῶν μνημεῖα	tomb (28:1) τὸν τάφον
the holy city (27:53)[87] εἰς τὴν ἁγίαν πόλιν	the city (28:11) εἰς τὴν πόλιν
centurion (27:54)—ὁ ἑκατόνταρχος	those guarding (28:4)— οἱ τηροῦντες the guards (28:11)— τῆς κουστωδίας soldiers (28:12)— τοῖς στρατιώταις

---

[87] Note the *inclusio* with Matt. 4:5—εἰς τὴν ἁγίαν πόλιν. Previously, after the baptismal scene in which God the Father identifies Jesus as the beloved Son with whom he is pleased (3:17), Satan challenged Jesus, attempting to incite him to take the initiative to identify himself as "the Son of God"—εἰ υἱὸς εἶ τοῦ θεοῦ—but Jesus refused (4:6–7). Similarly, the scene prior to the pericope under consideration reads like an antibaptismal scene—reversing the scene that precedes Jesus' temptation in the wilderness. Formerly, Jesus had spoken (3:15), the Spirit descended on him (3:16), and the Father audibly testified from heaven to his identify (3:17); now, after crying out with a loud voice twice (27:46, 50) an unnerving silence pervades the scene before Jesus yields the Spirit and dies (27:50). It is only after Jesus' death that Matthew notes how

fear (27:54) ἐφοβήθησαν	fear (28:4, 5, 8, 10) φόβου ... φοβεῖσθε ... φόβου ... φοβεῖσθε
genuine profession (27:54)	false profession (28:13–15)
Mary Magdalene and Mary (27:56) Μαριά ἡ Μαγδαληνὴ καὶ Μαρία	Mary Magdalene ... Mary (28:1) Μαριὰμ ἡ Μαγδαληνὴ ... Μαρία
Joseph of Arimathea before Pilate (27:57)	the chief priests before Pilate (27:62)
great stone (27:60) λίθον μέγαν	the stone (28:2) τὸν λίθον
attempt to guard the tomb (27:62–66)	inability to guard the tomb (28:4)

First, King Herod (Matt. 2:1) is literarily paralleled with Jesus, the newborn King of the Jews (Matt. 2:2). The archetype of the longed-for Davidic king has arrived in Jesus; unlike Herod's reign, Christ's kingdom is not frustrated by "rival" rulers. Second, the beginning of Jesus' earthly ministry is literarily paralleled with the beginning of John the Baptist's earthly ministry—both have wilderness experiences (Matt. 3:1; 4:1) and both begin their homiletical endeavors by heralding the same message: "Repent, for the kingdom of heaven is at hand" (Matt. 3:2; 4:17). The prophet like Moses has come *in* the person of Jesus (Deut. 18:15–22; John 6:14). He is greater than John. He leads righteously through the wilderness

---

the Father testified to Jesus' identity as the "the Son of God" by means of the cosmological and apocalyptic imagery that dominates this historical scene.

without succumbing to temptation as did Adam and Moses (Gen. 3:6; Num. 20:10–13).

Third, scenes surrounding Jesus' birth are literarily paralleled with scenes surrounding his death. Thus, when Jesus was born, children were slaughtered (Matt. 2:16); when Jesus died, the dead were raised to life (Matt. 27:52). Fourth, Matthew has employed literary parallelism by contrasting characters and scenes not only within his narrative but also in the structure of his work as a whole.[88]

---

[88] Lohr argues for a similar structure of Matthew's Gospel. See Charles H. Lohr, "Oral Techniques in the Gospel of Matthew," *CBQ* 23 (1961): 427. He, too, places Matt. 23 in the eschatological sermonic discourse. For a critique of Lohr's position, see Jerome Murphy-O'Connor, "The Structure of Matthew XIV–XVIII," *RB* 82 (1975): 369–71. Murphy-O'Connor's strongest contention is that placing Matt. 23 with Matt. 19–22 accentuates the correspondence between the first sermonic discourse, Matt. 5–7, and the last sermonic-discourse, Matt. 24–25. In this case, both sermonic discourses would be addressed to Jesus' disciples; his disciples would be, according to Murphy-O'Connor, distinguished from the crowds within Matthew's Gospel. Additionally, Murphy-O'Connor contends that this makes obvious the deliberate intention of Matthew to make the five sermonic discourses one of the major components of his Gospel. Murphy-O'Connor argues that this is indisputable by the phrase καὶ ἐγένετο ὅτε ἐτέλεσσεν ὁ Ἰησοῦς, which is used only fives times throughout the Gospel. However, for a defense of Lohr's position, see Jason Hood, "Matthew 23–25: The Extent of Jesus' Fifth Discourse," *JBL* 3 (2009): 527–43. Contra Murphy-O'Connor, Hood suggests that the inclusion of Matt. 23 in the eschatological sermonic discourse "encourages investigation of the oft-ignored close correlations of chap. 5 and chap. 23 (particularly the 'blessings and curses' and their contexts) and the important correlation of the first and fifth discourses in their entirety." Jonathan Pennington also notes that chap. 13 forms the chiastic center of Matthew. For Pennington, this accentuates "the centrality of the message of the coming of the Kingdom of God." Jonathan T. Pennington, *Heaven and Earth in the Gospel of Matthew* (Grand Rapids: Baker Academic, 2009), 280–81. Further, via Pennington, table 1.2 manifests a "sermon" then "narrative" structure throughout the Gospel rather than "narrative" then "sermon." Though preceding interpreters have noted that the discourses were either sermons or material collected from several of Jesus' sermons, the phrase "sermonic discourse" is original to this dissertation's author. The phrase is used intentionally to emphasize the homiletical nature of the Matthean discourses.

Table 1.2. Macro-Chiastic Structure of Matthew's Gospel

					1–4	Introduction: Birth and Beginnings of Jesus' Earthly Ministry
				5–7		Sermonic Discourse: Sermon on the Mount / Entering the Kingdom of Heaven
			8–9			Narrative Discourse: The Authority of Jesus to Heal
		10				Sermonic Discourse: Missiological Sermon to the Community
	11–12					Narrative Discourse: Rejection of Jesus as the Christ by This Generation
13						Sermonic Discourse: Parabolic Sermon on the Kingdom of Heaven
	14–17					Narrative Discourse: Recognition of Jesus as the Christ by the Disciples
		18				Sermonic Discourse: Ecclesiological Sermon to the Community
			19–22			Narrative Discourse: The Authority of Jesus Challenged
				23–25		Sermonic Discourse: Eschatological Discourse/Coming of the KOH
					26–28	Conclusion: Death and End of Jesus' Earthly Ministry

The Resurrected Saints

The question, then, is *why* Matthew employed this intentionality in Matthew 27:45–28:15. It seems his literary parallelism is intended to accentuate Jesus' identity as the Son of God—the earth he created mourns (Matt. 27:45) and breaks (Matt. 27:51) at his death, giving back the dead as a testimony to his dominion as the Son of God (Matt. 28:18). Further, Matthew's intentionality in literary parallelism is intended to accentuate the mission his death necessitates—his death is life-giving and ultimately salvific for persons from every nation who profess faith in his name (Matt. 28:16–20; cf. 27:54). By dying and being buried in a tomb, Jesus bears much fruit, just as the seed of wheat does by falling to the earth (John 12:24).[89] The eschatological significance(s) embedded in the rending of the temple veil have missiological import. Thus, Matthew concludes his Gospel with an *inclusio* that has missiological implications, for Jesus "bears fruit" through the disciples he promises to be with until the end of the age as they are on mission for the renown of the triune name (Matt. 28:20; cf. 1:23).

This is significant both for our interpretation of the discourse (they are sermons/sermonic) as well as for our proclamation of the text—Matthew's Gospel was intended to model one aspect of *how* to preach about the kingdom of heaven now that it has been πληρῶσαι in Christ (Matt. 5:17). It seems, then, that the homiletical goals of Matthew informed his composition of the sermonic discourse in that he crafted his Gospel (1) to solicit a certain type of response to the kingdom of heaven and (2) to model for his readers how to preach authoritatively, like Jesus, about the kingdom of heaven—ἦν γὰρ διδάσκων αὐτοὺς ὡς ἐξουσίαν ἔχων (Matt. 7:29). Though referring to the Sermon on the Mount, Pelikan notes that homileticians can take their sermonic cues from the great Rhetor, Jesus Christ, who perfectly wed form with content. This model is seen in the sermonic discourses crafted by Matthew in his Gospel. See Jaroslav Pelikan. *Divine Rhetoric: The Sermon on the Mount as Message and Model in Augustine, Chrysostom, and Luther* (Crestwood, NY: St. Vladimir's Seminary Press, 2000), 48.

[89] Matthew is clear, though, that it is only a life-giving death for those who love God instead of mammon (Matt. 28:11–15; cf. 6:24).

Conclusion

This dissertation suggests that bifurcating the Matthean resurrection pericopes places undue interpretive stress on each of the five individual portents within Matthew 27:51–54, which has led to a separation of the historicity of the act itself and its placement in the Gospel from its theological meaning. Moreover, interpretive stress has guided interpreters to focus on minor speculative questions related to Matthew 27:52b–53 (What kind of bodies did the resurrected dead possess? Who were they? How many people saw them?) rather than how Matthew 27:51–54 is functioning in the death-resurrection scene and the three theological foci of the pericope—Christology, missiology, and eschatology. A literary reading of the death-resurrection scene mitigates this interpretive stress. For what many interpreters have often taken to be the central portent (Matt. 27:52b–53) is merely one of five portents within the death-resurrection conclusion of Matthew's Gospel.

2

Translating Matthew 27:51–54

The interpretive predicament in the pericope under consideration is obviated by recognizing that both Matthean resurrection pericopes (Matt. 27:51–54 and 28:1–10) must be fused and read together in order to understand the theological significance of Matthew 27:51–54. When this connection is not maintained and Matthew's intentional narrative placement and strategy are not observed, the interpretation of Matthew 27:51–54 is obscured and inordinate interpretive stress is placed on the five divine portents, particularly the resurrection of the sleeping saints (Matt. 27:52b–53). This has led to an an interpretive dichotomy that separates the historicity of the act itself from its theological meaning.

Therefore, it is necessary to address the issue of translation in relation to Matthew 27:51–54.[1] That is, "What is the most natural

---

[1] I would like to thank Charles Quarles in allowing me to view a pre-published version of his paper presented at the 2014 annual ETS conference in San Diego, CA. See Charles Quarles, "Matthew 27:51–53 as a Scribal Interpolation: Testing a Recent Proposal," paper presented at the Evangelical Theological Society National Conference, San Diego, California, November 19–21, 2014. In this academic address, Quarles skillfully demonstrates that the pericope under consideration in this dissertation is original to the Matthean narrative. Furthermore, his address, contra Craig Evans, amply demonstrates awareness of this pericope among early church interpreters such as Ignatius of Antioch, Egerton Papyrus 3, Tertullian, Clement of Alexandria, Julius

translation of the Matthean pericope?" Since there is currently no Matthean pericope more ferociously debated in contemporary evangelicalism than this scene surrounding Jesus' death on the cross, it is necessary to examine the translation of Matthew 27:51–54. This chapter will argue, contra Wenham, that a comma at the end of Matthew 27:51 is more grammatically appropriate because it links the five signs that occur as a result of Jesus' death on the cross after he yields τὸ πνεῦμα (Matt. 27:50).[2] Furthermore, a semicolon at the end of Matthew 27:52 will be advocated since it suggests a close relationship between the resurrection of the saints and their emergence from their graves that a period does not sufficiently indicate.[3]

Africanus, and Origen. He concludes that both internal as well as external evidences testify to the originality of this Matthean pericope, making a theory of interpolation highly doubtful. Therefore, this chapter will assume the originality of the Matthean text and will not discuss external evidence relating to the textual tradition of this pericope.

[2] Blaine Charette contends that Jesus' yielding his τὸ πνυεμα in Matt. 27:50–54 is a reference to the Spirit of God rather than an anthropological indirect reference to Jesus' life. See Blaine Charette, *Restoring Presence: The Spirit in Matthew's Gospel*, JPTSup 18 (Sheffield: Sheffield Academic Press, 2000), 92–97. Additionally, Charette connects the τὸ πνυεμα released by Jesus in Matt. 27:50 with the τὸ πνυεμα that descended on him at his baptism in Matt. 3:16, arguing, "It is important to recall that earlier at the temptation the term [τοῦ πνεύματος] clearly refers to the Spirit of God [i.e., τὸ πνυεμα] which had come upon Jesus at his baptism. It is therefore at least possible Matthew is now describing the 'letting go' of that same Spirit at the moment of Jesus' death." See Blaine Charette, "'Never Has Anything like This Been Seen in Israel': The Spirit as Eschatological Sign in Matthew's Gospel," *JPT* 8 (1996): 31–51. Interestingly, careful readers will notice that the temptation narrative and the signs surrounding the crucifixion scene are further linked by the phrase εἰς τὴν ἁγίαν πόλιν (Matt. 4:5; 27:53). France, however, suggests there is no evidence in the scene for any reference to the Holy Spirit. See R. T. France, *The Gospel of Mark*, NIGTC (Downers Grove, IL: InterVarsity Press, 1989), 655.

[3] The connection between the resurrection of the saints and their entrance εἰς τὴν ἁγίαν πόλιν (Matt. 27:53; cf. 4:5) will be discussed more fully when exploring Ezek. 37:12–14 as the primary Old Testament passage Matthew is relying on in the composition of his Gospel narrative. Though interpreters

Translating Matthew 27:51–54

A reading that tethers the signs in Matthew 27:51–54 with the events of Good Friday accentuates the three theological foci Matthew is featuring in his Gospel's conclusion: Christology, missiology, and eschatology. Indeed, for Matthew, the βασιλεία has broken into the present *in* the person of Jesus (Matt. 4:17; cf. 3:2; 10:7). Thus, by virtue of his identity (Matt. 27:54; cf. 3:17; 16:16; 17:5), his life (as well as his life-giving death) necessitates a mission to the ends of the earth because his death and resurrection has implications for the world.[4]

J. W. Wenham

In 1981, J. W. Wenham published his article "When Were the Saints Raised? A Note on the Punctuation of Matthew xxvii. 51–53,"

---

point to a number of texts that informed Matthew's composition of this pericope—2 Sam. 22:8; Jer. 8:1–3; 15:9; Ezek. 37:12–14; Dan. 12:2; Amos 8:9; Zech. 14:4–5—this dissertation contends Ezek. 37 is the primary text informing Matthean Gospel composition. For those proposing numerous influences, see the following resources: Charette, *Restoring Presence*, 84–97; Rafael Monasterio, *Exegesis de Mateo, 27, 51b–53: para una teologia de la muerte de Jesus en el Evangelio de Mateo* (Vitoria: Eset, 1980); and Charles Quarles, "Matthew 27:51–53: Meaning, Genre, Intertextuality, Theology, and Reception History," *JETS* 59, 2 (2016): 271–86.

[4] Not only is the narration of Jesus' divine identity replete throughout the Gospel, it is proclaimed from the lips of both Jewish and pagan characters in Matthew's Gospel. Careful readers will observe in the Matthean narrative of Jesus' death that the profession of Jesus' divine identity is on the lips of the Gentile crowd—ἀληθῶς θεοῦ υἱός (Matt. 27:54). This is the same profession that was uttered from the mouths of Jesus' disciples earlier in Matthew's Gospel—ἀληθῶς θεοῦ υἱός (Matt. 14:33). Matthew's intentionality in placing this profession in the mouths of both Jewish and Gentile audiences in his Gospel underscores the missiological, salvation-historical significance of Jesus' work on the cross. As Gentiles were grafted into his genealogical line—Rahab and Ruth (Matt. 1:5)—so they are grafted into his eschatological kingdom by placing faith in his name (Matt. 27:54; 28:16–20; cf. Rom. 11:11–24). Ironically, what the high priest questioned—ἡμῖν εἴπῃς εἰ σὺ ὁ υἱὸς τοῦ θεοῦ (Matt. 26:63)—the centurion affirms (Matt. 27:54).

which argued for a full-stop punctuation in the middle of Matthew 27:52.[5] He suggested that it was inappropriate for translators to translate ἀνεῴχθησαν without punctuation because it wrongly ties the resurrection of τῶν . . . ἁγίων to events that occurred on Good Friday after Jesus yielded up τὸ πνεῦμα on the cross (Matt. 27:50). According to Wenham, the resurrection of the saints is an event "which no one could pretend to have witnessed."[6] For Wenham, it is absurd to conclude that Matthew is implying that these resurrected dead sat invigorated with life yet dormant in their respective crypts for three days while Jesus lay in his tomb.

To substantiate his thesis, Wenham argues that καὶ ἐξελθόντες . . . πολλοῖς forms a partial parenthesis that invades the narrative of Good Friday but narrates events that took place *after* Jesus' resurrection.[7] The words καὶ ἐξελθόντες . . . πολλοῖς are parenthetical, but they lack a subject within the versification in which they are currently found. Rather, he argues that the subject is found in the previous verse (πολλὰ σώματα; Matthew 27:52) and postulates that it makes more linguistic sense for the subject to be tied to the events that follow it instead of the events that precede it.[8] Consequently, he contends that this tidily places the resurrection of the saints with the events that follow instead of the events that precede—namely, he claims that the saints are both resurrected *and* come out of the tombs on Easter Sunday *after* Jesus' resurrection from the dead.[9] This reading of the Matthean crucifixion narrative alleviates Wenham's interpretive concern that the saints were resurrected while remaining in or around their respective tombs until Jesus is raised from the dead in his narrative (Matt. 28:1–10). He writes,

---

[5] J. W. Wenham, "When Were the Saints Raised?," *JTS* 32, 1 (1981): 150–52.
[6] Ibid., 150.
[7] Ibid., 151.
[8] Ibid.
[9] Ibid.

Translating Matthew 27:51–54

Then the succession of events on Good Friday is clearly delineated, and the whole episode of the resurrected saints is placed after the resurrection of Jesus, thus *absolving* the evangelist from the charge of depicting living saints cooped up for days in tombs around the city. Admittedly Matthew would have *expressed himself with greater elegance and lucidity* if he had placed his μετὰ τὴν ἔγερσιν αὐτοῦ at the beginning of the sentence. But do we not all from time to time start sentences which *threaten to prove misleading* and then *clumsily* modify them?[10]

According to Wenham's hypothesis, then, the most accurate translation of Matthew 27:51–53 would read as follows: "Behold, the curtain of the temple was torn in two from top to bottom and the earth quaked and the rocks split and the tombs were opened. And, many bodies of the saints who had fallen asleep were raised and came out of the tombs after [Jesus'] resurrection and they went into the holy city and appeared to many." According to Wenham's translation of the passage, the crucifixion pericope should be pictorially diagrammed as below (see fig. 2.1).

---

[10] Ibid., 151 (emphasis mine). Though striving for interpretive clarity is admirable, Wenham's (false) assumption that Matthew would compose his crucifixion scene so carelessly contradicts the idea that the biblical author was exceptionally intentional in crafting his Gospel narrative. Currently, a broad scholarly consensus affirms Matthean intentionality in his Gospel-prose composition. He did not mince words, record useless phrases, or haphazardly cobble together his Gospel. For more on the compositional intentionality of this literary Gospel-artist, see Richard B. Hays, *Reading Backwards: Figural Christology and the Fourfold Gospel Witness* (Waco, TX: Baylor University Press, 2014), 35–53; Timothy Wiarda, *Interpreting Gospel Narratives: Scenes, People, and Theology* (Nashville: B&H Publishing, 2010), 180–87, 216–28; Peter J. Leithart, *The Four: A Survey of the Gospels* (Moscow, ID: Canon Press, 2010), 117–48; Peter J. Leithart, *Deep Exegesis: The Mystery of Reading Scripture* (Waco, TX: Baylor University Press, 2009); and Jonathan Pennington, *Reading the Gospels Wisely: A Narrative and Theological Introduction* (Grand Rapids: Baker, 2012), 169–82.

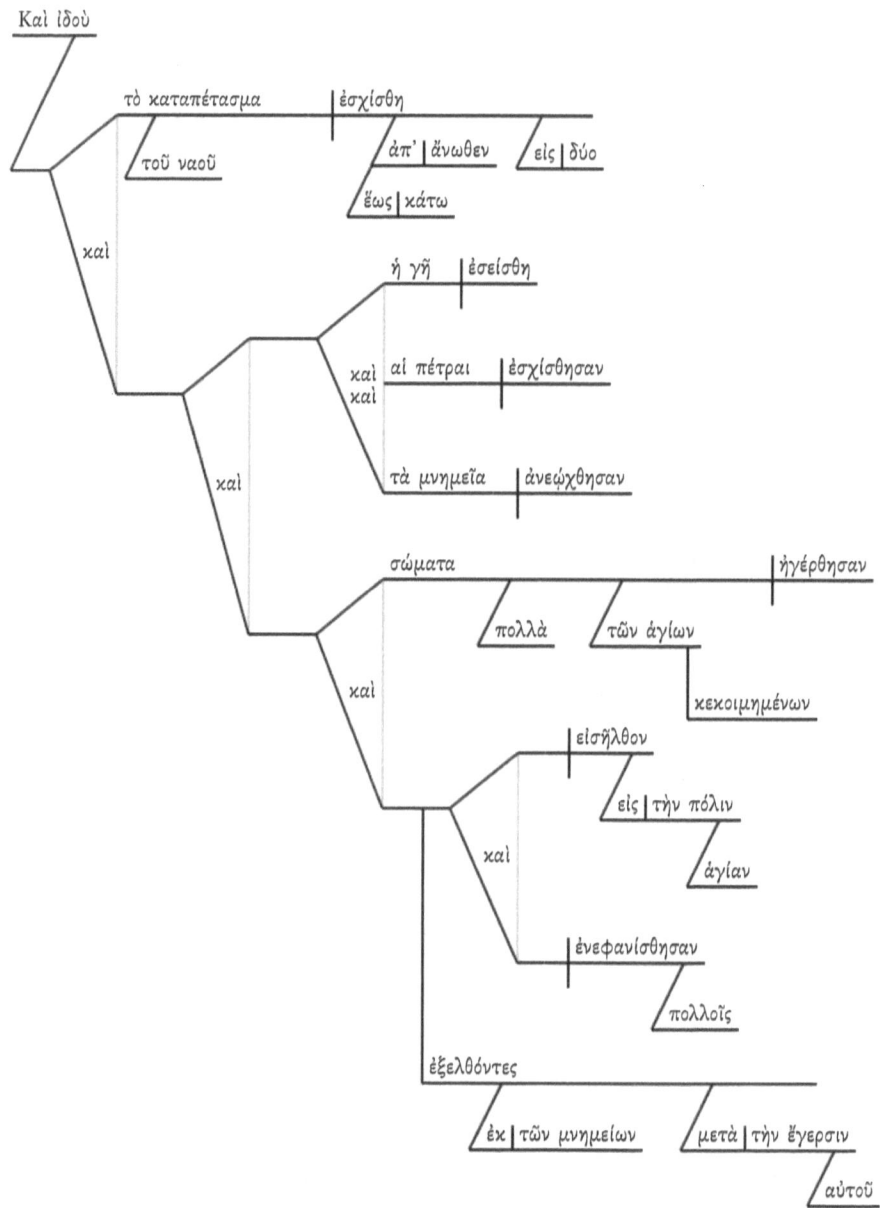

Fig. 2.1. Displacement Diagram of Matthew 27:51–54

Wenham's concerns are twofold. First, the temporal lapse between the splitting rocks caused by the earthquake in Matthew 27:51 and the subsequent resurrection of the many sleeping saints neatly places the latter events after Jesus' resurrection and maintains his title as the firstborn from the dead—ἀπαρχὴ τῶν κεκοιμημένων (1 Cor. 15:20; cf. Col. 1:18; Rev. 1:5).[11] Second, he wants to tie the resurrection of the saints with Jesus' vindicating resurrection from the dead in Matthew 28:1–10. According to Wenham, their resurrection is caused by Jesus' resurrection. This causal relationship accentuates the power of Jesus' resurrection from the dead, a resurrecting power accessible to "all who fall asleep in Jesus."[12] Therefore, he connects the resurrection of the saints with the resurrection of Jesus to emphasize his "victory," which is proclaimed and promised to all who die in him.[13]

The impact of Wenham's proposal cannot be overstated. Though his article is short (only two pages), his contribution is pervasive in contemporary evangelicalism in relation to the interpretation of Matthew 27:51–54 because his thesis persuades many well-known modern commentators. For example, D. A. Carson contends that Wenham has

---

[11] Wenham, "When Were the Saints Raised?," 151. Wenham ties the temporal lapse between the splitting of ἡ γῆ and the opening of τὰ μνημεῖα with the Bible's "third day" motif because, according to Wenham, this motif highlights the two foci accentuated as Matthew narrates Jesus' saving work in Matt. 27–28: the sacrificial death of Jesus and the vindicating resurrection of Jesus. For a recent treatment of the "third day" motif, see Stephen G. Dempster, "From Slight Peg to Corner Stone to Capstone: The Resurrection of Christ on 'the Third Day' according to the Scriptures," *WTJ* 76, 2 (2014): 371–409.

[12] Wenham, "When Were the Saints Raised?," 152.

[13] Ibid., 151. Wenham continues by contending that the climax of Jesus' saving work has two central foci: his death on the cross, which blots out sin and defeats the renegade powers of evil, and his resurrection by which his victory is proclaimed to all and promised to those who die in him. He interprets each of the five signs that occur as a result of Jesus' yielding the Spirit in Matt. 27:50 as corresponding to one of these two foci: "The rending of the curtain of the Holy of Holies and the opening of the graves corresponds to the first event and the appearance of the resurrected saints to the second" (ibid., 151).

convincingly argued that a full stop should be placed, not after "split" (v. 51), but after "broke open" (v. 52). . . . The resurrection of "the holy people" begins a new sentence and is tied up only with Jesus' resurrection. So Matthew does not intend his readers to think that these "holy people" were resurrected when Jesus died and then waited in their tombs till Easter Sunday before showing themselves. The idea is a trifle absurd anyway: there is no more reason to think they were impeded by material substance than was the resurrected Lord, the covering rock of whose grave was removed to let the witnesses in, not to let him out. The "holy people" were raised, came out of the tombs, and were seen by many after Jesus rose from the dead. There is no need to connect the earthquake and the breaking open of the tombs with the rising of "the holy people": the two foci must be differentiated.[14]

Carson, then, in accord with Wenham, assumes that the Matthean pericope is displaced within his Gospel. That is, the resurrection of the sleeping-saints belongs chronologically in Matthew 28, *after* Jesus' resurrection from the dead. He gives three reasons for advocating this interpretation: (1) The pericope would be disruptive to the flow of the narrative in chapter 28, (2) the pericope's current placement links the cross and the empty tomb, communicating that Jesus' death on the cross is one work, and (3) the pericope, along with the other signs occurring on Good Friday, points to Jesus' future vindicating resurrection in Matthew 28:1–10.[15]

Similarly, in accord with Wenham by way of citation, Craig Blomberg states,

---

[14] D. A. Carson, *The Expositor's Bible Commentary with the New International Version*, vol. 2, *Matthew 13–28*, ed. Frank E. Gaebelein (Grand Rapids: Zondervan, 1995), 581–82.

[15] Carson, *Expositor's Bible Commentary*, 2:582.

Translating Matthew 27:51–54

The [Matthean] text should probably be punctuated with a period after "tombs broke open." Then the rest of vv. 52b-53 would read, *And the bodies of many holy people who had died were raised to life, and, having come out of the tombs after Jesus' resurrection, they went into the Holy City* [i.e., Jerusalem]. Contra the NIV rendering of v. 53, there is no "and" in the Greek nor any reason to pause between "tombs" and "after."[16]

Unfortunately, Blomberg, when advocating for this translation, is reading Matthew in light of the Pauline corpus rather than reading Matthew in light of his Gospel narrative.[17] He states, "As the NIV [translation] stands, Matthew's account contradicts Paul, inasmuch as the saints actually precede Christ out of the tomb."[18] For Blomberg, the resurrection of the saints in Matthew 27:52–53 is an illustration of Paul's teaching in 1 Corinthians 15:20–22. According to him, this confirms that Jesus is "the firstfruits of a new age, guaranteeing the bodily resurrection of all his people."[19] Carson and Blomberg are two of many that Wenham's thesis has persuaded.

As has been previously noted, Wenham's interpretive instinct to connect the resurrection of τῶν κεκοιμημένων ἁγίων (Matt. 27:52–53) with Jesus' resurrection (Matt. 28:6) is correct. Close examination of the narrative manifests that Matthew has placed the pericopes parallel to each other in order to make clear the christological, missiological, and eschatological foci of the passage. Wenham, however, incorrectly assumes that the raising of τῶν κεκοιμημένων ἁγίων threatens Jesus' right as ἀπαρχὴ τῶν κεκοιμημένων (1 Cor.

---

[16] Craig L. Blomberg, *Matthew*, NAC, vol. 22 (Nashville: Broadman Press, 1992), 421.

[17] This dissertation proposes that a Pauline reading of Matthew's Gospel does not necessarily force the interpretive dilemma Blomberg suggests, which stems from interpreters not reading Matthew closely enough. A good reading *begins* with Matthew's Gospel and *then* reads the Gospel in light of the entire New Testament corpus, not vice versa.

[18] Blomberg, *Matthew*, 421.

[19] Ibid.

15:20) and occurs when Jesus is raised.[20] Rather, Matthew intends for his readers to interpret the raising of the sleeping saints similarly to Lazarus's resurrection. Just as Jesus' power was demonstrated and his naysayers were silenced when he restored the life of the sleeping-dead girl (Matt. 9:24–25), his divine power is displayed through the cosmic portents as the dead are raised to life (Matt. 27:52–53), confirming his identity as the Son of God (Matt. 27:54). As Jesus' fame was heralded for overturning death previously in the Gospel (Matt. 9:26), so now Matthew recounts that his fame is heralded in τὴν ἁγίαν πόλιν and, ultimately, to the ends of the earth (Matt. 28:16–20).

Assessing Bible Translation and Revisiting the Translation of Matthew 27:51–54

Due to the interpretive confusion caused by this elusive Matthean pericope, and as a consequence of the popularity of a thesis like Wenham's among contemporary evangelical linguistic scholars, Bible translations are manifold in their renderings of this pericope, offering a smorgasbord of interpretive possibilities. This is most clearly visualized in table 2.1.

On the one hand, the chart reveals that, like Wenham, many recent modern English Bible translations—the ESV, NASB, NIV, and HCSB—punctuate Matthew 27:51–54 similarly. These translations,

---

[20] Preceding Wenham and for different reasons, Fuller contended that it was inaccurate to assume the holy dead were raised on Good Friday because their resurrection would conflict with Paul's teaching in 1 Cor. 15:20. In contrast to others, however, Fuller does not take the resurrection of the saints after Christ's death in Matt. 27:51–53 to mean they were granted glorified bodies on Easter Sunday. Rather, he contends they had to wait until the Last Day to take possession of those. For him, then, the purpose of the resurrection pericope is to inspire hope in readers of the Matthean narrative as they pine for resurrection on the Last Day: "The purpose of the appearance of these bodies was no doubt to show visibly that Christ has raised us from the death of sin and that at the Last Day we shall possess glorified bodies, as Christ did on Easter Sunday" (R. H. Fuller, "The Bodies of the Saints, Mt 27:52–3," *Scripture* 3 [1948]: 86–87).

Table 2.1. Parallel of English Bible Translations

English Standard Version	King James Version	New American Standard Bible: 1995 Update	New International Version	New King James Version	Revised Standard Version	Holman Christian Standard Bible
51 And behold, the curtain of the temple was torn in two, from top to bottom. And the earth shook, and the rocks were split.	51 And, behold, the veil of the temple was rent in twain from the top to the bottom; and the earth did quake, and the rocks rent;	51 And behold, the veil of the temple was torn in two from top to bottom; and the earth shook and the rocks were split.	51 At that moment the curtain of the temple was torn in two from top to bottom. The earth shook, the rocks split	51 Then, behold, the veil of the temple was torn in two from top to bottom; and the earth quaked, and the rocks were split,	51 And behold, the curtain of the temple was torn in two, from top to bottom; and the earth shook, and the rocks were split;	51 Suddenly, the curtain of the sanctuary was split in two from top to bottom; the earth quaked and the rocks were split.
52 The tombs also were opened. And many bodies of the saints who had fallen asleep were raised,	52 And the graves were opened; and many bodies of the saints which slept arose,	52 The tombs were opened, and many bodies of the saints who had fallen asleep were raised;	52 and the tombs broke open. The bodies of many holy people who had died were raised to life.	52 and the graves were opened; and many bodies of the saints who had fallen asleep were raised;	52 the tombs also were opened, and many bodies of the saints who had fallen asleep were raised,	52 The tombs also were opened and many bodies of the saints who had fallen asleep were raised.
53 and coming out of the tombs after his resurrection they went into the holy city and appeared to many.	53 And came out of the graves after his resurrection, and went into the holy city, and appeared unto many.	53 and coming out of the tombs after His resurrection they entered the holy city and appeared to many.	53 They came out of the tombs after Jesus' resurrection and went into the holy city and appeared to many people.	53 and coming out of the graves after His resurrection, they went into the holy city and appeared to many.	53 and coming out of the tombs after his resurrection they went into the holy city and appeared to many.	53 And they came out of the tombs after His resurrection, entered the holy city, and appeared to many.

aside from the NIV, place a period, indicating a full stop, after ἐσχίσθησαν at the end of Matthew 27:51. Of these four, the ESV and NIV divide Matthew 27:52 into two separate sentences by placing a period after ἀνεῴχθησαν, which would seem to separate the opening of the tombs from the resurrection of the saints. These two translations are more ambiguous in their interpretive gloss of the Greek text, allowing readers to take the opening of the crypts of the righteous dead with the events that precede Good Friday *or* the events that follow on Easter Sunday. The other translations, however, clearly impose an interpretation that separates the resurrection of the saints from the events of Good Friday and securely locates them on Easter Sunday.

On the other hand, the chart reveals that older modern English Bible translations—the KJV, RSV, and NKJV—also punctuate Matthew 27:51–54 similarly. The KJV and RSV, however, place a semicolon at the end of Matthew 27:51 and connect the events in Matthew 27:52 with a comma. Their main difference is in the suggested sequence of the signs after the yielding of Jesus' τὸ πνεῦμα by the use of a semicolon or comma throughout their respective translations. The KJV places a semicolon after δύο ἐσχίσθησαν and ἀνεῴχθησαν, indicating that the sequence of the signs was the tearing of the veil, the quaking and breaking of the earth, the opening of the sepulchers, and *then* the raising of the saints. The RSV places a semicolon after δύο and ἐσχίσθησαν, which indicates that the sequence of the signs was the tearing of the veil, then the quaking and breaking of the earth, and then the opening of the sepulchers, which was coterminous with the raising of the saints. The NKJV differentiates the sequence in that it places a semicolon after δύο and ἀνεῴχθησαν and ἠγέρθησαν, indicating that the first sign was the tearing of the veil, then the quaking and breaking of the earth as coterminous with the opening of the sepulchers, and *then* the raising of the saints.[21]

Moreover, this interpretive translation phenomenon is not

---

[21] Analysis of these interpretive decisions made by translation committees for each of these respective translations echoes Moises Silva's work on

relegated merely to English Bible translations. In the German translation Schlachter 2000, one observes the gloss in figure 2.2.

---

51 Und siehe, der Vorhang im Tempel riss von oben bis unten entzwei,[g] und die Erde erbebte, und die Felsen spalteten sich.

52 Und die Gräber öffneten sich, und viele Leiber der entschlafenen Heiligen wurden auferweckt

53 und gingen aus den Gräbern hervor nach seiner Auferstehung und kamen in die heilige Stadt und erschienen vielen.

54 Als aber der Hauptmann und die, welche mit ihm Jesus bewachten, das Erdbeben sahen und was da geschah, fürchteten sie sich sehr und sprachen: Wahrhaftig, dieser war Gottes Sohn!

Fig. 2.2. Schlachter 2000

The Schlachter 2000—like the English ESV, NASB, NIV, and HCSB—punctuates Matthew 27:51–54 with a period, indicating a full stop, after ἐσχίσθησαν at the end of Matthew 27:51. Then, like the NASB, NIV, and HCSB, the Schlachter 2000 clearly imposes an interpretation that separates the resurrection of the saints from the events of Good Friday and firmly locates them on Easter Sunday. The rending of the temple veil and the quaking and breaking of the earth are coterminous, while (1) the opening of the tombs, (2) the resurrection of the saints, and (3) their exit from the graveyard is postponed to Easter Sunday. The entirety of the resurrection scene is

---

translation as a form of interpretive treason. See Moises Silva, "Are Translators Traitors? Some Personal Reflections," in *The Challenge of Bible Translation: Communicating God's Word to the World (Essays in Honor of Ronald F. Youngblood)*, ed. Glen G. Scorgie, Mark L. Strauss, and Steven M. Voth (Grand Rapids: Zondervan, 2002), 37–50.

displaced in the Matthean narrative according to the German translation.

In contrast to the translations above, this dissertation suggests that a comma at the end of Matthew 27:51 is more grammatically appropriate, linking the cosmic portents that occur after Christ's dereliction cry (Matt. 27:50). Furthermore, rather than using a period at the end of Matthew 27:52, a better rendering of the verse employs a semicolon to suggest a close relationship between the resurrection of the saints and their emergence from the grave.[22] Therefore, the translation of Matthew 27:51–54 that this dissertation is proposing is as follows:

> Behold, the curtain of the temple was torn in two from top to bottom, the earth quaked, and the rocks split, the tombs, also, were opened and the bodies of many saints who had died were raised to life; coming out of the tombs, they went into the holy city after his resurrection, appearing to many people. When the centurion and those guarding Jesus with him saw the earthquake and the things that took place they were terrified and said, "This really was the Son of God!"

According to this translation of the passage, the crucifixion pericope should be pictorially diagrammed as below (see fig. 2.3).

This rendering finds an advocate in a dynamic equivalent

---

[22] When discussing the multiplicity of punctuation possibilities in relation to Matt. 27:51–54, Quarles wisely remarks, "Modern readers must remember that the original manuscripts of the New Testament were written in a script called *scriptio continua*. This consisted of one Greek letter after another with no punctuation and no space between paragraphs, sentences, or words. Punctuation decisions must be made by modern editors of the Greek New Testament and modern translators. The decisions of these editors and translators are subject to challenge." See Charles L. Quarles, "Matthew 27:51–53: Meaning, Genre, Intertextuality, Theology, and Reception History," *JETS* 59, 2 (2016): 274.

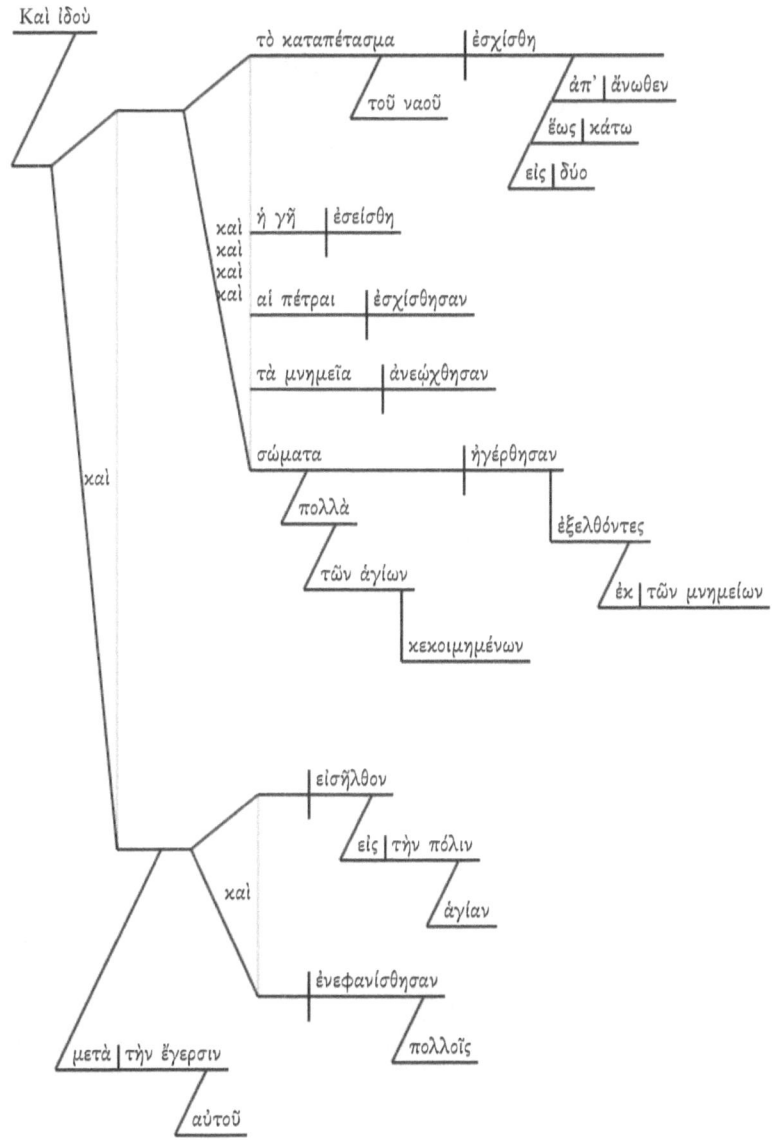

Fig. 2.3. Literary Reading Diagram of Matthew 27:51–54

translation, the NLT.[23] The NLT offers, in a footnote, a rendering similar to the one suggested in this dissertation. The NLT's alternative translation is as follows: "At that moment the curtain of the Temple was torn in two, from top to bottom. The earth shook, rocks split apart, tombs opened, and the bodies of many godly men and women who had died were raised from the dead. After Jesus' resurrection, they left the cemetery, went into the holy city of Jerusalem, and appeared to many people."

Like the ESV, NASB, NIV, and HCSB, the NLT places a period, indicating a full stop, in Matthew 27:51. The NLT, however, places its full stop after δύο. The NLT's alternative translation suggests that the latter four signs are coterminous—the quaking and breaking of the earth, the opening of the sepulchers, and the raising of the saints. In the NLT's substitute translation, the latter four signs occur on Good Friday rather than Easter Sunday. There is a full-stop punctuation between Matthew 27:52 and Matthew 27:53. The resurrected saints exit their graveyard, enter Jerusalem, and manifest themselves to others on Easter Sunday.[24]

This interpretive gloss finds support outside of English Bible translations as well. In the French translation in figure 2.4, one can observe a rendering akin to the NLT's alternative translation. The period, however, is placed after ἠγέρθησαν in Matthew 27:52, indicating that the sequence of the signs was the tearing of the veil, the quaking and breaking of the earth, and the opening of the sepulchers as coterminous with the raising of the saints. In this rendering, then, it is natural for a reader of the French text to understand the five

---

[23] The NLT is not represented in Table. 2.1.

[24] Though he lobbied for a translation that would look more like Wenham's understanding of Matt. 27:51–54, I am thankful to Craig Blomberg. In a private correspondence, he kindly took the time to explain to me how the translation committee for the NLT—Grant Osborne, Craig Blomberg, Donald Hagner, and David Turner—went about forming the initial draft of the NLT in 1996. Unfortunately, none of Blomberg's textual translation notes are available, as this translation committee did their work in a time before electronic correspondence would have been prevalent.

> 51 Et voici que le voile du temple[e] se déchira en deux depuis le haut jusqu'en bas, la terre trembla, les rochers se fendirent,
>
> 52 les tombeaux s'ouvrirent et les corps de plusieurs saints[f] qui étaient morts ressuscitèrent.
>
> 53 Etant sortis des tombes, ils entrèrent dans la ville sainte après la résurrection de Jésus et apparurent à un grand nombre de personnes.
>
> 54 A la vue du tremblement de terre et de ce qui venait d'arriver, l'officier romain et ceux qui étaient avec lui pour garder Jésus furent saisis d'une grande frayeur et dirent: «Cet homme était vraiment le Fils de Dieu.»

Fig. 2.4. Segond 21

signs as happening on Good Friday right after Jesus died. Moreover, the most natural reading of the grammar in Matthew 27:53 is to understand that they entered the city *after* Jesus' resurrection. Their resurrection at the time of Jesus' death is assumed from the structure of Matthew 27:51–52.[25]

Summary

Bible translations, English and beyond, offer a variety of glosses of Matthew 27:51–54. Many, this dissertation has argued, fall in accord with Wenham's thesis, which bifurcates the pericope's signs—particularly the resurrection of the dead saints—from Good Friday and displaces them to Easter Sunday. It has been argued that this is not the most natural rendering of the Greek and that this

---

[25] Rob Plummer, in a private conversation, confirmed the understanding of the French grammar of this Matthean pericope.

interpretive gloss reads and translates Matthew in light of the Pauline corpus rather than in light of Matthew's Gospel.

Syntactical and Grammatical Features

As signs surrounded the birth of Jesus, so also, careful readers will notice, signs surrounded his death (Matt. 1:18–2:23; 27:51–53).[26] The question, then, is *why* did Matthew intentionally employ this imagery in his narrative? Syntactical and grammatical analysis of this pericope will manifest that the narrative structure is intended to accentuate Jesus' divine identity—at his birth, wise men are confounded as a star guides them to the Lord of heaven and earth (Matt. 2:1–12). At his death, the heavens mourn in darkness (Matt. 27:45), the earth heaves and breaks (Matt. 27:51), and the dead are brought back to life as a testimony to his dominion as the Son of God (Matt. 28:18). As the Son of God, he saves people from their sins (Matt. 1:21): Jewish people (Matt. 14:33) and Gentile people (Matt. 27:54) who recognize him to be the Son of God regardless of where they reside on the planet (Matt. 28:18–20). His death cry (Matt. 27:50) is a proclamation from the cross. Like Lazarus, those who hear his voice are restored to life and come forth from their graves (Matt. 27:52–53; cf. John 5:25, 28). Further, Matthew's intentionality in his narrative structure is intended to accentuate the mission Jesus' death necessitates—his death is life-giving and ultimately salvific for persons from every nation who profess faith in his name (Matt. 28:16–20; cf. 27:54). Since Jesus is the Son of God

---

[26] Similarly, Brown highlights that "Matthew did not hesitate to have the moment of Jesus' birth marked by a star in the sky; the moment of his death is even more climactic, marked by signs in the heavens, on the earth, and under the earth." Raymond E. Brown, *A Crucified Christ in Holy Week: Essays on the Four Gospel Passion Narratives* (Collegeville, MN: Liturgical Press, 1984), 44. For a recent analysis studying the affinity between the beginning and ending of Matthew, see Jason Hood, *The Messiah, His Brothers, and the Nations (Matthew 1:1–17)* (London: T&T Clark, 2011), 139–56.

and his life is unlike any other life, his death is a life-giving death (Matt. 27:52) and has meaning for the nations when the temple cultus is rendered obsolete (Matt. 27:51, 54; 28:16–20).

Despite the theological import of this pericope, some consider Matthew 27:51–54 an inelegant chronological problem that exists because of clumsy scribal interpolation.[27] Interpretive confusion has caused some to overlook the passage's textual features (parataxis, divine passives, and extensive parallelism) as well as its "catchword connexions [sic] with the immediate context and repetitive vocabulary" such as earth (Matt. 27:45, 51), torn/split (Matt. 27:51a, 51c), many (Matt. 27:52, 53), and holy (Matt. 27:52, 53) in the pursuit of interpretive clarity.[28] The aim of this section, therefore, is to shed

---

[27] Craig A. Evans, *Matthew*, NCBC (Cambridge: Cambridge University Press, 2012), 466–67. Evans goes on to say that Matt. 27:51–54 is a "strange story" resulting from a "clumsy gloss" that has created "chronological awkwardness" in the Matthean narrative. Interestingly, he admits, "we possess no textual evidence or witness that suggests vv. 52–53 are a gloss. But one will recall that it was not until older manuscripts were discovered that glosses were recognized." He then likens Matt. 27:51–54, without textual or manuscript evidence to support his claim, to the perspiring blood of Jesus and the appearance of the angel in Luke 22:43–44, the angelic agitation of the pool in John 5:3b–4, the longer Gospel ending in Mark 16:9–20, and the story of the adulterous woman brought before Jesus in John 8:1–11. Without warrant, Evans predicates the charge of scribal interpolation on this Matthean pericope.

[28] W. D. Davies and Dale C. Allison Jr., *A Critical and Exegetical Commentary on the Gospel according to Saint Matthew*, ICC, vol. 3, *Matthew 19–28* (New York: T&T Clark, 2004), 628. No major grammar deals with the pericope under consideration, specifically Matt. 27:51b–53. See Daniel B. Wallace, *Greek Grammar beyond the Basics: An Exegetical Syntax of the New Testament* (Grand Rapids: Zondervan, 1996), 803; F. Blass and A. Debrunner, *A Greek Grammar of the New Testament and Other Early Christian Literature*, trans. Robert W. Funk (Chicago: University of Chicago Press, 1961), 304; Herbert W. Smyth, *Greek Grammar* (Cambridge, MA: Harvard University Press, 1984); and Steven E. Runge, *A Discourse Grammar of the Greek New Testament*, Lexam Bible Reference Series (Bellingham, WA: Lexham Bible Reference, 2010). Furthermore, Metzger does not even mention this text at all in his textual commentary. See Bruce M. Metzger, *A Textual Commentary on the Greek New Testament* (New York: United Bible Societies, 1994), 59. This does not mean, however, that there

interpretive light into Matthew's "inelegant chronological problem" by analyzing the syntax and structure of this pericope.

Matthew 27:51 begins with the dramatic καὶ ἰδού, which serves as a connector between the death of Jesus in 27:50 and the extraordinary events that follow in Matthew 27:51–53.[29] Additionally, καὶ ἰδοὺ demarcates what precipitates in Matthew 27:51–54 as the aftermath of Jesus' death in Matthew 27:50. The apostle strings together five short main clauses with the conjunction καὶ; in each of these five clauses the subject is first and the verb is in the aorist passive.[30] Though the clauses are connected by καὶ and each one is associated with the events of Good Friday, they should not be read as sequential in their respective occurrences. Rather, τὸ καταπέτασμα ... ἐσχίσθη ἡ γῆ ἐσείσθη and αἱ πέτραι ἐσχίσθησαν are coterminous in their occurrence as a result of Jesus' death cry from the tree

---

are no noteworthy text-critical issues surrounding Matt. 27:51–53. Quarles has demonstrated that an increasing number of scholars wrongly argue that the prepositional phrase μετὰ τὴν ἔγερσιν αὐτοῦ is a scribal interpolation. For example, see Willoughby C. Allen, *The Gospel according to Matthew* (New York: Charles Scribner's Sons, 1907), 296. See also Adalbert Merx, *Die vier kanonischen Evangelien nach ihrem ältesten bekannten Texte: Übersetzung und Erläuterung der syrischen im Sinaikloster gefundenen Palimpsesthandschrift; Zweiter Teil, erste Hälfte, Erläuterung. Matthaeus* (Berlin: Reimer, 1902), 427–29. For a thorough exploration of the issue, see Charles L. Quarles, "ΜΕΤΑ ΤΗΝ ΕΓΕΡΣΙΝ ΑΥΤΟΥ: A Scribal Interpolation in Matthew 27:53?," *TC* 20 (2015): 1–15.

[29] R. T. France, *The Gospel of Matthew*, NICNT (Grand Rapids: Eerdmans, 2007), 1079; and Davies and Allison, *Critical and Exegetical Commentary*, 3:630. Concerning καὶ ἰδού, Pearson contends that it is an idiom containing special significance as a narrative marker in Matthew's Gospel by distinguishing the introduction or conclusion of significant gospel events. She notes that this pericope is one of "the most noticeable areas in the Gospel where this usage occurs." Brook W. R. Pearson, "New Testament Literary Criticism," in *Handbook to Exegesis of the New Testament*, ed. Stanley E. Porter (Leiden, Netherlands: Brill, 1997), 256.

[30] Ulrich Luz, *Matthew 21–28*, trans. James E. Crouch, ed. Helmut Koester, Hermeneia (Minneapolis: Fortress Press, 2005), 560. Luz, too, notes that the structure of Matt. 27:51–54 demarcates it from the previous section. Further, he notes that the signs in Matt. 27:51–52 are lumped together syntactically. Thus, Matt. 27:54 is the acclamatory conclusion of the signs preceding it.

after unleashing τὸ πνεῦμα (Matt. 27:50–51), and τὰ μνημεῖα ἀνεῴχθησαν is the result of the cosmological portents preceding it, which allows the πολλὰ σώματα ... ἠγέρθησαν to exit their tombs.[31] In the narrative, the tearing of the veil (Matt. 27:51) is the first in a series of signs that climaxes in the raising of the dead from their open tombs (Matt. 27:52) and results in the acclamation of the centurion and those with him (Matt. 27:54).[32]

The first of the five clauses, τὸ καταπέτασμα τοῦ ναοῦ ἐσχίσθη ἀπ' ἄνωθεν ἕως κάτω εἰς δύο, introduces the first divine

[31] Despite the fact that the first three signs are simultaneously coterminous and the latter two are simultaneously coterminous in Matt. 27:52, all five uses of the *passivum divinum* are eschatological victory signs occurring subsequent to Jesus' victory cry on the cross. The former three cosmological signs preceded the latter two resurrection signs after Jesus yielded the Spirit. Hill, likewise, suggests this Matthean pericope is a narrative vehicle toward a theological and eschatological interpretation of Jesus' death. Regrettably, Hill claims that concerns about the passage's historicity "involve a host of pseudo-problems and cause us to lose sight of the true meaning." David Hill, "Matthew 27:51–53 in the Theology of the Evangelist," *IBS* 7 (1985): 76. Senior suggests the signs in Matt. 27:51–54 are the author's polyvalent interpretation of the death of Jesus. He sees three layers to this Matthean pericope: (1) a confessional layer (Jesus is vindicated in his claim to be the Son of God), (2) a salvation-historical layer (Jesus' death is the crucial turning point in the history of salvation), and (3) a soteriological layer, since Jesus' death triggers the resurrection of the saints in Matthew's narrative, saving power (i.e., life-giving) is ascribed to his death. See Donald Senior, "The Death of Jesus and the Resurrection of the Holy Ones (Mt 27:51–53)," *CBQ* 38 (1976): 325–29; and Donald Senior, *The Passion of Jesus in the Gospel of Mark* (Wilmington, DE: Michael Glazier, 1984), 128. Osborne, too, notes the salvation-historical significance of Jesus' death in this pericope: "The darkness, the tearing of the curtain, the earthquake, the raising of the saints" all demonstrate the intersection of human history by divine power. Following Wenham, however, Osborne contends that Matt. 27:51–54 serves to "unite Jesus' death and resurrection into a single event in salvation history." Grant R. Osborne, *Matthew*, Zondervan Exegetical Commentary on the New Testament (Grand Rapids: Zondervan, 2010), 1044.

[32] Contra Sim's contention that the portents surrounding Jesus' death were not sufficient for the centurion to make a positive profession of faith. See David C. Sim, "The 'Confession' of the Soldiers in Matthew 27:54," *HeyJ* 34 (1993): 416.

passive[33] encountered in the pericope, indicating that these events are signs from God rather than the people.[34] This signals the reader to recognize the subsequent uses of the *passivum divinum* in the pericope. The doctrine of the atonement is pictured in God's action of rending the veil after the penetrating divine silence pervading the scene of Jesus' mocking and death (27:32–50).[35] Matthew's

---

[33] There are instances, especially in the Gospels, where the unspecified agent is implied to be God. According to Porter, this is referred to as the "divine or theological passive," or *passivum divinum*. See Stanley E. Porter, *Idioms of the Greek New Testament* (London: Sheffield Academic Press, 2005), 65–66. Wallace argues that the "passive is used when God is the obvious agent." Wallace, *Greek Grammar*, 437–38. According to this definition in relation to this text, the following five verbs can be classified as divine passives: ἐσχίσθη, ἐσείσθη, ἐσχίσθησαν, ἀνεῴχθησαν, and ἠγέρθησαν. Thus, it is none other than God who tore the curtain in two, shook the earth, split the rocks, opened the tombs, and raised the righteous dead who then entered the holy city to testify, along with the Gentile crowd, that Jesus is the Son of God.

[34] Osborne notes that there "were two veils in the temple, one separating the Holy Place from the Most Holy place and the other separating the sanctuary as a whole from the court." Additionally, he contends that the "imagery [in Matt. 27:51] and in Hebrews 6:19; 9:12–13; 10:19–20 favors the inner curtain, signifying opening up a new entrance to the presence of God" even though he admits that the outer veil fits the text's imagery of a public sign (Osborne, *Matthew*, 1043). Contra Osborne, Benedict Green suggests the outer veil was torn since it would have served as an obvious omen of the temple's future destruction among the people. See H. Benedict Green, "The Gospel according to Matthew in the Revised Standard Version: Introduction and Commentary" (Oxford: Oxford University Press, 1975), 224. Though interpreters often cite Hebrews as definitive textual data to clarify which veil was rent in the passion narrative, even Hebrews commentators do not affirm a conclusive allusion to the tearing of the veil after Jesus' death. For example, though Bruce and Hagner suspect an allusion, they admit that it is not certain. See F. F. Bruce, *The Epistle to the Hebrews*, NICNT (Grand Rapids: Eerdmans, 1964), 244–49; and Donald Hagner, *Hebrews*, New International Biblical Commentary (Peabody, MA: Hendrickson, 1990), 164. For a thorough treatment of the tearing of the temple veil in Matthew's Gospel, see Daniel M. Gurtner, *The Torn Veil: Matthew's Exposition of the Death of Jesus* (Cambridge: Cambridge University Press, 2007), 97–137.

[35] Following Davies and Allison, Frederick Bruner describes the signs in Matt. 27:51–54 as an "explosion of the supernatural." Interestingly, he terms

directional emphasis in his word order when recounting the rending of the temple veil—ἀπ' ἄνωθεν ἕως κάτω εἰς δύο—connotes a tear from heaven to earth and forcefully inserts God into the narrative as the divine actor after the death of his Son. Although commentators speculate as to which veil is alluded to in Matthew 27:51, there is broad consensus that the Matthean pericope does not contain specificity in regard to which veil—the inner veil or the outer veil—was torn.[36] Though the imagery in textual data of Hebrews (6:19; 9:12–13; 10:19–20) favors the inner curtain, the textual imagery of Matthew 27:51–54 favors the more public outer veil as a visible sign for the populace. For many, the rending of the inner veil is preferred for its theological import (i.e., a new way to God's presence has been opened up through Jesus' death; now Christians are able to enter the holy place by means of the nail-pierced flesh and shed blood of Jesus). Charles Quarles, however, has convincingly argued, "The rending of any of the temple curtains would have signified the temple was now open and vulnerable to desecration. Its courts were no longer sacrosanct."[37] The temple's

---

this explosion "The Prodigia"; he suggests that Matt. 27:55–56 may need to be added to the scene of Matt. 27:51–54, although he gives no justification for his suggestion (though it seems he is adding the women to the list of witnesses). See Frederick Dale Bruner, *The Churchbook: Matthew 13–28* (Grand Rapids: Eerdmans, 2004), 756. Davies and Allison link the "shower of astounding miracles" in Matt. 27:51–54 primarily with Zech. 14:4–5. For them, Matt. 27:53 "narrates the realization of Zechariah's prophecy." See Davies and Allison, *Critical and Exegetical Commentary*, 3:629.

[36] M. de Jonge contends not only that the Gospel author is uninterested with the question as to which of the two curtains of the temple is meant but also that it should not even be discussed in the exegesis of the text. See M. de Jonge, "Matthew 27:51 in Early Christian Exegesis," *HTR* 79 (1986): 67–68.

[37] Quarles, "Matthew 27:51–53," 272. Interestingly, Quarles strengthens the tie of Matt. 27:51–54 to Ezekiel's prophecy by postulating that the "ripping of the veil may have even signified the departure of divine glory from the temple (Ezek. 10:18–19)." Similarly, Bruner suggests that "the violent ripping of the curtain would thus confirm Jesus' pronouncement in Matthew 23:38, 'Behold, your house is left to you desolate.'" Bruner, *The Churchbook*,

split veil communicates an end to the temple cultus and the accessibility of salvation for all who profess faith in Christ.³⁸

The phrase καὶ αἱ πέτραι ἐσχίσθησαν elaborates on one of the effects of the violent earthquake—καὶ ἡ γῆ ἐσείσθη—recounted in Matthew 27:51. The trembling of the earth and the splitting of rocks should be read as signs coterminous with the splitting of the veil.³⁹ The mention of καὶ αἱ πέτραι ἐσχίσθησαν completes the only two uses of σχίζω in Matthew's Gospel narrative. Both are located in Matthew 27:51: ἐσχίσθη and ἐσχίσθησαν. The former is mentioned in relation to the rending of the temple curtain, the latter in relation to the rending of rocks as the land reeled because of the divine σεισμός after Jesus yielded the Spirit.⁴⁰ The earthquake

---

759. Bruner connects the rending of the veil with both "the veil that is spread over all nations" in Isa. 25:7 and "the dividing wall of hostility" in Eph. 2:13–16 (Ibid.). Spurgeon, however, connected the ripping of the veil with the ripping of Jesus' flesh to emphasize the atoning aspects of Jesus' death: "The body of Christ being rent, the veil of the temple was torn in twain from the top to the bottom. Now was there an entrance made into the holiest of all, by the blood of Jesus; and a way of access to God was opened for every sinner who trusted in Christ's atoning sacrifice." C. H. Spurgeon, *Spurgeon's Popular Exposition of Matthew* (Grand Rapids: Baker, 1979), 251.

³⁸ For a helpful survey of the interpretation of the rending of the temple veil among early Christian exegetes, see M. de Jonge, "Two Interesting Interpretations of the Rending of the Temple-Veil in the Testaments of the Twelve Patriarchs," in *Jewish Eschatology, Early Christian Christology and the Testaments of the Twelve Patriarchs: Collected Essays of Marinus De Jonge*, NovTSup 63 (Leiden, Netherlands: Brill, 1991), 220–32.

³⁹ Though I came to this conclusion independently of Quarles, he also notes, "It is likely that the first three clauses described events that were simultaneous rather than consecutive" (Quarles, "Matthew 27:51-53," 273).

⁴⁰ When surveying the synoptic parallels, one notes that Mark's Gospel, too, only has two uses of the verb σχίζω. His two uses of σχίζω, however, connect the end with the beginning of his Gospel narrative. He begins his Gospel with the heavens (σχιζομένους) followed by the Spirit's descent (Mark 1:10) and concludes his narrative with the temple curtain being ἐσχίσθη in two (Mark 15:38). Motyer, noting the *inclusio* between the "splitting" in Mark 1:10 and 15:38 contends that the rending of the veil is "a Markan Pentecost, a proleptic bestowal of the Spirit analogous to the proleptic destruction of the

in Matthew 27:51 alerts readers to the divine theophany occurring as a result of Jesus' death. The earthquake is a prelude to the opening of the tombs and resurrection of the saints in Matthew 27:52.⁴¹ The reference to the land—ἡ γῆ (frequently translated "the earth")—points the reader back to Matthew 27:45. As darkness enveloped *the land* of Israel, so now an earthquake occurs in *the*

---

temple."S. Motyer, "The Rending of the Veil: A Markan Pentecost?," *NTS* 33 (1987): 155–57. Though I do not affirm Motyer's conclusions of a proleptic Pentecost, this may give insight into Matthew's use of τὸ πνεῦμα in Matt. 27:50–54 as a reference to the Spirit of God rather than an indirect anthropological reference to Jesus' life. Read together, both Gospels communicate that the Spirit is linked with the revelatory signs surrounding the birth and death of Jesus. In Matthew's Gospel, the Spirit conceives the child—Jesus—in Mary's womb (Matt. 1:20); the Spirit descends and rests on Jesus at his baptism (Matt. 3:16); Jesus yields the Spirit at his death (Matt. 27:50); and the yielding of the Spirit in Matt. 27:50 causes the signs in Matt. 27:51–54. In Mark's Gospel, the Spirit tears through the heavens to rest on Jesus after he is baptized (Mark 1:10), and the temple curtain is torn after Jesus yields his Spirit (though Mark does not record this detail) in Mark 15:38. For more on σχίζω in relation to the tearing of the veil in Mark's Gospel, see Harry L. Chronis, "The Torn Veil: Cultus and Christology in Mark 15:37-39,"*JBL* 101, 1 (1982): 97–114. For more on Mark's relationship to Matthew, especially Matt. 27:51–54, see J. Andrew Doole, *What Was Mark for Matthew? An Examination of Matthew's Relationship and Attitude to His Primary Source*, Wissenschaftliche Untersuchungen zum Neuen Testament 2 Reihe 344 (Tübingen: Mohr Siebeck, 2013), 33, 97, 99, 104.

⁴¹ Bauckham states that in "very many Old Testament and intertestamental texts an earthquake accompanies a theophany." Richard Bauckham, "The Eschatological Earthquake in the Apocalypse of John," *NovT* 19 (1977): 224–33. He goes on to note that theophanic tremors are "cosmic quakes" in many of their contexts, accompanying end-time events (ibid., 224). Similarly, Matthew's death-resurrection scenes are replete with cosmological imagery: darkness, dereliction cries, earthquakes, and resurrections. Calvary has become another revelatory mount for Matthew. As Sinai trembled and was enveloped in darkness as YHWH revealed his Word to his people (Ex. 19:16–20; 20:18–21), so now, on a hill outside of Jerusalem, YHWH once again reveals himself through his Word—the eschatological Word (John 1:1), the Son of David (Matt. 1:1–17), the bloodied and crucified Messiah (Matt. 27:26–44), the Son of God (Matt. 27:54)—as the earth totters in darkness and spews forth its dead (Matt. 27:45–53).

land of Israel. This localizes the catastrophe, insinuating judgment on Israel.⁴²

In Matthew 27:52 one again notices the conjunction καὶ, which closely connects the two signs in this verse with the three signs in Matthew 27:51 as the immediate effect of Jesus' yielding the Spirit (Matt. 27:50). The uses of the *passivum divinum* continue to assert that God is the primary actor in the signs as a response to the death of Jesus. The divine σεισμός results in tomb-opening bedrock fissures—τὰ μνημεῖα ἀνεῴχθησαν—exposing the dead buried within (Matt. 27:52). The Matthean narrative recounts a peculiar episode as the climactic event in this series of signs surrounding Jesus' death: καὶ πολλὰ σώματα τῶν κεκοιμημένων ἁγίων ἠγέρθησαν. "Sleep"—τῶν κεκοιμημένων—is a euphemism for death in the Matthean narrative. As Jesus raised the sleeping-dead girl⁴³ in Matthew 9:25 as a testimony to his divine identity,⁴⁴ so now the sleeping saints are raised at his death as a sign testifying to his divine identity as the Son of God.⁴⁵ Though the resurrection of the

---

⁴² Bauckham notes that the shaking of the creation frequently occurs before the coming of God to judge in biblical revelation. See Bauckham, "Eschatological Earthquake," 224. Old Testament texts referring to the quaking of the earth as a sign of God's impending judgment are Isa. 13:13; 24:18–20; Jer. 51:29; Ezek. 38:20; Joel 2:10; Nah. 1:5.

⁴³ Matt. 9:24 states ἀναχωρεῖτε, οὐ γὰρ ἀπέθανεν τὸ κοράσιον ἀλλὰ καθεύδει.

⁴⁴ In Matt. 9, Jesus is "the Son of Man" (9:6), the soul physician (9:12–13), the eschatological bridegroom (9:15), the resurrectionist of the dead (9:25), and the "Son of David" healing the blind (9:30) and casting out demons so that the mute can speak (9:33).

⁴⁵ Matthew is not concerned with the identity of the resurrected saints. Thus, any attempt to specify their identity is speculative, at best. Further, it is a misunderstanding to assume those participating in resurrection prior to the resurrection of Jesus participated in glorified/end-time resurrection. Additionally, it is a misunderstanding to assume that resurrection scenes prior to the resurrection of Jesus necessarily contradict the teaching that he was the firstborn from the dead (1 Cor. 15:20; Col. 1:18; Rev. 1:5). Both testaments have examples of persons being raised prior to the resurrection of Jesus. In the Old Testament, Elijah raises the widow's son after stretching himself on him

sleeping saints is the climactic sign, the crescendo of the series of revelatory signs is the confession of the centurion, and his entourage, that Jesus is the Son of God in Matthew 27:54.[46] The five short main clauses, which began in Matthew 27:51 with the subject first and the verb in the aorist passive, end here.

It is crucial to notice, however, that the thought of Matthew 27:51–52 does not conclude until the end of Matthew 27:53. The latter is a longer sentence containing two main verbs introduced by a participle. Rather, it narrates the events of the resurrected saints, who have emerged from their opened crypts: καὶ ἐξελθόντες ἐκ τῶν μνημείων μετὰ τὴν ἔγερσιν αὐτοῦ εἰσῆλθον εἰς τὴν ἁγίαν πόλιν καὶ ἐ'νεφανίσθησαν πολλοῖς. The temporal participle, ἐξελθόντες, does not introduce a new subject; its action is antecedent to the main verbs—εἰσῆλθον and ἐ'νεφανίσθησαν.[47] The

---

three times (1 Kings 17:17–24), and a man was raised to life when his body touched the bones of the prophet Elisha (2 Kings 13:21). Neither of these Old Testament resurrections were glorified/end-time resurrections; both recount the testimonial raising of someone via the prophet who would die again. In Matthew's Gospel, Jesus raised a girl to life; surely, she too would die again (Matt. 9:25). Similarly, John recounts Jesus' raising Lazarus back to life (John 11:43–44), who we assume would die again. How could the Pharisees plot to kill a person raised to everlasting life (John 12:10–11)? Like the author of 1 Kings, 2 Kings, and John, Matthew records a Lazarus-like resurrection occurring as a result of Jesus' death on the cross so that the doubting city may believe Jesus to be the Son of God the Father, sent into the world to save people from their sins (Matt. 1:21; cf. John 11:14–15, 42).

[46] Thus, Senior states, "All of these events are tied together (all are linked by καὶ, 'and . . .') and lead to the acclamation by the soldiers, a point Matthew explicitly makes by stating that their witness of the 'earthquake and what took place' prompted both their 'fear' and their confession of Jesus as Son of God (27:54; cf. Mark 15:39)." Donald Senior, *Matthew*, ANTC (Nashville: Abingdon Press, 1998), 333. Similarly, Witherup states that the climax of the signs "inevitably leads to v. 54, the acclamation by the centurion and his companions." Ronald D. Witherup, "The Death of Jesus and the Raising of the Saints: Matthew 27:51–54 in Context," SBLSP 26 (1987): 578–79.

[47] Similarly, Luz states, "It does not introduce a new subject. Its greater detail shows that this conclusion—that is, the statements about the dead—is what is most important." Luz, *Matthew*, 560. See also Robert H. Gundry, *Matthew:*

phrase μετὰ τὴν ἔγερσιν αὐτοῦ[48] is the most difficult phrase in the pericope.[49] It is the source of chronological problems for interpreters and the cause of the translation smorgasbord in relation to Matthew 27:51–54. Careful analysis, though, shows that had Matthew wanted to make it clear that the resurrection of τῶν κεκοιμημένων ἁγίων occurred only after Jesus' resurrection, the phrase could have preceded the participle ἐξελθόντες.[50]

Grammatically, it is best to read ἐξελθόντες as modifying ἠγέρθεσαν. Similarly, Quarles suggests, "The dead were raised and exited the tombs at the time of the crucifixion, but did not enter the city of Jerusalem until after Jesus' resurrection."[51] In support of this

---

A Commentary on His Handbook for a Mixed Church under Persecution (Grand Rapids: Eerdmans, 1994), 576. Contra Luz, Gundry asserts that it seems as if Matthew is relatively unconcerned with the resurrected saints. Rather, they rise as *one* of five signs testifying to the identity of Jesus.

[48] Schweizer wrongly considers this comment to be a later addition. See Eduard Schweizer, *The Good News according to Matthew*, trans. David E. Green (Atlanta: John Knox Press, 1975), 516. Oddly, Davies and Allison agree with Schweizer even though they admit that it appears in nearly all manuscripts and versions (Davies and Allison, *Critical and Exegetical Commentary*, 3:634). Similarly, Evans calls this scribal interpolation (Evans, *Matthew*, 466–67).

[49] Not only does Brown recognize this phrase as the *crux interpretum* of the pericope, he also asserts that "we should reject attempts to remove or neutralize" this phrase. Raymond E. Brown, *The Death of the Messiah: From Gethsemane to the Grave—A Commentary on the Passion Narratives in the Four Gospels*, ABRL (New York: Doubleday, 1994), 1127–29.

[50] Donald A. Hagner, *Matthew 14–28*, WBC 33B, vol. 2 (Nashville: Thomas Nelson, 1995), 850. Though France locates the departure of the raised dead from their graves after Jesus' resurrection, he notes that the Greek word order allows "after his resurrection" to be read either with ἐξελθόντες or with εἰσῆλθον and ἐνεφανίσθησαν. See France, *Gospel according to Matthew*, 1073. According to France, then, contra Wenham, the saints were raised immediately as a result of Jesus' death on the cross. The difference, then, is that they either (1) waited in their tombs until after Jesus was resurrected from the dead and then entered Jerusalem or (2) waited in the surrounding countryside until after Jesus was resurrected from the dead, and then entered the city.

[51] Quarles notes that nothing in the grammar of Matt. 27:51–54 precludes this punctuation of the passage. Nothing prohibits interpreters from

reading, David Wenham writes, "μετὰ τὴν ἔγερσιν αὐτοῦ in verse 53 may be taken as applying primarily to the main verb that follows it rather than as defining the time of the saints' exit from the tomb; in this case the saints may be supposed to have been raised and to have left their tombs on Good Friday, though they did not appear until after Easter."[52] Temporally, the sleeping dead were raised and exited their graves on Good Friday but did not enter εἰς τὴν ἁγίαν πόλιν until *after* Jesus was resurrected on Easter Sunday.[53] This reading of Matthew 27:53 reinforces the interpretation that Matthew 27:52 is connected to Matthew 27:51 in its occurrence and communicates that the saints were both raised from and exited their respective tombs on Good Friday.[54]

As Matthew concludes the pericope, readers are once again pointed to the missiological purpose behind the scene (as well as the entire Gospel): because of his identity, Jesus' death is a life-giving death and has meaning for the nations. Thus, as Gentile magi expressed faith at his birth (Matt. 2:1–12), so now Gentile militia profess faith at his death (Matt. 27:54).[55] Matthew's mention of

---

understanding μετὰ τὴν ἔγερσιν αὐτοῦ to modify the verbs that follow it rather than the preceding participle. He notes that normal Matthean style suggests that the prepositional phrase modifies the verb that follows it. See Quarles, "Matthew 27:51–53," 275.

[52] Admittedly, however, Wenham suggests μετὰ τὴν ἔγερσιν αὐτοῦ modifies only εἰσῆλθον whereas this dissertation suggests μετὰ τὴν ἔγερσιν αὐτοῦ modifies both εἰσῆλθον and ἐνεφανίσθησαν. See David Wenham, "The Resurrection Narratives in Matthew's Gospel," *TynBul* 24 (1973): 21–54, esp. 46.

[53] This will be discussed more fully when exploring Matthew's reliance on Ezek. 37:12–14 in the composition of his crucifixion scene.

[54] Again, though I came to these conclusions independent of Quarles, he also notes, "Overall, the best solution to the perceived chronological problem is to punctuate the text in such a way that the phrase 'after his resurrection' refers only to the entrance [and appearance] of the saints into the holy city" (Quarles, "Matthew 27:51–53: Meaning, Genre, Intertextuality, Theology, and Reception History," 275). Their resurrection, and subsequent entrance and appearance in the city of Jerusalem, was a sign pointing to the divine identity of the Crucified One.

[55] Green states, "The representatives of the Gentile world are witnesses of

τὸν σεισμὸν in Matthew 27:54 harkens the reader to ἐσείσθη in Matthew 27:51 and brings the pericope to a close, but not before the confession of the Roman centurion and his entourage—ἀληθῶς θεοῦ υἱὸς[56]—which is the result of the divine signs testifying to Jesus' divine identity following his death. Their profession of his identity is the reversal of the sarcastic ridicule Jesus received from his enemies in Matthew 27:40, 43.

Conclusion

In the prosecution of this dissertation's thesis, it was necessary to address the issue of translation in relation of Matthew 27:51–54. This chapter has argued that the most natural translation of the Matthean pericope is as follows:

> Behold, the curtain of the temple was torn in two from top to bottom, the earth quaked, and the rocks split, the tombs, also, were opened and the bodies of many saints who had died were raised to life; coming out of the tombs, they went into the holy city after his resurrection, appearing to many people. When the centurion and those guarding Jesus with him saw the earthquake and the things that took place they were terrified and said, "This really was the Son of God!"

This reading tethers the signs in Matthew 27:51–54 with the events of Good Friday and accentuates the three theological foci Matthew is featuring in his Gospel's conclusion: Christology,

---

the death of the Son of God and its earth-shattering character, as they were of the signs which accompanied his marvelous birth" (Green, *Gospel according to Matthew*, 224). See also Bruner, *Matthew*, 764.

[56] Though there is no article with θεοῦ or with υἱὸς in the Greek text, and even though the phrase can be translated either "the Son of God" or "a Son of God," it is clear from the context that "the Son of God" is the correct reading/translation according to Colwell's Rule.

missiology, and eschatology. Because the βασιλεία has broken into the present *in* the person of Jesus (Matt. 4:17; cf. 3:2; 10:7), Jesus dies like no other in history. Accompanying his death are signs testifying to his divine identity as the Son of God; they underscore the missiological implications of his death—it has meaning for the nations (Matt. 27:54; 28:16–20).[57] Therefore, it has been argued that a proper understanding of the pericope's translation removes the inordinate interpretive stress placed on the five divine portents—particularly the resurrection of the sleeping saints (Matt. 27:52b–53).

---

[57] Senior powerfully captures this: "The crucifixion scenes also express Matthew's view of Jesus' death as redemptive. Through the death of Jesus, the dead are liberated from their tombs, and the salvific mission of Jesus, implicit in his very name and enacted in his ministry of healing, comes to its most powerful expression" (Senior, *Matthew*, 336).

3

From Rigor Mortis to Resurrection: Matthean Dependence on Ezekiel 37:1–14 in the Composition of Matthew 27:51–54

> Behold, the curtain of the temple was torn in two from top to bottom, the earth quaked, and the rocks split, the tombs, also, were opened and the bodies of many saints who had died were raised to life; coming out of the tombs, they went into the holy city after his resurrection, appearing to many people. When the centurion and those guarding Jesus with him saw the earthquake and the things that took place they were terrified and said, "This really was the Son of God!"

A proper understanding of Matthew 27:51–54 mandates an examination of the pericope's translation. The suggested translation above helps interpreters ascertain: (1) How Matthew 27:51–54 is functioning in the death-resurrection scene and (2) the three theological foci of the pericope—Christology, missiology, and eschatology. Further, the translation suggests that the five signs recounted in Matthew 27:51–53 occur as a result of Jesus' death on the cross after he unleashes the Spirit (τὸ πνυεμα) in Matthew 27:50. Literally, the events of Good Friday are tethered closely with the events occurring on Easter Sunday in Matthew 28:1–15. Matthew brings the pericopes together because Jesus' death and resurrection is viewed as one evil-defeating, death-defying event in his Gospel narrative as they inaugurate a new age. But the looming question is, From where did Matthew draw his literary inspiration in the composition of this Matthean pericope? Therefore, a proper understanding of the pericope under consideration also requires consideration of the primary Old Testament referent utilized in Matthew 27:51–54.

Though Matthew's use of the Old Testament has been much debated, this chapter will argue that the pericope, laced with divine signs testifying to Jesus' divine identity as the Son of God (i.e., Matt. 27:51–54), finds its principal origins in Ezekiel 37:1–14. Brevard Childs, though referring specifically to Matthew's formula citations within his Gospel, helps elucidate the theological context that the Old Testament provides in the Matthean narrative as well as the homiletical interests behind its deployment in the Gospel when he states,

> First, the Old Testament citations provide a theological context with the divine economy of God with Israel by which to understand and interpret the significance of Jesus' life and ministry. The entire Old Testament is viewed as a prophetic revelation of God's purpose pointing to the future which has now been fulfilled in Jesus Christ, God's promised Messiah. The term "reflexion citation" is helpful in emphasizing the role of the citation in evoking an activity of reflection, meditation, and interpretation on the part of the reader in striving to grasp the relationship between Old Testament prophecy and New Testament fulfillment. The New Testament technique of citing a passage is badly misunderstood if one concludes that Matthew's interests are narrowly construed or largely apologetic. Rather, the specific text functions as a transparency into the larger prophetic dimension represented by the entire Old Testament. Secondly, the formula citations are a form of Christian proclamation. The gospel [*sic*] writer bears witness from the context of Israel's prior experience of God

to the realization of the divine will, now through the Messiah. On the one hand, Matthew reads the Old Testament from the perspective of the gospel, and testifies to the unity of the one plan of God within the scheme of prophecy and fulfillment. On the other hand, the very meaning of the gospel to which he bears witness receives its definition from the Old Testament.[1]

As he was in the beginning of his narrative, Matthew is concerned with anchoring Jesus' life in Old Testament cotext,[2] for "everything written about [Jesus] in the Law of Moses and the

---

[1] I agree with his conclusions and would apply them to instances where Scripture is both explicitly identified and implicitly alluded to within Matthew's Gospel, whether cognizantly referred to or incognizantly echoed in the Matthean narrative. See Brevard S. Childs, *The New Testament as Canon: An Introduction* (Philadelphia: Fortress Press, 1984), 70–71. Similarly, Quarles states, "Matthew regards the Scriptures, the Word of God, as the message about Jesus. Jesus was the fulfillment of the Old Testament message." Charles Quarles, *A Theology of Matthew: Jesus Revealed as Deliverer, King, and Incarnate Creator*, Explorations in Biblical Theology, ed. Robert Patterson (Phillipsburg, NJ: P&R Publishing, 2013), 28. This chapter, then, will contend the prophetic revelation portended in Ezek. 37:1–14 (especially 37:11–14) was fulfilled, at least partially, in Jesus Christ.

[2] To comprehend the context of the Matthean pericope, interpreters must not merely situate it within Matt. 27 or the conclusion to Matthew's Gospel or within the entirety of Matthew, but also within the canonical context, the theological context of resurrection, and the homiletical context of textual application. The "cotext," then, of Matt. 27:51–54 is the series of expanding interpretive frameworks providing layers of interpretive meaning. See Graeme Goldsworthy, *Gospel-Centered Hermeneutics: Foundations and Principles of Evangelical Biblical Interpretation* (Downers Grove, IL: InterVarsity Press, 2006), 206. According to Cotterell, the cotext is "the total text ... within which we may expect to locate the clues which might serve to resolve our inescapable exegetical uncertainties." Peter Cotterell, "Hermeneutics: Some Linguistic Considerations," *Evangel* 13, 3 (Autumn 1995): 78–83. Admittedly, Cotterell is combating postmodernist deconstructionist hermeneutics that dissects meaning at the level of the sentence rather than at the level of the utterance. But his article helps us to see the multiple interpretive frameworks working

Prophets and the Psalms must be fulfilled" (Luke 24:44).[3] This chapter will endeavor to identify the location of these Matthean motifs in the Ezekielian Old Testament prophetic narrative.

The Genesis of Matthew 27:51–54

Scholars have often debated the origins of Matthew 27:51–54; their pontifications have not been scarce.[4] On the one hand, some suggest that the Matthean pericope finds its background in

---

together to produce context and meaning.

[3] France has compellingly argued that Matthew was cognizant of differing levels of sensibility to discern allusions to the Old Testament among his hearers and readers. See R. T. France, "The Formula-Quotations of Matthew 2 and the Problem of Communication," *NTS* 27 (1981): 233–51. This dissertation suggests, though, that even without an explicit fulfillment formula quotation in Matt. 27:51–54, the Gospel writer directs our attention to Ezekiel's prophecy. Matthew created a plain meaning in the construction of this pericope by including signs that identify Jesus as the eschatological Son of God (Matt. 27:54; cf. 3:16; 16:16; 17:5) *and* embedded a deeper meaning by connecting the events of Jesus' life-giving death to Ezek. 37:1–14—the Davidic Servant (Matt. 1:1), Jesus, leads the resurrected dead into the land to fulfill what was spoken by the prophet. Because Matthew begins his Gospel by echoing both the Genesis narrative as well as the life of David—Βίβλος γενέσεως Ἰησοῦ Χριστοῦ υἱοῦ Δαυὶδ υἱοῦ Ἀβραάμ (Matt. 1:1)—and, because he carefully weaves fulfillment quotations throughout his Gospel narrative (Matt. 1:22; 2:5, 15, 17, 23; 4:14; 8:17; 12:17; 13:35; 21:4; 26:56; 27:9), his readers are granted hermeneutical "license" to look to the Old Testament for how the life (and death and resurrection and ascension) of Jesus fulfills the Scripture we are told is written about him (Luke 24:44). Similarly, Leithart, using John's Gospel as an example, states, "I read John 1:1 and I hear echoes of Genesis 1:1, and I begin to suspect that John wants to teach that the gospel story is a story of new creation." Peter J. Leithart, *Deep Exegesis: The Mystery of Reading Scripture* (Waco, TX: Baylor University Press, 2009), 132. The "license" is given to readers by virtue of explicit Old Testament quotations in the Gospel narrative. The more familiar readers are with the biblical narrative, the more adept will be their sensibility to discern intertextual connections between the New Testament and Old Testament, even when they are not explicitly identified.

[4] Three examples from reputable scholars will suffice to illustrate this point. Senior suggests Matt. 27:51b–53 is solely dependent on Ezek. 37, in Donald P.

a mixture of a plethora of Old Testament passages, with some of the more prominent allusions being Isaiah 26:19, "Your dead shall live; their bodies shall rise," and Daniel 12:2, "And many of those who sleep in the dust of the earth shall awake, some to everlasting life, and some to shame and everlasting contempt."[5] Less conspicuous Old Testament influences include Psalm 77:19; Psalm 104:30; Jeremiah 15:9; Joel 2:10; Amos 8:9; Nahum 1:5–6; Haggai 2:6; and Zechariah 14:4–5.[6]

On the other hand, others suggest Matthew's pericopal hapax finds its roots in an extrabiblical, pre-Matthean tradition. The

---

Senior, *The Passion Narrative according to Matthew: A Redactional Study*, BETL 39 (Leuven, Belgium: Leuven University Press, 1975), 207–23. Allison, taking issue with Senior's claim that Matt. 27:51b–53 is based solely on Ezek. 37, contends that Zech. 14:4–5, at least in part, directly informs the composition of Matt. 27:51–54, in Dale C. Allison Jr., *The End of the Ages Has Come: An Early Interpretation of the Passion and Resurrection of Jesus* (Philadelphia: Fortress Press, 1985), 40–46. Throughout his exposition of the Matthean pericope, Brown supports a mixture of scriptural passages—some of the more prominent being Isa. 26; Ezek. 37, and Zech. 14—informing the composition of Matt. 27:51–54, in Raymond E. Brown, *The Death of the Messiah: From Gethsemane to the Grave—A Commentary on the Passion Narratives in the Four Gospels*, ABRL (New York: Doubleday, 1994), 2:1118–33.

[5] Riesenfeld suggests that passages such as Isa. 26:19 and Dan. 12:2 manifest that the idea of bodily resurrection was not foreign to the religious beliefs of the Jewish people six centuries prior to Christ. See Harald Riesenfeld, *The Resurrection in Ezekiel XXXVII and in the Dura-Europos Paintings* (Leipzig: Otto Harrassowitz, 1948), 3. For a recent discussion on a biblical theology of resurrection in the Old Testament, see Mitchell Lloyd Chase, "Resurrection Hope in Daniel 12:2: An Exercise in Biblical Theology" (PhD diss., The Southern Baptist Theological Seminary, 2013). Nickelsburg contends that Dan. 12:1–3 is the earliest datable reference to a resurrection from the dead in the Hebrew Bible in which eschatological resurrection is expressed. See George W. E. Nickelsburg, *Resurrection, Immortality, and Eternal Life in Intertestamental Judaism and Early Christianity*, HTS 56 (Cambridge, MA: Harvard University Press, 1972), 23.

[6] Beale and Carson suggest the following textual concoction shaping Matt. 27:45–54: Ex. 10:22; 26:31–35; Ps. 69:21; Ezek. 37:12; Dan. 12:2; Joel 2:10; Amos 8:9; Zech. 14:4–5. G. K. Beale and D. A. Carson, eds., *Commentary on the New Testament Use of the Old Testament* (Grand Rapids: Baker, 2007), 98.

trembling of the celestial Watchers in response to the great quaking of the earth at the revelation of God in 1 Enoch 1:3–8 is suggested as one of the more prominent influences:

> The Great Holy One will come forth from his dwelling, and the eternal God will tread from thence upon Mount Sinai. He will appear with his army, he will appear with his mighty host from the heaven of heavens. All the watchers will fear and [quake], and those who are hiding in all the ends of the earth will sing. All the ends of the earth will be shaken, and trembling and great fear will seize them (the watchers) unto the ends of the earth. The high mountains will be shaken and fall and break apart, and the high hills will be made low and melt like wax before the fire. The earth will be wholly rent asunder, and everything on the earth will perish, and there will be judgment on all. With the righteous he will make peace, and over the chosen there will be protection, and upon them mercy.[7]

Fourth Ezra 7:32 is also noted for its conspicuous resurrection imagery: "And the earth shall give back those who are asleep in it, and the dust those who rest in it and the treasuries shall give up the souls which have been committed to them."[8] Less evident

---

[7] George W. E. Nickelsburg and James C. VanderKam, *1 Enoch: A New Translation Based on the Hermeneia Commentary* (Minneapolis: Fortress Press, 2004), 19–20.

[8] The translation from 4 Ezra was taken from Michael E. Stone, *Fourth Ezra: A Commentary on the Book of Fourth Ezra*, Hermeneia (Minneapolis: Fortress Press, 1990). I was made aware of the connection between the Matthean narrative and 4 Ezra 7:32 by Weren. See Wim J. C. Weren, *Studies in Matthew's Gospel: Literary Design, Intertextuality, and Social Setting* (Leiden, Netherlands: Brill, 2014), 210–21. He contends that Matthew's Gospel and 4 Ezra are linked by eschatology. The resurrection of the saints in Matt. 27:51–54, then, manifests that "Jesus' death and resurrection form the beginning of the age to come." Weren differs, however, in that he suggests the "text chain"

extrabiblical, pre-Matthean influences include the Gospel of Peter, the Testament of Levi, and 4 Ezra.[9] In 4 Ezra 4:35–42, the souls of the righteous are pining for release from sheol; their confinement—which is likened to a child in the womb of a woman—cannot persist beyond a predetermined allotted time. Likewise, neither can sheol prevent the righteous from their impending resurrection and release.

Scrutiny of these various suggestions, however, reveals that verbal and thematic connections between certain Old Testament or extrabiblical influences and the Matthean narrative are weak. Rather, an examination of Ezekiel 37:1–14 in its Septuagintal form manifests numerous links to Matthew's Gospel. The aim of this section of the chapter will be to situate Ezekiel 37:1–14 within the entirety of its Ezekielian context and to examine Ezekiel 37:1–14 (LXX) as the primary text on which Matthew is relying in the composition of Matthew 27:51–53.[10] There is plenty of evidence contending that Matthew read and made use of the Greek Old Testament in the composition of his Gospel.[11] This chapter will suggest that the

---

informing Matt. 27:51–54 is a combination of Isa. 26:19, Dan. 12:3, and Ezek. 37:1–14 along with other extrabiblical texts such as Pseudo-Ezekiel.

[9] I was made aware of the connections between Matt. 27:51–54 and both 4 Ezra and T. Levi 3:9 in Brown, *Death of the Messiah*, 2:1122, 1127.

[10] Matthew relied heavily on the Old Testament in the composition of his Gospel. The intent of this chapter, then, is not to suggest that Matthew is *solely* dependent on Ezek. 37:12–14 in the composition of Matt. 27:51–53, for Allison has convincingly argued that Matt. 27:51–54 is at least partially reliant on Zech. 14:4–5 (LXX). He gives four reasons for this assertion: in both Matthew and Zechariah there is (1) a resurrection that occurs immediately outside of Jerusalem, (2) an earthquake, (3) the verb σχίζω used in the passive, and (4) the resurrected dead identified as οἱ ἅγιοι. See Allison, *End of the Ages Has Come*, 44. Rather, it is the aim of this chapter to suggest that Matthew has Ezek. 37:12–14 (LXX) as his *primary* Old Testament referent when composing this resurrection pericope. The importance of this claim will soon become evident.

[11] Text-type in relation to the Matthean formula quotations as well as Matthean textual allusions throughout his Gospel have been vehemently debated. France contends the LXX is not "Matthew's Bible" and "to speak of 'the Hebrew' and 'the LXX' as the main or only textual resources available

connection between Matthew 27:51–54 and Ezekiel 37:1–14 (LXX) is another example of Matthew's making use of a Greek Old Testament in his Gospel.

Ezekiel 37:1–14 in Prophetic Context

Ezekiel, a prophet heralding in exile from Babylon, the land of Israel's judgment, speaks of restoration in Ezekiel 36:16–37:14. In the latter portion of his prophecy, a return from exile is promised in Ezekiel 36:24: "I will take you from the nations and gather you from all the countries and bring you into your own land" (cf. Ezek. 11:17; 20:42; 37:12, 21). Before the people can enter "their own land," they must be cleansed. Israel is contaminated and unclean as a consequence of their defiling deeds, idol worship, and exile in a foreign land (Ezek. 36:17–20). As God rakes in the castaways from the various countries to which they have been scattered, the people are

---

to Matthew is at least an oversimplification." Rather, it seems that Matthew made use of Hebrew, LXX, and "his own creative paraphrasing," as his scriptural reflections enabled him to insert quotations that would best suit the contexts into which he placed them. See R. T. France, *Matthew: Evangelist and Teacher* (Eugene, OR: Wipf & Stock, 1989), 172–76. Similarly, Soares Prabhu suggests that Matthew's text-type is a combination of LXX, Hebrew, and Matthean redaction. See G. M. Soares Prabhu, *The Formula Quotations in the Infancy Narrative of Matthew* (Rome: Biblical Institute Press, 1976), 73–77. This dissertation, then, does not claim that Matthew made use of only the LXX but rather that he made use of the LXX, broadly defined as Greek versions of the Old Testament, while composing his Gospel. Again, it is France who argues that it is not unreasonable to suggest that the Gospel writers generally refer to the LXX when making use of the OT, especially "where the LXX was a fair translation of the version quoted by Jesus, [since] it would be natural for the Greek translator to use the LXX words familiar both to himself and to his readers." R. T. France, *Jesus and the Old Testament: His Application of Old Testament Passages to Himself and His Mission* (Vancouver: Regent College Publishing, 1998), 25. Like Gundry (though he is discussing Matthew's use of the Old Testament), I aim to manifest that a discernable thought connection exists between Matt. 27:51–54 and Ezek. 37:12–14. See Robert H. Gundry, *The Use of the Old Testament in St. Matthew's Gospel: With Special Reference to the Messianic Hope* (Leiden, Netherlands: Brill, 1967), 1–5.

washed by water: "I will sprinkle clean water on you, and you shall be clean from all your uncleanness, and from all your idols I will cleanse you" (Ezek. 36:25).[12] The water cleansing is not perfunctory. It is essential because of the people's impurity. The prophet does not just promise cleansing; he prophesies a new heart for God's people (Ezek. 36:26).[13] The new heart will come with a new eschatological

---

[12] The "sprinkling" foretold in Ezek. 36:25 is redemptive washing—atonement and forgiveness of sins. Isaiah tells us this cleansing is for the nations, not just the rejected house of Israel: "Behold, my servant shall act wisely; he shall be high and lifted up, and shall be exalted . . . so shall he sprinkle many nations" (Isa. 52:13–15). Those who were put to shame in exile for forsaking "the Lord, the fountain of living water" (Jer. 17:13) will replenish their thirsty spiritual palates by believing in God's Messiah as the Scripture has said (John 7:38) since the Davidic Servant will be wounded for their transgressions (Isa. 53:5) so they may receive the new hearts Ezekiel promises to those who are cleansed: "And I will give you a new heart, and a new spirit I will put within you. And I will remove the heart of stone from your flesh and give you a heart of flesh" (Ezek. 36:26).

[13] Commenting on Ezek. 36–37, Gentry and Wellum state, "There will be a new covenant to renew the relationship with God and his people, a covenant that will deal effectively with hearts stubbornly bent on sin (36:24–32)." Peter J. Gentry and Stephen J. Wellum, *Kingdom through Covenant: A Biblical-Theological Understanding of the Covenants* (Wheaton, IL: Crossway, 2012), 472–73. Likewise, Hamilton, while commenting on Ezek. 37:24, argues that a new heart will be given when the new David reigns and Yahweh has delivered his people from the judgment of exile. See James M. Hamilton Jr., *God's Glory in Salvation through Judgment: A Biblical Theology* (Wheaton, IL: Crossway, 2010), 229. For a Reformed and Baptistic understanding of the new covenant, see Pascal Denault, *The Distinctiveness of Baptist Covenant Theology: A Comparison between Seventeenth-Century Particular Baptist and Paedobaptist Federalism* (Birmingham, AL: Solid Ground Christian Books, 2013), 35–154. Denault demonstrates that Reformed Baptists have insisted that the covenant of grace never had an outward administration that included unbelievers under the old covenant; rather, it was the promise of the new covenant to save God's elect people, which was progressively revealed under the old covenant and formally actualized with the death of Jesus in the new covenant. The covenant of grace is God's promise, which was extended immediately after the fall in Gen. 3:15, to save his elect people because of Jesus' work in the covenant of redemption, in which he kept the law Adam failed to keep in the covenant of works.

shepherd in the land—the Davidic Servant—who will replace the false shepherds of Israel (Ezek. 34:1–10; 37:24–25).[14] A new heart, according to Ezekiel, enables the people to be covenantally faithful to God by means of obedience to his Word—"I will remove the heart of stone from their flesh and give them a heart of flesh, that they may walk in my statutes and keep my rules and obey them" (Ezek. 11:19–20).[15] Like the resurrection in Ezekiel 37:1–14, the creation of a new heart is the result of divine initiative (Ezek. 36:26; cf. 18:31). Speaking of the messianic theme in Ezekiel, Stephen Dempster writes,

> Even the divided kingdom of exiles is reunited under a new leader, who is said to be "my servant David" (Ezek. 37:24–25; cf. 34:23–24). But he is also described as one who will come to power through relative obscurity. In a remarkable allegorical passage, a Davidic descendant is compared to a tender shoot plucked from a tall tree, taken to Mount Zion and planted there to grow into a huge tree, bearing fruit and providing shade for all the birds of the forest (17:22–24). Thus all the trees of the forest (peoples of the word) will know

---

[14] House contends, "Creating the remnant, then, is a task the Lord must perform." His initiative will place the people under Davidic leadership. The new leadership will result in a new covenant, which will result in permanent, new protection for God's people. As in Jeremiah's prophecy, the presence of God's Davidic servant is the catalyst for a new, permanent covenant (Jer. 31:31–34; Jer. 33:14–26; Ezek. 37:24–28). See Paul R. House, *Old Testament Theology* (Downers Grove, IL: InterVarsity Press, 1998), 341.

[15] As in Matt. 27:45–54, the presence of the Spirit is prevalent in the passage. The new heart comes to the exilic people by the agency of God's Spirit in Ezek. 36. The role of the Spirit is prominent in the vision of dry bones—the Spirit creates people from nothing when not even a stone heart exists! The Spirit who enlivens the people and enables obedience (Ezek. 36:26–27) is the same Spirit who anoints Ezekiel to preach (Ezek. 37:1), gives life to the dead (Ezek. 37:4–10), empowers Israel to return to the land (Ezek. 37:11–14), and creates a new humanity cleansed from idolatry (Ezek. 37:15–23). See House, *Old Testament Theology*, 342.

that "I the Lord lower the tall tree and raise the low tree. I dry up the green tree and make the dry tree flourish" (17:24). Later, this "David" who will come to power is remembered for his humble origins as a shepherd (34:23); he will provide true leadership, as opposed to past leaders, who are symbolized as corrupt and destructive shepherds. Both these motifs of Davidic rule (a tender shoot and a shepherd) echo Jeremiah's prediction of a "plant growth" from the line of David, which will bring good shepherds—justice for the nation (Jer. 23:1–8). Ezekiel states that it is during this period of future Davidic leadership that a covenant of shalom will bring a flourishing prosperity and fertility to the land (34:23–31), which will be a new Eden (36:35).[16]

---

[16] Stephen G. Dempster, *Dominion and Dynasty: A Biblical Theology of the Hebrew Bible*, NSBT 15, ed. D. A. Carson (Downers Grove, IL: InterVarsity Press, 2003), 170–71. Additionally, Dempster notes that the spiritual plight of the people requires nothing less than restorative resurrection. The vision, then, of resurrection inspired by the Spirit is one of a new humanity placed in the new Eden (Gen. 2:7; Ezek. 37:7–10; John 20:19–23). Not only are the aforementioned passages linked conceptually, they are linked linguistically. The same verb, ἐμφυσάω, is used in the LXX in Gen. 2:7 and Ezek. 37:9 as well as in John 20. In all three biblical texts the verb is accompanied by either an accusative or dative auxiliary structure, which should encourage translators to understand that something is being breathed into, toward, or on. In Gen. 2 in the LXX, God ἐνεφύσησεν into Adam's face; the accusative substantive, εἰς τὸ πρόσωπον αὐ᾽τοῦ πνοὴν ζωῆς, is the auxiliary structure. Thus, the structure is verb plus preposition plus accusative substantive. In Ezek. 37 in the LXX, the prophet ἐμφύσησον to the wind; the auxiliary structure in this prophetic passage is εἰς τοὺς νεκροὺς τούτους. Thus, the structure is verb plus preposition plus accusative substantive. And in John 20 Jesus ἐνεφύσησεν onto the disciples. The auxiliary structure is αὐτοῖς; the form of the structure is verb plus dative object. Thus, αὐτοῖς seems to be playing double duty for both the verb ἐνεφύσησεν and the verb λέγει in 20:22—it functions as the indirect object of both verbs. For more on ἐμφυσάω, consult BDAG (Chicago: University of Chicago Press, 2000), s.v. "ἐμφυσάω." Compare with L&N, 2nd ed., ed. Ronald B. Smith and Karen A. Munson (New York: United Bible Societies, 1989), s.v. "ἐμφυσάω." Consult also LSJ, 9th ed., ed. Henry S. Jones and Roderick McKenzie (Oxford: Clarendon Press, 1940), s.v. "ἐμφυσάω."

The prophecy of Israel's future is hopeful. But, lest the people be confused, the restorative cleaning is for the exaltation of Yahweh's name, not because of Israel's inherent worth (Ezek. 36:32). Because the reputation of Yahweh is at stake, three times in Ezekiel 36:21–23 the prophet asserts that redemption and restoration are for God's name alone:

> *But I had concern for my holy name*, which the house of Israel had profaned among the nations to which they came. "Therefore say to the house of Israel, Thus says the Lord God: It is not for your sake, O house of Israel, that I am about to act, *but for the sake of my holy name*, which you have profaned among the nations to which you came. And I will vindicate the holiness of *my great name*, which has been profaned among the nations.

The end result of cleansing and restoration is that the people will know that Yahweh is God: "The nations will know that I am the Lord, declares the Lord God, when through you I vindicate my holiness before their eyes.... Then they will know that I am the Lord" (Ezek. 36:23, 38).[17]

The narrative context of Ezekiel's dry bones vision is one of new covenant promise amid exilic despair. Throughout Ezekiel, the revelation of God's salvation comes to his people by means of "the word of the Lord," as it does throughout the entirety of the biblical narrative.[18] As God formerly revealed himself at Sinai through his

---

[17] The refrain "they will know that I am the Lord" is repeated eighteen times throughout Ezekiel (LXX): 6:14; 24:27; 25:11, 17; 26:6; 28:23, 26; 29:9, 16, 21; 30:8, 19, 26; 32:15; 33:29; 35:15; 36:38; 38:23.

[18] In LXX of Ezekiel, "word of the Lord" occurs fifty-nine times—Ezek. 1:3; 3:16; 6:1, 3; 7:1; 11:14; 12:1, 8, 17, 21, 26; 13:1; 14:2, 12; 15:1; 16:1, 35; 17:1, 11; 18:1; 20:2; 21:1, 3, 6, 13, 23; 22:1, 17, 23; 23:1; 24:1, 15, 20; 25:1, 3; 26:1; 27:1; 28:1, 11, 20; 29:1, 17; 30:1, 20; 31:1; 32:1, 17; 33:1, 23; 34:1, 7; 35:1; 36:1, 4; 36:4, 16; 37:4, 15; 38:1.

word (Ex. 19:16–20; 20:18–21)—and as God would, in the future, reveal himself on a hill outside of Jerusalem through the eschatological Word (Matt. 27:54; cf. John 1:1)—so, too, in Ezekiel the prophesied new heart comes by means of God's Word: "Then he said to me, 'Prophesy over these bones, and say to them, O dry bones, hear the word of the LORD.'" (Ezek. 37:4; cf. Rom. 10:17).[19] For Ezekiel, resurrection from the dead is likened to a return from exile (Ezek. 37:12–14).[20] The vision of dry bones signifies rebirth of the entire people "in a way which radically transcends the hope of Jeremiah."[21]

---

[19] Leithart also contends the prophecy of Ezek. 36:24–29 will come to fruition when Jesus, the Messianic Davidic Servant, comes. The vision in Ezek. 37, then, like the prophecy in Ezek. 36, is "first of all about a resurrection from the death of exile." Peter J. Leithart, *A House for My Name: A Survey of the Old Testament* (Moscow, ID: Canon Press, 2000), 218–19. Additionally, Leithart connects the blessings foretold with nations outside of Israel. He notes that the messages to the seven Gentile nations in Ezek. 25–32 indicate that, once again, "Yahweh provokes Judah to jealousy by sending His word to the Gentiles."

[20] Interestingly, Hamilton links the revelatory vision of Ezek. 37 with the book of Revelation—"The sequence of events in Rev. 20–22 matches the sequence of events in Ezek. 37–48 as follows: resurrection of God's people (Ezek. 37:1–14; Rev. 20:4–6); Christ's reign over the land restored from war (Ezek. 37:24; 38:8, 11; Rev. 20:4–6); satanic attack by Gog and Magog (Ezek. 38:1–4, 8, 11; Rev. 20:7–8); defeat of Gog and Satan (Ezek. 38:16–39:24; Rev. 20:9–10); new heaven and new earth presented as a cosmic temple (Ezek. 40–48; Rev. 21–22)." James M. Hamilton Jr., *With the Clouds of Heaven: The Book of Daniel in Biblical Theology*, NSBT 32 (Downers Grove, IL: InterVarsity Press, 2014), 219. Though this dissertation will not labor to connect Ezekiel with John's apocalypse, it is worthwhile to note the eschatological overtones Hamilton notices within Ezekiel's vision. This, then, gives further credence to the eschatological foci that this dissertation's thesis argues is central in the Matthean pericope under consideration.

[21] Brevard S. Childs, *Biblical Theology of the Old and New Testaments: Theological Reflection on the Christian Bible* (Minneapolis: Fortress Press, 1993), 178. Childs notes, "Ezekiel can also make use of the Davidic hope, the one true shepherd (34.23) and of an everlasting covenant which calls forth a new heart (11.19; 18.31; 36.26; 39.29)" (ibid.). Additionally, House highlights that Ezekiel's employment of the Spirit links the king and servant images found in Isaiah and Jeremiah "as well as those prophets' teachings about the everlasting and new covenants" (House, *Old Testament Theology*, 342).

Ezekiel 37:1-14 (LXX)

Probably no portion of Ezekiel's prophecy is as well known as "the valley of dry bones." Throughout the pericope, despondence threatens the existence of the people of Israel. They are, the Scripture says, both hopeless in their faith and oppressed in their exile: καὶ αὐτοὶ λέγουσιν Ξηρὰ γέγονεν τὰ ὀστᾶ ἡμῶν, ἀπόλωλεν ἡ ἐλπὶς ἡμῶν, διαπεφωνήκαμεν (Ezek. 37:11 LXX). Despite their despair, the prophetic vision recounted in Ezekiel 37:1-14 is an oracle of hope for their future salvation, their return from exile.[22] Yahweh, via the prophet, upends their pessimistic premise and proclaims a new salvation syllogism.

Table 3.1. A Divine Ezekielian Enthymeme

Israel	God
Dry bones *cannot* live (37:3)	Dry bones *can* live (37:1–10)
Israel is dry bones (37:11a)	Israel is dry bones (37:12a)
Therefore Israel cannot live (37:11b)	Therefore Israel can live (37:12b–14)

---

[22] Allen argues that the notion of hope can even be seen in the compositional intentionality of the prophetic vision. He contends that "structurally there is a double movement in the vision account from a negative orientation [vv. 1–3] to a positive one [vv. 4–8]; this is matched by a single movement in the accompanying oracle of salvation [vv. 8–10]. In terms of tradition history this movement echoes the metaphorical creedal statement that Yahweh both kills and makes alive, in order to affirm his positive purpose to restore his exiled people [vv. 11–14]." Leslie C. Allen, "Structure, Tradition and Redaction in Ezekiel's Death Valley Vision," in *Among the Prophets: Language, Image and Structure in the Prophetic Writings*, ed. Philip R. Davis and David J. A. Clines, JSOTSup 144 (Sheffield: Journal for the Study of the Old Testament Press, 1993), 127–42.

As in Matthew 27:51–54, table 3.1[23] above illustrates that the compositional parallelism of the passage delivers a rhetorical "punch" to Ezekiel's (re)readers.[24] The persuasive force of the Ezekielian passage does not reside, then, in its rational argumentation—though, as the chart manifests, the prophecy is not devoid of rational argumentation. Rather, the persuasive force of the pericope resides in the dramatic images it conjures to arrest the prophet's (re)readers through its enthymematic structure. This section will endeavor, then, to (1) exegete the passage, (2) show the internal logic of the prophetic argument coursing throughout the oracle, and (3) crystallize the oracle's thought connections to Matthew 27:51–54.

Interpreting Ezekiel 37:1–14

A close reading of the Septuagintal version of Ezekiel 37:1–14 will manifest that repetition is a literary device utilized by the prophet to underscore and emphasize the vision's theological import in this well-known fourteen-verse pericope. First, "live" is used six

---

[23] Table 3.1 is an adapted version of that found in Michael V. Fox, "The Rhetoric of Ezekiel's Vision of the Valley of Dry Bones," *HUCA* 51 (1980): 1–15. Fox observes that auditors could not appreciate the complex rhetorical structure devices. So he labors to accentuate rhetorical devices more readily observable to auditors beyond the level of structure: in the vision, Ezekiel is not merely a prophetic messenger but a prophetic spectator; unstated absurdity of corporeal resurrection persists throughout the pericope; the death is so complete that it takes two steps to complete the process of resurrection. But, contra Fox, Ezek. 37 is a literary text that permits reading, and rereading. The persuasive force of the prophecy's structure is enhanced when placed on the examination table of the reader/interpreter.

[24] For Petersen, this is one of the main premises for not delaying the resurrection of the sleeping dead in Matt. 27 to after Jesus' resurrection: "The resurrection—and, therefore, the appearance—of the resurrected persons is placed here, at the death of Jesus on the cross, as one of the natural wonders which accompanied Jesus' death, and which signified its gravity. To delay their appearance until 'after his resurrection' defeats the entire purpose of place the report at this point in the [Matthean] narrative." William L. Petersen, "Romanos and the Diatessaron," *NTS* 29 (1983): 500.

times throughout the fourteen verses in Ezekiel 37:3, 5, 6, 9, 10, 14.²⁵ Second, the passage underscores its pneumatological overtones through the use of πνεῦμα cognates.²⁶ "Spirit" or "breath" is used nine times throughout the pericope in Ezekiel 37:1, 5, 6, 8, 9a, 9b, 9c, 10, 14 (cf. Ezek. 36:26–27).²⁷ Like its Hebrew counterpart (רוּחַ), πνεῦμα is multivalent and therefore has a range of meaning and "can mean 'breath, wind, spirit,' both human and divine."²⁸ The divine activity of "the Spirit" is conspicuous as he enlivens the people and enables obedience (Ezek. 36:26–27), anoints Ezekiel to preach (Ezek. 37:1), gives life to the dead (Ezek. 37:4–10), empowers Israel to return to the land (Ezek. 37:11–14), and creates a new humanity cleansed from idolatry (Ezek. 37:15–23). Third,

---

²⁵ The passage employs various Greek conjugations that are translated "live": ζήσεται, ζωῆς, ζήσεσθε, ζησάτωσαν, ἔζησαν, ζήσεσθε.

²⁶ Homing in on the pneumatological theme coursing throughout the passage, Allen, commenting on the MT, argues that the Ezekielian pericope "functions as an elaboration of the gift of Yahweh's spirit promised in 36.27a." Thus, he states, "[Ezek. 37:1–14's] ninefold occurrence of רוּחַ 'breath/spirit' [is] an illustration of the restoring power of God in 36.27a. It intends to focus particularly on the reference to the giving of the רוּחַ in v. 6." Allen, "Structure, Tradition and Redaction," 141–42. Olley, commenting on the LXX, remarks on the pneumatology of the pericope. Yet he notices how the pericope's placement, along with the repetition of "Spirit/breath," after Ezek. 36 underscores this theological theme: "In the traditional position following ch. 36 [Ezek. 37:1–14] vividly promises the spiritual and physical renewal of the nation through the Lord's Spirit." John W. Olley, *Ezekiel: A Commentary Based on Iezekiēl in Codex Vaticanus*, Septuagint Commentary Series (Boston: Brill, 2009), 488.

²⁷ The passage employs the following pneuma words: πνεύματι (1x), πνεῦμα (3x), τὸ πνεῦμα (3x), τῷ πνεύματι (1x), πνευμάτων (1x).

²⁸ BDB is inconclusive as to whether the references in 37:6, 8, 9a–c, 10, 14 should be "breath" or "spirit"; they fail to even suggest "Spirit" as an option. They do, however, lump these seven references into a broad category—"symbol of life." Interestingly, BDB does not even mention the two occurrences in 37:1, 5. See F. Brown, S. Driver, and C. Briggs, *The Brown-Driver-Briggs Hebrew and English Lexicon*, 11th ed. (Peabody, MA: Hendrickson Publishers, 2007), s.v. "רוּחַ." In Ezek. 37:6, 14, Olley suggests the phrases containing πνεῦμα should be translated "my Spirit." See Olley, *Ezekiel*, 488.

the Ezekielian phrase "you shall know that I am the Lord" is used three times throughout the fourteen verses of the pericopal unit in Ezekiel 37:6, 13, 14.[29] Fourth, the passage is bracketed by references to τίθημι and the "Spirit" (Ezek. 37:1, 14). Together, the references to ἔθηκεν in Ezekiel 37:1 and θήσομαι in Ezekiel 37:14 form an *inclusio*; the same Spirit that sets Ezekiel in the valley also functions as the catalyst for resettling the resurrected in their ἐπὶ τὴν γῆν ὑμῶν (Ezek. 37:14). Further, a close reading of Ezekiel 37:1–14 manifests that the pericope can be divided into two larger sections with a transition verse connecting the two sections (see table 3.2).[30]

Table 3.2. Structure of Ezekiel 37:1–14

The vision of dry bones	1–10
Interpretive comments referring to 37:1–10 and to 37:12–14	11
Divine explication of the vision	12–14

---

[29] καὶ γνώσεσθε ὅτι εἰμι κύριος is used twice; καὶ γνώσεσθε ὅτι ἐγὼ κύριος is used once. Like "word of the Lord" in Ezekiel, this is a refrain that is used repeatedly throughout his prophecy. It occurs twenty-three times in the LXX of Ezekiel—Ezek. 6:7, 13; 11:10, 12; 12:20; 13:9, 14, 21, 23; 14:8; 16:62; 17:21; 20:42, 44; 22:16, 22; 23:49; 35:4, 12; 36:36; 37:6, 13, 14.

[30] The intent of table 3.2 is not to suggest a chiastic arrangement to Ezek. 37:1–14. Rather, it is merely to accentuate the transitional importance of Ezek. 37:11 as it refers backward to Ezek. 37:1–10 and forward to Ezek. 37:12–14. Fishbane, however, commenting on the Hebrew text, argues for a chiastic structure that likewise confirms the crucial interpretive role of Ezek. 37:11 in the prophetic pericope. For him, Ezek. 37:11, chiastically placed in its "broader structural perspective," is "preparatory to the more forceful repetition of the meaning of the vision in vv. 12–14." Michael Fishbane, *Biblical Interpretation in Ancient Israel* (Oxford: Clarendon Press, 1988), 451–52.

In the first section, Ezekiel 37:1–10, the prophetic address to the dead house of Israel begins with divine activity, leading the reader to expect a dramatic series of events. Though the χεὶρ κυρίου guided Ezekiel early in the prophetic narrative (Ezek. 1:3; 3:14, 22; 8:1), its relative absence is striking throughout the majority of the prophecy. The phrase reappears when Jerusalem was struck down in her exile (Ezek. 33:21).[31] The question is, What is the Lord about to do? Formerly, Ezekiel had been transported by the "hand of the Lord" (χεὶρ κυρίου) to witness the atrocities occurring within the Jerusalem temple (Ezek. 37:1; cf. Ezek. 8–11); the last time that he had been led to "the valley" (πεδίον), he was confronted with the vision of Yahweh's glory (Ezek. 3:22–23; cf. Ezek. 37:1–2; 8:4). Now the prophet is led "in the Spirit" (ἐν πνεύματι) to an Israeli boneyard (Ezek. 37:1). The grisly scene confronting Ezekiel is appalling as an avalanche of skeletal remains unearthed in a field overtakes his vista—καὶ τοῦτο ἦν μεστὸν ὀστέων (Ezek. 37:1). The priest cannot merely glance at the cadaverous remains of his people and be on his merry way. Rather, he has to peruse the bones scattered throughout the countryside as the hand of God leads him along—περιήγαγέν με ἐπ' αὐτὰ κυκλόθεν κύκλῳ (Ezek. 37:2).[32] The remains of this bone hoard were ξηρὰ σφόδρα, implying that their sun-bleached bones have been exposed for a lengthy amount of time. Reflecting on the horror of the scene in the battlefield turned graveyard, Christopher Wright states, "These bones, then, are not just evidence of death, but of death under curse. These bones proclaim that their 'owners' had been the victims not only of battle, but also of divine judgment."[33] The vision intentionally exaggerates the consequence

---

[31] χεὶρ κυρίου will appear once more in the LXX of Ezekiel, Ezek. 40:1.

[32] The scene is even more shocking when read in light of the law for Levitical priests mentioned in Ezek. 44:25—"They shall not defile themselves by going near to a dead person" (cf. Lev. 21:1).

[33] Wright asserts this is the destiny of the truly accursed. See Christopher J. H. Wright, *The Message of Ezekiel: A New Heart and a New Spirit*, The Bible

of the people of Israel's unrepentant sinful folly.

While standing in the midst of the deadest bones imaginable, the prophet is asked an incomprehensible question—εἰ ζήσεται τὰ ὀστᾶ ταῦτα (Ezek. 37:3).[34] What follows the incomprehensible question, then, is an absurd command—Προφήτευσον ἐπὶ τὰ ὀστᾶ ταῦτα καὶ ἐρεῖς αὐτοῖς Τὰ οσ'τᾶ τὰ ξηρά, ἀκούσατε λόγον κυρίου . . . καὶ ζήσεσθε (Ezek. 37:4–6). Despite the detail that ears have bones, but bones do not have ears, Ezekiel is given a preaching exercise more preposterous than preaching to the deaf and blind (Ezek. 37:4–10; cf. Isa. 42:18).[35] Though Ezekiel has his doubts, the text is clear: God is not halted by death. Battling unbelief, Ezekiel obeys the command by speaking the unadulterated "word of the Lord"—καὶ ἐπροφήτευσα καθὼς ἐνετείλατό μοι (Ezek. 37:7). Following the compliant prophetic pronouncement, there is a σεισμός (Ezek. 37:7) and the undoing of death as the bones became skeletons and the skeletons became cadavers—καὶ προσήγαγε τὰ ὀστᾶ ἑκάτερον πρὸς τὴν ἁρμονίαν αὐτοῦ. καὶ εἶδον καὶ ἰδοὺ ἐπ' αὐτὰ νεῦρα καὶ σάρκες ἐφύοντο, καὶ ἀνέβαινεν ἐπ' αὐτὰ δέρμα ἐπάνω (Ezek. 37:7–8). Despite the stunning vision of death reversal, Ezekiel is quick to note that the hoard still remains a heap

---

Speaks Today (Downers Grove, IL: InterVarsity Press, 2001), 304. Many of the observations made below from Ezek. 37:1–14 are dependent on Wright's contribution.

[34] Ezekiel, a prophet and priest, surely would have known Deut. 32:39: "See now that I, even I, am he, and there is no god beside me; I kill and I make alive; I wound and I heal; and there is none that can deliver out of my hand." Interestingly, Wright suggests Ezekiel would have recalled the other rare Old Testament resurrection stories: "the resuscitation of the dead through the powerful prayer of Elijah and Elisha, and the startling revival of a corpse upon contact with the bones of Elisha" (ibid., 305). It seems plausible, then, to propose that as the resurrection vision would have conjured Old Testament resurrection appearances for Ezekiel, so reflection on the resurrection sign at Jesus' death would have conjured the most dramatic picture of resurrection in the Old Testament for Matthew: Ezek. 37:1–14.

[35] Wright drew my attention to the contrast between Isaiah's preaching ministry and Ezekiel's. See Wright, *Message of Ezekiel*, 306.

of lifeless corpses—καὶ πνεῦμα οὐκ ἦν αὐτοῖς (Ezek. 37:8). The observation is followed by a second absurd command: καὶ εἶπεν πρός με Προφήτευσον . . . καὶ ζησάτωσαν (Ezek. 37:9). With brevity, Ezekiel narrates his obedience—καὶ ἐπροφήευσα καθότι ἐνετείλατό μοι (Ezek. 37:10). The result of Ezekiel's obedience to the divine voice is breathtaking: καὶ εἰσῆλθεν εἰς αὐτους τὸ πνεῦμα, καὶ ἔζησαν (Ezek. 37:10). The vitality associated with the Lord is bequeathed to the dead; it is imparted by proclamation and animated by the Spirit. What was πολλὰ σφόδρα (Ezek. 37:2) has become, through the Spirit-filled proclamation of Ezekiel, a συναγωγὴ πολλὴ σφόδρα (Ezek. 37:10).[36]

In the second section of the prophecy, as the divine voice speaks to Ezekiel for the fourth time in the pericope,[37] interpretive comments are given in the first part of Ezekiel 37:11 that identify who the skeletal remains figuratively referred to—τὰ ὀστᾶ ταῦτα πᾶς οἶκος Ισραηλ ἐστίν. In the second part of Ezekiel 37:11, divine interpretive comments continue by narrating the despondent exilic situation that the people of Israel find themselves in—Ξηρὰ γέγονεν τὰ ὀστᾶ ἡμῶν, ἀπόλωλεν ἡ ἐλπὶς ἡμῶν, διαπεφωνήκαμεν.[38] It is these comments by the prophet to his (re)readers that lead them to the optimistic comments located in Ezekiel 37:12–14. In Ezekiel 37:12, the visionary panorama rapidly shifts from the boneyard to

[36] Olley observes an intentional decision by the LXX translator to avoid militaristic language in Ezek. 37:14. He proposes the translator avoids δυνάμις or ἰσχύς, the normal LXX matches for the Hebrew חיל, to mitigate militaristic overtones leading readers of Ezek. 37:1–14 to assume the pericope is primarily about Israel's "rise" to military prominence over the surrounding nations. See Olley, *Ezekiel*, 490.

[37] καὶ εἶπεν πρός με in Ezek. 37:3, 4, 9 (LXX) and καὶ ἐλάλησεν κύριος πρός με in Ezek. 37:11 (LXX).

[38] This is the only reference to διαφωνεω in Ezekiel (LXX). It appears to have a sense not only of being "cut off" but of spiritually "lost." See LSJ, 9th ed., ed. Henry S. Jones and Roderick McKenzie (Oxford: Clarendon Press, 1940), s.v. "διαφωνεω." This further underscores the metaphorical and symbolic overtones of the prophetic pericope.

the graveyard, and one learns that the previous vision was both metaphorical and symbolic. Ezekiel will preach not to the literally dead but to the house of Israel, the living dead in exile.[39] Even though the banished people are διαπεφωνήκαμεν (Ezek. 37:11) and despite the anticipation of burial in tombs located in a foreign land (Ezek. 37:12),[40] hope is portended of a day when God will burst open their sepulchers and raise them to life—᾽Ιδοὺ ἐγω ἀνοίγω ὑμῶν τὰ μνήματα καὶ ἀνάξω ὑμᾶς ἐκ τῶν μνημάτων ὑμῶν (Ezek. 37:12). Even though the presence of hope is deferred to a future day, the magnitude of the promise is not diminished. God does not simply promise them life, but life in their homeland—καὶ εἰσάξω ὑμᾶς εἰς τὴν γῆν τοῦ Ισραηλ (Ezek. 37:12). Their exile will go from bad to worse—Israel will certainly die in exile—but God promises resurrection to Israel, resurrection that will confirm his identify among the people of his possession: καὶ γνώσεσθε ὅτι ἐγὼ κύριος ἐν τῷ ἀνοῖξαί με τοὺς τάφους ὑμῶν τοῦ ἀναγαγεῖν με ἐκ τῶν τάφων τὸν λαον μου (Ezek. 37:13). As the people can be certain that the sun will rise after the dark of night or that gravity will exert its force on any who attempt to defy it, so they should be confident that the Lord's promise of resurrection will come to pass: λελάληκα καὶ ποιήσω, λέγει κύριος (Ezek. 37:14).[41]

---

[39] In some LXX manuscripts, according to Lust, Ezek. 37 follows Ezek. 38–39. This placement, however, mitigates the theological interests that informed the placement of Ezek. 37:1–14 prior to prophecy against Gog. The traditional placement accentuates Israel's morally and spiritually dead state. See J. Lust, "Major Divergences between LXX and MT in Ezekiel," in *Messianisms and the Septuagint: Collected Essays*, ed. K. Hauspie (Leuven, Belgium: Leuven University Press, 2004), 207–8.

[40] τὰ μνήματα in Ezek. 37:12; τοὺς τάφους in Ezek. 37:13. Olley suggests that the mention of "graves/tombs" can imply individual resurrection rather than eschatological, glorified resurrection. See Olley, *Ezekiel*, 488.

[41] Fensham notes that the dry bones' becoming living beings manifests that the curse of death is translated into a blessing in the Ezekielian prophetic vision; death is translated into life. See F. C. Fensham, "The Curse of the Dry Bones in Ezekiel 37:1–14: Changed to a Blessing of Resurrection," *JNSL* 13 (1987): 59–60.

From Rigor Mortis to Resurrection

Ezekielian Thought Connections to Matthew 27:51–54

In working to establish Matthean dependence on Ezekiel 37:1–14 (LXX) in the composition of Matthew 27:51–54, it is imperative to note that numerous hermeneutical thought connections exist between the two pericopes. A careful perusal of the Matthean passion narrative alongside Ezekiel's oracle manifests a conclusive parallelism used by the Gospel author. This parallelism can be visualized in the chart below (see table 3.3).

Though many interpreters lament literary readings connecting Old Testament and New Testament pericopes that overextend themselves hermeneutically, Matthew's intentionality in connecting his passion narrative to Ezekiel's prophetic narrative is manifest.[42] As he has done at other points within his Gospel, Matthew utilizes parallelism to import theological truth as well as to concretize Jesus' identity.[43]

---

[42] While discussing the overinterpretation of texts, Eco helps one to see the question is not "By what criterion do we decide that a given textual interpretation is an instance of over-interpretation?" Rather, he postulates that readers who have postured themselves to pay careful attention to the details of the text are able to discern "which [readings] are 'bad.'" Sensitive readers, then, are able to ascertain what is being "evoked [even unconsciously] by the text." Thus, for Eco, sensitive readings do "not contradict other explicit aspects of the text." See Umberto Eco and Stefan Collini, eds., *Interpretation and Over-interpretation* (Cambridge: Cambridge University Press, 1992), 52, 62. This dissertation, therefore, suggests that Matthew's compositional intentionality makes the best sense of all the relevant facts with which this difficult pericope is concerned. Namely, it makes the best interpretive sense of the relationship existing between Matt. 27:51–54 and Matt. 28:1–10 as well as the relationship existing between Matt. 27:51–54 and Ezek. 37:1–14.

[43] For more on Matthew's use of parallelism within his Gospel narrative, see my comments in chap. 1 in which I illustrate his literary intentionality with two character examples from the Gospel's introduction along with one example from the scenes surrounding Jesus' birth and death as well as one macro-structural example of the Gospel. These manifest his intentionality in the use of parallelism as a literary device. Further, they manifest that meaning, for Matthew, is often embedded in the presentation of his narrative.

Table 3.3. Thought-Connection Parallelism between Matthew 27:51–54 and Ezekiel 37:1–14

Matthew 27:50–54	Ezekiel 37:1–14
the Spirit (27:50) τὸ πνεῦμα	my Spirit (37:1)—ἐν πνεύματι my Spirit (37:6)—πνεῦμά μου my Spirit (37:14)—τὸ πνεῦμά μου[44]
many bodies (27:52) πολλὰ σώματα	many corpses (37:2) πολλὰ σφόδρα[45]
Behold … the earth quaked … earthquake (27:51, 54) Καὶ ἰδοὺ … ἐσείσθη … σεισμόν	Behold, an earthquake (37:7) καὶ ἰδοὺ σεισμός[46]
the tombs, also, were opened (27:52) καὶ τὰ μνημεῖα ἀνεῴχθησαν	Behold, I will open your graves (37:12) Ἰδοὺ ἐγὼ ἀνοίγω ὑμῶν τὰ μνήματα[47]

[44] Though the pericope employs nine pneumatic words, it is contextually clear that the references in Ezek. 37:1, 6, 14 are references to the divine Spirit, the Lord's Spirit.

[45] Quarles suggests the difference between Matt. 27:52 and Ezek. 37:2 (LXX) is accounted for since the adjective πολλὰ refers to the ὀστέων in Ezek. 37:1. Thus, translators should translate πολλὰ σφόδρα as "many corpses." Charles Quarles, "Matthew 27:51–53 as a Scribal Interpolation: Testing a Recent Proposal," paper presented at the Evangelical Theological Society National Conference, San Diego, California, November 18–20, 2014.

[46] Rabbinic commentator Rabbi Eliezer interpreted σεισμός as "earthquake," not "shaking." Rabbi Eliezer, *Pirke de Rabbi Êlizer*, trans. G. Friedlander (New York: Hermon Press, 1970), 248–51.

[47] This is the only reference to the opening of tombs/graves in the entirety of the Old Testament narrative.

they went into the holy city after his resurrection (27:53) μετὰ τὴν ἔγερσιν αὐτοῦ εἰσῆλθον εἰς τὴν ἁγίαν πόλιν	and [I will] raise you from your graves and lead you into the land of Israel (37:12) καὶ ἀ'νάξω ὑμᾶς ἐκ τῶν μνημάτων ὑμῶν καὶ εἰσάξω ὑμᾶς εἰς τὴν γῆν τοῦ Ισραηλ[48]

In Matthew's Gospel, then, there is a multilayered context. At one level, meaning is present in the narrative proper. At another level, meaning is present in the Matthean presentation, or structure, of his narrative. In the case of our pericope, this is evident in the parallelism existing between Matthew 27:51–54 and Matthew 28:1–10 as well as the parallelism existing between Matthew 27:51–54 and Ezekiel 37:1–14. Awareness of Matthew's presentation enables readers to see that the Gospel's author is primarily evoking Ezekiel 37—not 1 Corinthians 15:20, Colossians 1:18, Revelation 1:5, Isaiah 26:19, Daniel 12:1–3, or Zechariah 14:4–5—by placing the resurrection of the sleeping saints on the day of Jesus' death.

Scrutiny of the two Greek texts manifests that a σεισμός preceded the resurrection of those in the Ezekielian boneyard as well as πολλὰ σώματα τῶν κεκοιμημένων ἁγίων in the Judean countryside (Ezek. 37:7; Matt. 27:51–52).[49] The use of σεισμός in Ezekiel

---

[48] In Ezek. 37:13 (LXX) there is a shift from τὰ μνήματα and ἐκ τῶν μνημάτων το τοὺς τάφους for "graves/tombs." This creates another thought connection between the two resurrection pericopes since τὸν τάφον is used in Matt. 28:1.

[49] Ezek. 37:7 (LXX) employs the noun σεισμός, while Matt. 27:51 employs the aorist passive ἐσείσθη. In both Ezekiel (LXX) and Matthew, σεισμός is used four times—Ezek. 3:12, 13; 37:7; 38:19 and Matt. 8:24; 24:7; 27:54; 28:2. In Matthew's Gospel, σεισμός is rendered "earthquake" in the latter three instances. In Matt. 8:24, however, it is typically glossed as "storm" when referring to the tumultuous waters on which Jesus slept before he rebuked the tempest (Matt. 8:25–27).

37:7 (LXX), according to John Olley, insinuates a fiercer "shaking" than its Hebrew counterpart רעש.⁵⁰ Further, σεισμός was utilized in Ezekiel (LXX) previously and associated with the earlier prophetic theophanies (Ezek. 3:12, 13). For Olley, the revelatory nature of these verses make it "probable that these verses . . . have influenced the enigmatic Mt 27:52–53."⁵¹ As God was not halted by the long-term deaths of the skeletal hoard in Ezekiel 37:1–10, so Jesus' resurrection power over mortality was not halted by the deaths of those embedded in the Judean countryside who were raised at his crucifixion (Matt. 27:51–54). As the miracle of resurrection is performed through prophetic mediation in Ezekiel 37:7–10, so resurrection is facilitated through the One mediator between God and man in Matthew 27:51–54—the eschatological prophet, Jesus. The ground of Ezekiel's proclamation of the resurrection of the bodies, even after they have been utterly decomposed under the sun, is the revelation of Yahweh in Israel; so, in Matthew's Gospel, the revelation of Yahweh in the incarnate Jesus is tantamount. One of the events revealing Jesus to be Yahweh's Christ is the raising of the saints caused by his crucifixion, which results in the centurion's christological confession of Jesus to be θεοῦ υἱός (Matt. 27:54).⁵² As in Ezekiel 37 (LXX) the Spirit infuses life into a heap of corpses (Ezek. 37:10), so in Matthew 27 the Spirit is the divine catalyst unleashed by Jesus from the cross, resulting in the five divine signs (Matt. 27:50).⁵³ Finally, as in Ezekiel 37

---

⁵⁰ Olley, *Ezekiel*, 490.

⁵¹ Ibid., 491.

⁵² Robert Martin-Archard, *From Death to Life: A Study of the Doctrine of the Resurrection in the Old Testament* (Edinburgh: Oliver and Boyd, 1960), 102.

⁵³ Commenting on Ezek. 37:7–10, Martin-Archard states, "The [Spirit] of God alone makes a living man out of the dead." Ibid., 96. He goes on to connect Ezekiel's image of the Spirit animating life with Gen. 2:7. As the divine breath made Adam a living being, so it transformed the lifeless into an exceedingly great multitude. John, too, utilizes the image of Spirit-animated life in John 20:22. For more on John 20:19–23, see Raymond Johnson, "The Church's Mission: John 20:19–23 Reconsidered," *CurTM* 43, 4 (October 2016): 22–28.

the reception of Spirit-animated life leads to life in the land (Ezek. 37:14; cf. 36:27–30), so in Matthew 27:52–53 Spirit-animated life leads to entrance into the land.

Other interpreters have noted Matthean dependence on Ezekiel 37:1–14 in the composition of his death-resurrection pericope in Matthew 27:51–54. Daniel Block, commenting on "into the land" (Ezek. 37:12) and "your own land" (Ezek. 37:14), states, "The description of the resurrection scene after the death of Jesus in Matt. 27:51–54 suggests that this event may have been interpreted in the light of Ezek. 37:1–14."[54] Thus, entrance "into the holy city" in Matthew 27:53 was Matthew's (re)interpretation of the Ezekielian resurrected dead reentering the land (cf. Ezek. 37:12–14).

Additionally, in his detailed exegetical study, Rafael Monasterio contends that Ezekiel 37 constitutes the fundamental biblical background for Matthew 27:51b–53.[55] One reason he argues for Matthean dependence on Ezekiel 37 is that in both Matthew 27:51–54 and Ezekiel 37:1–14 the Spirit is the active agent of resurrection:

> In Ezekiel 37 the Spirit of God is the one who produces life and brings about the resurrection of the dead: "I will put my Spirit within you and you will live" (Ezekiel 37, 14. Also v. 5. 6. 9. 10). In Matthew we find something similar: "[And Jesus cried out] again with a great voice and surrendered the Spirit. And, behold, the veil of temple was torn ... and many bodies of the dead saints were resurrected" (Mt. 27, 50 ff.).[56]

---

[54] Daniel I. Block, *The Book of Ezekiel: Chapters 25–48*, NICOT (Grand Rapids: Eerdmans, 1998), 389. Further, Block implies that YHWH's leading the raised corpses in Ezek. 37:1–14 into the land directly influenced Matthew's assertion that Jesus' resurrection preceded the entrance of the resurrected dead into the holy city. Thus, he states, "The Lord himself goes before a band of folk who have risen from their tombs into the holy city" (ibid.).

[55] Rafael A. Monasterio, *Exegesis de Mateo, 27, 51b–53: para una teologia de la muerte de Jesus en el evangelio de Mateo* (Vitoria, Brazil: Eset, 1980), 26.

[56] "En Ez. 37 el Espiritu de Dios es quien produce la vida y provoca la resurreccon de los muertos: 'Infundire mi espiritu en vosotros y vivireis (*dsesesthe*)'

Further, when discussing "los numerosos puntos de contacto entre el texto de Ezequiel 37 y la pericopa objeto de nuestro estudio,"[57] he puts forward six reasons contending that Matthew was conscious of the Ezekielian contextual background as he appropriated this text in his Gospel (see table 3.4).

Monasterio concludes that there is a "clear allusion in Mt. 27:51b-53 to Ezekiel's prophetic vision."[58] The allusion manifests that Matthew understood Jesus' crucifixion as a type of messianic salvation of God's eschatological in-breaking. The allusion, then, portrays Jesus' death and resurrection as the central moment in salvation history.

Table 3.4. Matthew's Conscious Use of Ezekiel

Matthew's Conscious Use of Ezekiel	
The spirit of God is the one who triggers the process that culminates in the resurrection of the dead.	Matt. 27's five portents occur as a direct result of Jesus' crucifixion. The presence of τὸ πνεῦμα in Matthew and Ezekiel connects the pericopes lexically.

(Ez. 37, 14. Tambien v.v. 5. 6. 9. 10). En Mateo encontramos la misma relacion: 'Diciendo una gran voz entrego el espiritu. Y he aqui que el velo del tempo se rasgo . . . y muchos cuerpos de los santos que habian muerto resucitaron (*egerthesan*)' (Mt. 27, 50 ss.)." Ibid., 184.

[57] His six points of contact can be found in Monasterio, *Exegesis de Mateo, 27, 51b–53*, 75–76. Monasterio, when noting the lexical thought connections linking the two pericopes also makes use of the LXX. Further, he observes that eschatology is a dominant theological theme present in the Matthean pericope.

[58] Rafael A. Monasterio, "Cross and Kingdom in Matthew's Theology," *TD* 29, 2 (1981): 149. Further, Monasterio notes that as Ezek. the prophetic vision's revelatory nature is twice referred to in Ezek. 37:12–14, so the centurion's profession emphasizes the revelatory nature of Jesus' death in Matt. 27:54.

God's intervention will be accompanied by an earthquake, a biblical sign of the eschatological action of God.	The Matthean portents manifest both divine intervention and the fulfillment of the Ezekielian prophecy.
The divine action culminates in the tombs being opened and those who were inside getting out (in the case of Ezekiel, speaking in a vision, the people; in the case of Matthew, many bodies of the saints that were dead).	Lexical cues signify Matthew's desire for interpreters to read the resurrection pericopes together, in light of each other.
Ezekiel's resuscitated village (restored) is led to the land of Israel. In Matthew, the resurrected saints enter the holy city (Jerusalem, the center of Israel).	The pericopes are not merely connected lexically; they are connected theologically by the theme of resurrection.
This divine action has a revelatory character.	The portents reveal the theological significance(s) of Jesus' crucifixion. The theological foci are Christology, missiology, and eschatology.
The sign of the resurrection is coupled with a new, more perfect sanctuary.	The rending of the temple veil signifies the end of the temple cultus.

Finally, the depiction of the resurrection in the Ezekiel cycle of the synagogue of Dura Europos notices thought connections between the two pericopes.[59] First, the fissure in the rocks—αἱ

---

[59] The content in this paragraph is reliant on Riesenfeld, *Resurrection in Ezekiel XXXVII*, 34–37. He notes that Ezek. 37 had a liturgical use for the Jewish

πέτραι ἐσχίσθησαν (Matt. 27:51)—is illustrated by the cloven Mount of Olives. Second, the quaking of the earth—ἡ γῆ ἐσείσθη (Matt. 27:51)—is depicted as a house hurled over a mountain slope. Third, the appearance of the resurrected saints in the city—καὶ πολλὰ σώματα τῶν κεκοιμημένων ἁγίων ἠγέρθησαν καὶ ἐξελθόντες ἐκ τῶν μνημείων μετὰ τὴν ἔγερσιν αὐτοῦ εἰσῆλθον εἰς τὴν ἁγίαν πόλιν καὶ ἐνεφανίσθησαν πολλοῖς (Matt. 27:52–53)—corresponds to the white-clad figures in the painting. The Ezekiel panel, then, connects the death and resurrection of Jesus with the fulfillment of Ezekiel's prophecy. As in Matthew's Gospel, the revelatory earthquake and the raising of the dead in the paintings are proofs of Jesus' christological identity—he is the Son of God.

Narrative Strategy—Using Ezekiel

After situating Ezekiel 37:1–14 in its context, the examination of Ezekiel 37:1–14 in its Septuagintal form has manifested a myriad of exegetical thought-connection links to Matthew's Gospel. These linguistic thought connections with Ezekiel 37:1–14 (LXX) reveal that the dry-bone resurrection vision in Ezekiel 37:1–14 is nearby in the compositional background of Matthew 27:51–54. This chapter, therefore, has suggested that Ezekiel 37:1–14 (LXX) is the primary text on which Matthew is relying in the composition of Matthew 27:51–54. It has been argued that Matthew 27:51–54 finds its principal origins in Ezekiel 37:1–14 (LXX). Cognizance of Matthean dependence on Ezekiel 37 (LXX), it has been suggested, crystalizes the theological foci of the Matthean pericopal hapax: Christology, missiology, and eschatology.

The sequential question, logically, to Matthew's deployment of Ezekiel in his Gospel narrative is, *Why* did Matthew make use

---

people during Passover. For him, this further links the pericopes since Jesus' crucifixion occurs during Jewish Passover.

of Ezekiel 37:1–14? The prophet Ezekiel is narrating Israel's story. And, at that time, disunity (Ezek. 9:9), disobedience (Ezek. 2:3), corrupt national leadership (Ezek. 13:1–14:11; 34:1–10), and polytheism characterized the nation's existence (Ezek. 6:4–7). As this was true of Israel's story when Ezekiel was prophesying, so it was when Matthew composed his Gospel. After the fissure between the northern and southern kingdoms (1 Kings 12), the people never reunited and regained their identity as the one people of God. Though "law-abiding" Pharisees and Sadducees roamed the land, law breaking and law circumvention abounded. In sharp contrast, Ezekiel 36:16–37:28 portends a day in which God repopulates the land, reunifies the people, induces heart change by the Spirit, and causes resurrection.[60] Thus, Douglas Stuart contends that "land, leadership, and people go together in the book of Ezekiel."[61] They go together because no nation can exist in an orderly manner without both a leader and a place to live.[62] Matthew employs the Ezekielian narrative knowing that evoking one portion actually evokes the entirety of the section. Evoking Ezekiel 37:12–14 in Matthew 27:51–53 evoked all of Ezekiel 36:16–37:28. The new leader, the new David, has come in the person of Jesus (Matt. 1:17; 12:23; 15:22; 20:30; 21:9). The new land that the new people of God populate is the ends of the earth (Matt. 28:18).

In Matthew's Gospel, the people's disunity is overturned as the new people of God are united *sola fide* in Christ (Matt. 4:17; 9:2); their disobedience is overturned as they come *sola gratia* to the One who has fulfilled the law (Matt. 5:17); they disavow their corrupt

---

[60] Stuart divides Ezek. 36:16–37:28 into three sections rather than four. He suggests the division is (1) Israel renewed as a people for God's holy name (36:16–38), (2) Israel revived as a people by God's Word and Spirit (37:1–14), and (3) Israel reunited as a people under the messianic king (37:15–28). See Douglas Stuart, *Ezekiel*, The Communicator's Commentary, vol. 18 (Dallas: Word, 1989), 334–50.

[61] Ibid., 334.

[62] Ibid.

national leadership by following the new David, God's Son, Jesus (Matt. 21:15; 27:54; 28:18–20);[63] and their polytheism is abandoned for Trinitarianism (Matt. 28:19). What Ezekiel's audience heard of, and read about, is provided through Jesus' crucifixion in the Matthean narrative. "Only in Him could the people of God be truly unified and obedient, and only His leadership was the sort that could" redirect their misplaced affections as they learn to worship the God who is one yet three.[64]

Additionally, Matthew evokes the Ezekielian context because the themes scattered throughout the entirety of Isaiah and Jeremiah's prophesies—the repopulation of the land, the reunification of the people, Spirit-induced heart change, and resurrection—are all in *one* place within Ezekiel's prophetic narrative, Ezekiel 36:16–37:28. What is chronicled in Matthew over the course of multiple chapters in Ezekiel is compressed into and evoked by one four-verse Matthean scene.[65] Matthew's literary details have didactic resonance; his Gospel communicates didactically. Matthew's premises are laden within his narrative's imagery and structure.[66] Matthew 27:51–54 refers to the entirety of Ezekiel 36–37 by way of the imagery populating the scene of Jesus' crucifixion. The scenarios are nearly identical. Matthew's deliberate compositional artistry calls the careful reader's attention to the Ezekielian prophetic narrative. It is the

---

[63] It is worth noting that as the beginning and end of Ezekiel are concerned with the new David (Ezek. 4:6; 37:24), so the beginning and end of Matthew's Gospel, too, are concerned with the new David (Matt. 1:1; 22:41–45).

[64] Stuart, *Ezekiel*, 350.

[65] I am indebted to Paul R. House for this observation.

[66] Like many, Sternberg contends the Bible is not purely a propositional or didactic document. It is a literary document with narrative features. Its interpretation often requires a literary approach. For example, though not dealing formerly with Matthew in his work, one can see that Matt. 27 makes use of an "analogical design" in the parallelism existing between Matt. 27:51–54 and 28:1–10; Matt. 27 makes use of poetic features with its reference to Ezekiel's dry-bones scene via descriptive resurrection imagery. See Meir Sternberg, *The Poetics of Biblical Narrative: Ideological Literature and the Drama of Reading* (Bloomington: Indiana University Press, 1985), 38–39, 41–57.

Gospel author's theological purposes, according to Robert Alter, that inspired Matthew's compositional intentionality.[67]

Telling the story backward from the perspective of the divine events realized in the person of Jesus, Matthew locates Jesus as the apex of God's revelation and promises foreshadowed in the Ezekielian prophetic narrative. Further, Matthew's evocation of Ezekiel is informed by his understanding of what the Scripture reveals about God in the Old Testament. God's saving purposes have come to their ultimate fulfillment in Jesus, the Son of God (Matt. 27:54). As Matthew interprets these events in light of God's saving purposes through Jesus' crucifixion, his homiletical intent is manifested: Jesus is the Christ (Matt. 27:54), his death necessitates a mission for those who respond to him by faith (Matt. 27:54; 28:18–20), and his crucifixion inaugurates the end of the temple cultus and the beginning of Spirit-filled life for mankind through Jesus (Matt. 27:51).[68] Discussing the *why* of Matthew's deployment of Ezekiel in his Gospel has poised us to now examine Matthean compositional intentionality and narrative strategy in chapter 4 of this dissertation.[69]

---

[67] Though I do not affirm all of his conclusions, and though he is focused on the Hebrew Bible rather than the Greek NT, Alter highlights the intentionality of employed narrative techniques by the biblical authors in their conveyance of truth. The Gospel authors, too, were pioneers in using intentionally crafted prose as a medium for truth. See Robert Alter, *The Art of Biblical Narrative* (New York: Basic Books, 1981), 155.

[68] Hahn, though dealing with the kingdom of God as it is revealed in 1–2 Chron., helps readers here by enabling them to see that Matthew, like the Chronicler, has a strategy in his composition. Theology informs not only the composition of the Matthean narrative but Matthew's interpretation of the Old Testament. The Gospel of Matthew's typologically interpreted history is theologically presented to accentuate Jesus' identity as the Christ, the mission his death necessitates, and eschatological overtones of his death on the cross. See Scott W. Hahn, *The Kingdom of God as Liturgical Empire: A Theological Commentary on 1–2 Chronicles* (Grand Rapids: Baker, 2012), 11–13.

[69] "Narrative strategy" will be discussed and defined in chap. 4.

Conclusion

This chapter has argued that there is textual and interpretive evidence that the resurrection vision in Ezekiel 37:1–14 is close in the background of Matthew 27:51–54.[70] Further, this chapter has argued that the pericope laced with divine signs testifying to Jesus' divine identity as the Son of God finds its primary origins in Ezekiel 37. As he was in the beginning of his Gospel, Matthew is concerned with anchoring Jesus' life in Old Testament cotext. The Old Testament cotext for Matthew 27:51–54 is in the Ezekielian Old Testament prophetic narrative.

Contra many scholars, this dissertation is arguing that the Matthean pericope does not find its background in a plethora of Old Testament passages. This dissertation rejects the suggestion that Matthew's pericopal hapax finds its primary roots in an extrabiblical, pre-Matthean tradition. Rather, this dissertation argues that an examination of Ezekiel 37:1–14 in its Septuagintal form manifests numerous links to Matthew's Gospel narrative. Awareness of Matthean dependence on Ezekiel 37 crystalizes the theological foci of Matthew 27:51–54—Christology, missiology, and eschatology. A proper understanding of the pericope's translation and primary Old Testament referent enables interpreters to ascertain how Matthew 27:51–54 is functioning in the death-resurrection scene and the theological meaning of the pericope. Thus, Matthew has Ezekiel 37:12–14 as his *primary* Old Testament referent when composing this resurrection pericope.

---

[70] Grassi also connects the two pericopes by observing the thought connections between the Dura Europos paintings and Matt. 27 as well as noting the numerous indirect references between Ezek. 37 (LXX) and Matt. 27:51–54. Thus, he states, "The early Christian tradition described the death and resurrection of Jesus in terms of Ezekiel's resurrection of the dry bones." J. A. Grassi, "Ezekiel 37, 1–14 and the New Testament," *NTS* 11 (1964–65): 164.

4

Matthean Narrative Strategy: Compositional Intentionality in Matthew's Death-Resurrection Scene—Matthew 27:45–28:20

Misunderstanding Matthew

This dissertation has argued that an interpretive chasm exists between exegetes and homileticians on both the precise function of Matthew 27:51–54 within the death-resurrection scene of Matthew's Gospel and the theological foci of this particular pericope—Christology, missiology, and eschatology. To bridge the apparent interpretive chasm, this dissertation has sought to demonstrate that interpreters must overcome three problems—mistranslation, misreferent, and misplacement—in the absence of interpretive consensus leading to an interpretive dichotomy that separates the historicity of the act itself and its placement in the Gospel from its theological meaning.

Therefore, chapter 2 argued that a proper understanding of Matthew 27:51–54 mandated an examination of the pericope's translation. The suggested translation enables interpreters to ascertain how Matthew 27:51–54 is functioning in the death-resurrection scene and the three theological foci of the pericope:

Behold, the curtain of the temple was torn in two from top to bottom, the earth quaked, and the rocks split, the tombs, also, were opened and the bodies of many saints who had died were raised to life; coming out of the tombs, they went into the holy city after his resurrection, appearing to many people. When the centurion and those guarding Jesus with him saw the earthquake and the things that took place they were terrified and said, "This really was the Son of God!"

To continue bridging the interpretive chasm of Matthew 27:51–54, this dissertation addressed the problem of misreference. Chapter 3 suggested that the failure to observe the abundant linguistic thought connections between Matthew 27:51–54 and Ezekiel 37:1–14 (LXX) obscures the interpretation of the Matthean pericope. An examination of the Septuagint's textual evidence reveals that the dry-bone resurrection vision in Ezekiel 37:1–14 is nearby in the compositional background of Matthew 27:51–54. Thus, this dissertation contends that Matthew 27:51–54 finds its primary origins in Ezekiel 37:1–14 (LXX).[1] Cognizance of Matthean dependence on Ezekiel 37 (LXX) crystalizes the theological foci embedded into Matthew 27:51–54. For it is Jesus, the Christ,[2] who executes the new covenant.[3] The new covenant has significance for the nations,

---

[1] Contra Stanton, who rejects Matthew employed the LXX in the composition of his Gospel. Stanton argues Matthew's allegiance is to the quotations as depicted in his sources, and when the references were Septuagintal in his sources, they appeared as such in his formula quotations. See Graham N. Stanton, *A Gospel of a New People: Studies in Matthew* (Edinburgh: T&T Clark, 1992), 353–58.

[2] Χριστός, or its cognates, are used as a descriptor of Jesus no fewer than ten times in Matthew's Gospel. See Matt. 1:1, 16, 18; 11:2; 16:16, 20; 26:63, 68; 27:17; 27:22. Christology is at the core of the Matthean narrative.

[3] The promise of the new covenant is the immediate context of Ezek. 37. Thus, Ezekiel writes, "And I will give you a new heart, and a new spirit I will put within you. And I will remove the heart of stone from your flesh and give you a heart of flesh. And I will put my Spirit within you, and cause you to walk in my statutes and be careful to obey my rules" (Ezek. 36:26–27; cf. Jer.

as the Gentile centurion's confession makes evident (Matt. 27:54).[4] The arrival of the new covenant coincides with the termination of the temple cultus (Matt. 27:51).[5] As he was in the beginning of his Gospel, so at the end of his narrative Matthew is concerned with anchoring Jesus' life in its Old Testament cotext, because "everything written about [Jesus] in the Law of Moses and the Prophets and the Psalms must be fulfilled" (Luke 24:44; cf. Matt. 5:17).

Awareness of Matthew's dependence on Ezekiel segues to our third interpretive problem: misplacement. Chapter 3 argued that the sequential question, logically, to Matthew's deployment of Ezekiel in his Gospel is, *Why* did Matthew make use of Ezekiel 37:1–14? Discussing the *why* of Matthew's deployment of Ezekiel in his narrative poises interpreters to examine Matthew's compositional intentionality and the placement of Matthew 27:51–54 in his passion narrative. The failure of interpreters to observe the purposeful narrative strategy and placement of Matthew 27:51–54 within the death-resurrection scene has impoverished the interpretation of this pericope and has separated the historicity of the act itself and its placement in the Gospel from its theological.

31:31–34; Heb. 8:8–12). Jesus executes the new covenant through his death and resurrection (Matt. 26–28).

[4] This dissertation, therefore, has proposed that the confession in Matt. 27:54 is the result of the centurion's conversion. It was the result of regeneration. For, the Matthean narrative says, ἰδόντες τὸν σεισμὸν καὶ τὰ γενόμενα ἐφοβήθησαν σφόδρα (Matt. 27:54). In positive response, then, to the signs surrounding Jesus' death, there is a salvific confession that Jesus truly was the Son of God; that Jesus' death has meaning for the nations (cf. Matt. 28:16–20). Likewise, Turner views the confession of the soldier and those with him as a positive response. See David Turner, *Matthew*, BECNT (Grand Rapids: Baker, 2008), 671.

[5] Contra Turner, who suggests it is "debatable that Matthew is thinking in terms of an absolute end of the temple" because Jesus stated he came to fulfill the Law and the Prophets, not abolish them (cf. Matt. 5:17–20; 24:2; 27:51). Turner, *Matthew*, 670. Rather, the symbolism of the pericope manifests the rending of the veil as a divine judgment from God. Thus, the hands of heaven tear the veil downward—καὶ ἰδοὺ τὸ καταπέτασμα τοῦ ναοῦ ἐσχίσθη ἀπ' ἄνωθεν ἕως κάτω εἰς δύο (Matt. 27:51).

Therefore, this dissertation suggests that a literary reading of Matthew 27:51–54 incorporates the entire scope of the death-resurrection narrative so that it is properly interpreted in light of the entire scene rather than isolated as a singular phenomenological occurrence. Recognizing how Matthew's compositional intentionality informs the structure and placement of Matthew 27:51–54 in the death-resurrection scene leads to interpretive clarity. Matthew's compositional intentionality manifests a deliberate narrative strategy to convey theological meaning.

Matthean Narrative Strategy—A Methodology

A literary reading of the passion narrative reveals that, for Matthew, the events of Good Friday are conjoined closely with the events occurring on Easter (cf. Matt. 28:1–15). This proposition is not novel. But the intimate connection between Matthew 27:51–54 and Matthew 28:1–15 can be observed only when one rejects its displacement in the Matthean passion narrative while simultaneously affirming its historicity.[6] Regarding displacement, W. F. Albright and C. S. Mann locate the signs surrounding Jesus' crucifixion on Good Friday in their translation of the pericope when they translate the passage as follows: "Then the curtain of the Most Holy Place was torn in two, from top to bottom, the earth shook, rocks were shattered, the tombs were opened as well, and many bodies of the saints who had died were raised, and coming out of the tombs at the time of his resurrection they went into the holy city and appeared to many people."[7] Further, David Turner writes, regarding historicity

---

[6] Contra Allison, who suggests Matt. 27:51–54 is "theological fancy" and one among many texts "composed to teach theological lessons, not record historical facts." Dale C. Allison Jr., *The Historical Christ and the Theological Jesus* (Grand Rapids: Eerdmans, 2009), 71–72.

[7] Contrary to the translation this thesis proposes, however, the translation of Albright and Mann seems to suggest that the resurrected dead remained in their former tombs until the time of Jesus' resurrection on Easter morning. Yet

in his exegesis of the pericope, "The opening of the tombs (Ezek. 37:13) is associated with Jesus's death, but the appearance of the saints (Zech. 14:15; Ezek. 37:1–14) in the holy city apparently will not occur until after Jesus's resurrection (27:53) . . . it is not helpful to take [this pericope] as a nonhistorical literary-theological creation."[8] Bringing the two pericopes in intimate narrative proximity enables readers to see that Jesus' death and victorious resurrection signal the inauguration of the new age.

Thus, to the question, Does Matthew have a narrative strategy coursing throughout the entirety of his Gospel? the answer being proposed is most certainly yes. Therefore, this dissertation must answer two questions. The first question is, What is meant by narrative strategy? or How is narrative strategy defined? This dissertation suggests that narrative strategy should be understood to convey the intentional use of authorial conventions that guides an audience's interpretation(s) of a text. Warren Carter articulates a similar definition of authorial conventions, though, admittedly, he does not use the phrase "narrative strategy."

> These conventions are "rules" or "practices" or "literary devices" that facilitate communication between author and audience and signal important dimensions of the text. They enable the audience to notice and attribute significance to important aspects of the text and to recognize a hierarchy of details and

---

Albright and Mann also connect the pericope under consideration with Ezek. 37 by way of the pneumatological imagery in the Matthean narrative's context (cf. 27:50) when Jesus unleashes τὸ πνεῦμα from the cross. See W. F. Albright and C. S. Mann, *Matthew: Introduction, Translation, and Notes*, AB, vol. 26 (New York: Doubleday, 1971), 349–51.

[8] Moreover, Turner notes that the pericope's syntax is ambiguous in Matt. 27:53. Thus, he too suggests that μετὰ τὴν ἔγερσιν does not necessarily modify ἐξελθόντες. Rather, according to Turner, it is reasonable to suggest that it modifies εἰσῆλθον. See Turner, *Matthew*, 670. As the diagram in chap. 2 indicates, this dissertation suggests that μετὰ τὴν ἔγερσιν modifies both εἰσῆλθον and ἐνεφανίσθησαν.

events. . . . The author assumes the audience has adequate skills to make appropriate use of these conventions.⁹

Therefore, because this dissertation suggests that Matthew does indeed have a narrative strategy, it will be argued that he assumes that the overall structure of his Gospel as well as the content within individual pericopes situated throughout his narrative denotes interpretive significance. Recognizing Matthean narrative strategy is imperative for interpretation because written texts are unable to generate all their meaning at one time. For literary texts like Matthew's Gospel, the meaning embedded in the structure of the material is grasped as the narrative progresses. Thus, the ordering and distribution of the Matthean Gospel material exercises significant influence over its interpretation(s).[10] "Fundamental to reading the narrative well," claims Wolfgang Iser, "is the relationship between Matthean structure and Matthean interpretation."[11] The arrangement of particular elements of the text material is, according to Menakhem Perry, determined by an author's "rhetorical or reader-oriented motivations."[12] Perry lumps the various motivations authors may have

---

[9] Warren Carter, *Matthew: Storyteller, Interpreter, Evangelist* (Peabody, MA: Hendrickson, 2004), 93. As was stated above, to my knowledge, "narrative strategy" is not a proper term/phrase to be defined. The phrase occurred to me while in a conversation with Paul House at ETS 2015 in Atlanta.

[10] I would like to thank my supervisor, Jonathan Pennington, for allowing me to view a prepublished version of his forthcoming book. Pennington contends that meaning is frequently embedded in the structure of Matthew's narrative. Thus, he states, "Paying attention to how the whole and the parts are structured is essential for good reading of Matthew." Jonathan T. Pennington, *The Sermon on the Mount and Human Flourishing: A Theological Commentary* (Grand Rapids: Baker Academic, forthcoming).

[11] Iser would say, "Central to the reading of every literary work is the interaction between its structure and its recipient." Wolfgang Iser, *The Act of Reading: A Theory of Aesthetic Response* (Baltimore: Johns Hopkins University Press, 1978), 20.

[12] Menakhem Perry, "Literary Dynamics: How the Order of a Text Creates Its Meaning [With an Analysis of Faulkner's 'A Rose for Emily']," *PT* 1, 1–2

for the final order of their respective narrative composition into two camps. On the one hand, his "'model'-oriented motivations" suggest that "the ordering of a group of textual elements is justified by regarding the text as adhering to some order familiar to the reader."[13] On the other hand, his "rhetorical or reader-oriented motivations" suggest that "the structure of the text-continuum . . . is supposed to be experienced. The sequence is justified through its effect on the reader. Its function is to control the reading process and to channel it in directions 'desirable' for the text."[14]

Matthew's Gospel falls into the latter category. Careful Gospel readers will observe that Matthew assumes that the presentation order of the pericopes throughout his Gospel denotes interpretive significance. In relation to presentation order, Perry has discussed what he calls the "primacy effect." That is, material situated at the beginning of the Gospel informs a reader's understanding of the whole Gospel. The organization of information determines how interpreters digest the material and justify meaning(s).[15] Similarly, Carter discusses what he calls the "latency effect," which for him regards "the impact of the Gospel's ending as the last thing that the audience encounters."[16] It is important to note that the literary

---

(1979): 40–41.

[13] Ibid., 36.

[14] Ibid., 40.

[15] According to Perry, "A perceiver does not wait for the end of a message in order to determine its understanding." Ibid., 53–55. For example, in Matthew's narrative it is the uniqueness of how Jesus' life begins—a virgin birth (1:18–25) and prophetic fulfillment (2:1–23)—that determines how readers interpret the meaning(s) and significance(s) of events related to his life recounted throughout the rest of Matthew's Gospel.

[16] Unfortunately, when discussing Matthew's Gospel, Carter incorporates only Matt. 28 rather than the entire death-resurrection conclusion, Matt. 27:45–28:20. See Carter, *Matthew*, 93. Regarding the latency effect, readers of Matthew's narrative observe that Jesus not only enters the world unlike any other man—he is born of a virgin (1:18–25) and fulfills prophecy in his infancy (2:1–23)—but he also dies unlike any other man: darkness canopies the landscape as his life wanes (27:45), he yields his own life after a dereliction

import of these two effects is often indiscernible or not fully grasped in the initial reading. However, Perry notes how the two effects may very well work together in the initial reading:

> Material appearing early in the text may determine "shades of meaning" to be activated in later material which is to be assimilated to it, accentuating certain aspects and weakening others; anticipating one bit of information about a character and delaying another, of a different nature entirely, may "prejudice" the reader in advance in favor (or against) the character, building up the "reservoir" of sympathy (or reservation) that will be hard to renounce and will condition details of a contrary nature later on in the text; the systematic repetition of a particular element in a typical position in the text-continuum (e.g. the final position in a line of verse; ends of chapters) will bring into prominence in the semantic hierarchy of the text.[17]

Recognizing the presence of Matthean narrative strategy enables readers to observe the structure of his Gospel as well as the content contained within individual pericopes that are intentionally situated throughout his narrative. Both structure and content denote interpretive significance.

The second question this dissertation must answer is, *How* does Matthew 27:51–54 fit within Matthew's whole narrative strategy? It is to this question that this dissertation now turns. To substantiate the reality of a narrative strategy within the Gospel of Matthew's passion narrative, this dissertation will argue that Matthew employs an intentional narrative strategy not only in his composition of Matthew 27:51–54 but also in his placement of Matthew 27:51–54 within Matthew 26–28.

---

cry (27:50), and observable portents ensue his death (27:51–54).

[17] Perry, "Literary Dynamics," 41.

Intentional Composition

A careful reading of the Matthean passion narrative manifests intentional composition. As table 4.1 (reproduced from chap. 1) demonstrates, this is apparent in the deliberate literary parallelism used by the Gospel's author.

Table 4.1. Literary Parallelism in Matthew 27–28

Matthew 27:45–66	Matthew 27:62–28:15
darkness (27:45) σκότος	dawn (28:1) τῇ ἐπιφωσκούσῃ
earth shook (27:51) ἡ γῆ ἐσείσθη	earthquake (28:2) σεισμὸς
raised (27:52) ἠγέρθησαν	risen (28:6) ἠγέρθη
tomb (27:52–53) τὰ μνημεῖα . . . τῶν μνημείων	tomb (28:1) τὸν τάφον
the holy city (27:53) εἰς τὴν ἁγίαν πόλιν	the city (28:11) εἰς τὴν πόλιν
centurion (27:54)—ὁ ἑκατόνταρχος	those guarding (28:4)—οἱ τηροῦντες the guards (28:11)—τῆς κουστωδίας soldiers (28:12)—τοῖς στρατιώταις
fear (27:54) ἐφοβήθησαν	fear (28:4, 5, 8, 10) φόβου . . . φοβεῖσθε . . . φόβου . . . φοβεῖσθε

genuine profession (27:54)	false profession (28:13–15)
Mary Magdalene and Mary (27:56) Μαριά ἡ Μαγδαληνὴ καὶ Μαρία	Mary Magdalene ... Mary (28:1) Μαριὰμ ἡ Μαγδαληνὴ ... Μαρία
Joseph of Arimathea before Pilate (27:57)	the chief priests before Pilate (27:62)
great stone (27:60) λίθον μέγαν	the stone (28:2) τὸν λίθον
attempt to guard the tomb (27:62–66)	inability to guard the tomb (28:4)

The chart enables readers to observe the intentional compositional correspondences between the two pericopes. Both Matthew 27:45–66 and Matthew 28:1–15 are tightly structured. Each pericope evokes the other. It is not by accident that readers encounter the dualistic imagery of "darkness" and "dawn" at the apex of the Matthean narrative in the precise moment when Jesus overthrows the dominion of darkness by means of his crucifixion (Matt. 27:45; 28:1; cf. Col. 1:13–14; 2:15).[18] Readers find the only pairs of earthquakes and resurrections recorded in the four New Testament passion narratives here at the end of Matthew's Gospel (Matt. 27:51, 52;

[18] In Matt. 27:45, τὴν γῆν should be understood to refer to the land of Israel rather than the entire earth. The cosmological imagery is localized. The imagery connotes God's judgment on those who have rejected his Son. Garland notes that first-century readers would have understood the darkness covering the land to be a cosmic portent that commonly attended the death of kings. See David Garland, *Reading Matthew: A Literary and Theological Commentary* (Macon, GA: Smyth & Helwys, 2001), 264. This phenomenon can be observed in Philo, *On Providence* 2:50; Dio Cassius, *Roman History* 56.29.3; and Josephus, *Ant.* 17:167.

28:2, 6).[19] Compositional forethought is on display in Matthew's narrative when one observes the triad of cries in the dark (Matt. 27:46, 50, 54),[20] the conquering of fear in the repentant (Matt. 27:54)[21]

[19] Similarly, Wenham notes that the earthquakes in Matt. 27:51 and Matt. 28:2 are parallel to each other in the conclusion of Matthew's Gospel. See David Wenham, "The Resurrection Narratives in Matthew's Gospel," *TynBul* 24 (1973): 21–54, esp. 42. However, there is an important distinction to make between the two. In Matt. 27, the earthquake was caused by Jesus' release of the Spirit in Matt. 27:50; the earthquake itself in Matt. 27:51 is the *reason* for the additional three signs that follow it in Matt. 27:51–53. In Matt. 28, however, the earthquake is not the cause of the resurrection. Rather, it is a side effect of the angel's activity (Matt. 28:2).

[20] The triad of cries in the dark is not represented in the chart above because all three "cries" occur in Matt. 27. Careful readers will observe a pair of dereliction cries by Jesus while suspended between heaven and earth in Matt. 27:46, 50 and a cry of repentant faith by the centurion in response to the signs accompanying Jesus' death in Matt. 27:54. In reference to the centurion's "cry," Verseput notes the affirmation—"This truly was the Son of God!"—comes from not only the centurion but also those guarding Jesus with him. This observation, therefore, raises the declaration to the level of a consensus testimony in response to the five portents. But he incorrectly suggests the affirmation is a "confession as witness to the vindication of God" rather than "the conversion of the Gentiles." Donald J. Verseput, "The Role and Meaning of the 'Son of God' Title in Matthew's Gospel," *NTS* 33 (1987): 532–56, esp. 48, 56. Menken suggests that Jesus dying as "the Son of God!" in Matthew is a theme derived from his reliance on Mark but expanded on in his Gospel. Maarten J. J. Menken, *Matthew's Bible: The Old Testament Text of the Evangelist*, BETL 173 (Leuven, Belgium: Leuven University Press, 2004), 235.

[21] In Matt. 27:54, the semantic range of ἐφοβήθησαν allows it to be rendered "they were filled with awe" instead of "they were fearful" or "they were terrified." The semantic range helps us see this as a "fear" leading to worship or praise. See *TDNT*, 9:208–12; and NIDNTT 4:609–14. Allison suggests that ἐφοβήθησαν σφόδρα is intended to refer the reader back to Matt. 17:6, its only other occurrence within the Gospel. According to Allison, "Common vocabulary encourages informed listeners to contemplate one scene in the light of another." Dale C. Allison Jr., "Anticipating the Passion: The Literary Reach of Matthew 26:47–27:56," *CBQ* 56 (1994): 701–14, esp. 707–10. Matthew, then, wants his readers to interpret Matt. 27:51–54 in light of Matt. 17:1–8. Likewise, Garland states, "In [Matt. 17], Jesus is confessed as the Son of God by a divine voice; in the second, by his executioners, Roman soldiers (27:54)."

and the provocation of fear among the unbelieving (Matt. 28:4), the competing testimonies about the meaning of Jesus' cross-work in the city of Jerusalem (Matt. 27:53; 28:11–15), the worship of the crucified (Matt. 27:54) and risen Christ (Matt. 28:9) by Gentiles (Matt. 27:54) and Jews (Matt. 28:9), the presence of the Marys—Mary Magdalene and Mary the mother of James—both at Jesus' death (Matt. 27:56) as well as his resurrection (Matt. 28:1),[22] and cognates of σείω and σεισμός linking Matthew 28:1–15 to 27:45–66 (see table 4.2).[23] For careful readers, then, the correspondences between Matthew 27 and Matthew 28 are manifest.

Table 4.2. Uses of σείω and σεισμός in Matthew 27:45–28:15

σείω (ἐσείσθη)	27:51
σεισμός (σεισμὸν)	27:54
σεισμός (σεισμὸς)	28:2
σείω (ἐσείσθησαν)	28:4

Garland, *Reading Matthew*, 185–86.

[22] This dissertation has noted that not all, however, affirm the historicity of these Matthean events. Therefore, assuming the symbolic significance of Matt. 27:51-54, Wüthrich suggests that even the women are included in both pericopes because, as mothers, they are watching for a symbolic "bringing forth" or "birth" of the one who will be called, "the first-born from the dead." According to Wüthrich, the "figures" are a "figurative expression of childbirth." Serge Wüthrich, "Naître de mourir: la mort de Jésus dans l'Évangile de Matthieu (Matt 27.51– 56)," *NTS* 56 (2010): 313–25. For a defense of Matt. 27:51–54's historicity, see Wenham, "Resurrection Narratives in Matthew's Gospel," 43.

[23] Though table 4.2 bears the resemblance of a chiasm, I do not detect any intentional chiasm by Matthew in his use of σείω and σεισμός. The arrangement of the chart is intended to distinguish the verbal forms of σείω from the noun forms of σεισμός and to suggest it is not by accident that both forms are found in both pericopes.

Matthean Narrative Strategy

Correspondences are not merely discernable. Rather, the correspondences are also intentionally situated. Matthew was not haphazard in his choice or placement of details in his narrative. By paying attention to Matthean narrative strategy, readers are able to observe the overall structure of his Gospel as well as the content within the individual pericopes situated throughout. Both structure and content denote interpretive significance.

Moreover, attention to Matthean narrative strategy enables careful readers to observe that both pericopes introduce their respective series of events with καὶ ἰδού (Matt. 27:50; 28:2) and then proceed with a similar sequence of events throughout the pericope (see table 4.3). The quaking of the earth,[24] the opening of the sepulcher(s), the fear of the guards, and the presence of women give compositional structure to each of the resurrection pericopes at the end of the Matthean narrative.[25]

Furthermore, there is an observable compositional intentionality not only in the manifest parallelism between Matthew 27–28 and the structuring of each respective pericope, but also in the dramatis

---

[24] Quarles notes this is a "localized catastrophe." In Matthew's Gospel-narrative, ἡ γῆ refers to the land of Israel rather than the entire earth (cf. Matt. 2:6, 20, 21; 9:26; 23:35; 24:30). See Charles Quarles, "Matthew 27:51–53: Meaning, Genre, Intertextuality, Theology, and Reception History," *JETS* 59, 2 (2016): 273. Similarly, Carter suggests the resurrection of the saints is "localized in Jerusalem" since it is not referring to "the general judgment and resurrection." Additionally, he notes this "is not the first time people have been raised in association with Jesus' ministry (9:18–19, 23–26; 10:8; 11:5)." See Warren Carter, *Matthew and the Margins: A Socio-Political and Religious Reading*, JSNTSup 204 (Sheffield: Sheffield Academic Press, 2000), 536.

[25] I owe this observation to Douglas Anderson. See Anderson, "The Origin and Purpose of Matthew 27:51b–53" (PhD diss., University of Otago Seminary, 2014), b–5 159. However, it is important to note that the conclusions in figs. 2.1 and 2.3 are my own. See Raymond Johnson, "Matthew 27:51–54 Revisited: A Narratological Re-appropriation," *SBJT* 18, 4 (2014): 31–50. I came upon Anderson's work after forming these conclusions independently and after the article's publication. Further, his analysis of the two pericopes is limited to Matt. 27:51b–3; 28:1–6.

Table 4.3. Parallel Sequence of Events in Matthew 27:45–66 and 28:1–15

Matthew 27	Matthew 28
καὶ ἰδού (27:50)[26]	καὶ ἰδού (28:2)
ἡ γῆ ἐσείσθη (27:51)	σεισμὸς (28:2)
τὰ μνημεῖα ἀνεῴχθησαν (27:52)	ἀπεκύλισεν τὸν λίθον (28:2)
ἐφοβήθησαν σφόδρα (27:54)	τοῦ φόβου . . . οἱ τηροῦντες (28:4)
γυναῖκες πολλαί (27:55)	ταῖς γυναιξίν (28:5)

personae of the Matthean passion narrative.[27] Every reference to specific characters functions as a compositional bridge between the two pericopes for Matthew. For example, Douglas Anderson notes that the "women are to be understood as a bridge linking the story of Jesus' crucifixion to the story of Jesus' burial and the Easter story. Since they were witnesses of Jesus' death, burial and resurrection

---

[26] Anderson puts too much interpretive weight on the καὶ ἰδού in Matt. 27:50. According to him, the presence of καὶ ἰδού indicates the end of the darkness referred to in 27:45. This is especially odd when one considers his suggestion that "both darkness (cf. 27:45) and earthquake (27:51b) may be understood to belong together as cosmic apocalyptic events." See Anderson, "Origin and Purpose of Matthew 27:51b–53," 165. The Gospel of Peter, too, suggests that the darkness of Matt. 27:45 persisted through the scene, through the cosmic portents recorded in Matt. 27:51–54. See Bart D. Ehrman and Zlatko Plese, *The Other Gospels: Accounts of Jesus from Outside the New Testament* (Oxford: Oxford University Press, 2014), 198.

[27] In reference to the pericope's characters, Herzer, following Gnilka, advocates for what he calls an "intra-textual" reading of Matt. 27 when laboring to identify the sleeping saints in Matt. 27:53. He connects Matt. 27:52 with Matt. 23:29 lexically. According to Herzer, the two pericopes are connected by

there is no possibility of mistake as to the reality of the death of the one who subsequently rose from the dead."²⁸

While it is possible to recall a plethora of proposed literary readings that have, in many ways, overextended themselves hermeneutically, Matthew's compositional intentionality in the parallelism within his Gospel's conclusion is discernable from the grammar. The observations made above concerning the pericopes in the Matthean passion narrative manifest a discernable level of compositional intentionality that makes Matthew 27:51–54 an integral pericope at the end of his Gospel. That Matthew directly connects the events of Good Friday with the events of Easter Sunday in his narrative is indisputable for the careful reader. Intentionally placed details forge a link between the two resurrection pericopes. Thus, Maria Riebl rightly states, "These [are] carefully placed [details] in relationship to one another, thereby making a direct connection between the events of Jesus' death and resurrection."²⁹ Further, as this thesis will argue,

---

the reference to τὰ μνημεῖα in Matt. 23:29 and 27:52, respectively. Further, he suggests that the resurrected dead in Matt. 27:53 are τῶν προφητῶν and τῶν δικαίων mentioned in Matt. 23:39, "who suffered and were killed, but now have been released from death by the death of Jesus and bear witness to the inhabitants of Jerusalem." Jens Herzer, "The Riddle of the Holy Ones in Matthew 27:51b–53: A New Proposal for a *Crux Interpretum*," in *"What Does the Scripture Say?" Studies in the Function of Scripture in Early Judaism and Christianity*, LNTS, ed. Craig Evans and H. Daniel Zacharias (New York: T&T Clark, 2012), 1:142–57, esp. 152. Cf. Joachim Gnilka, *Das Matthäusevangelium. Zweiter Teil: Kommentar zu Kapitel 14,1–28,20 und Einleitungsfragen* (Freiburg: Herder, 1988), 477. Admirably, Herzer wants exegetes to interpret Matt. 27:51–54 based on what has been revealed by Matthew in the Gospel's narrative. However, I find Herzer's exegetical conclusions unsatisfying and speculative. The catchword connection "tombs" (cf. Matt. 23:29; 27:52) is not a strong enough foundation to uphold his claims in reference to a group unidentified in the Gospel narrative.

²⁸ Oddly, he either fails to observe the presence of the guards in both pericopal units or fails to comment on the significance of their presence. Yet their presence also connects the two Matthean pericopes. See Anderson, "Origin and Purpose of Matthew 27:51b–53," 162.

²⁹ Maria Riebl, *Auferstehung Jesu in der Stunde seines Todes? Zur Botschaft von*

Matthew's compositional intentionality reveals theological truth about the meaning of Jesus' death while aiding our understanding of his identity.[30]

Intentional Placement

Table 1.2 (see chap. 1) suggested that Matthew employed a macro-structural compositional intentionality within his work as a whole.[31] It is reproduced here for convenience.[32]

Mt 27, 51b–53 (Stuttgart: Katholisches Bibelwerk, 1978), 66–67.

[30] At a macro-Gospel level, compositional intentionality is observed in the parallelism existing between the scenes surrounding Jesus' birth and death. One example will suffice: When Jesus was born, children were slaughtered (Matt. 2:16); when Jesus died, the dead were raised to life (Matt. 27:52).

[31] For a treatment of the Matthean sermonic discourses as catechesis, see David P. Scaer, *Discourses in Matthew: Jesus Teaches the Church* (St. Louis: Concordia Publishing, 2004), 9–32, 395–408. Scaer suggests that each of the five discourses builds on the foundation of the previous ones to culminate in the narrative of Jesus' death and resurrection. Further, he suggests that Matthew's Gospel was structured as a catechesis of what Christians were taught before being admitted by baptism into the full eucharistic membership of the church. Though I do not affirm Scaer's thesis, he does help readers see the discourses as integral to the Matthean narrative. Similarly, Barr suggests the discourses connect the narrative sections (i.e., Matt. 1–4, 8–9, 11–12, 14–17, 19–22, 26–28) of Matthew's Gospel. See David Barr, "The Drama of Matthew's Gospel: A Reconsideration of Its Structure and Purpose," *TD* 24, 4 (1976): 349–59.

[32] Similarly, Weren affirms the chiastic arrangement of the sermonic discourses throughout Matthew's Gospel. Further, he contends the discourses are "chiastically arranged in relation to one another" in Matthew's narrative. Therefore, he suggests the "programme" discourse at the beginning, the Sermon on the Mount, has a counterpart in the Eschatological Discourse; the Missionary Discourse and the Community Discourse discuss the disciples' mission and their mutual relationships; and the Parable Discourse has a central position and explains why the secrets of the kingdom are accessible to the disciples, while they are a mystery to outsiders. Wim J. C. Weren, *Studies in Matthew's Gospel: Literary Design, Intertextuality, and Social Setting* (Boston: Brill, 2014), 32. See also J. C. Fenton, "Inclusio and Chiasmus in Matthew," in *Studia Evangelica: Papers Presented to the International Congress on "The Four Gospels in 1957*," ed. Kurt Aland and F. L. Cross (Berlin: Akademie Verlag, 1959), 174–79, esp. 179.

Table 4.4. Macro-Chiastic Structure of Matthew's Gospel

					1–4	Introduction: Birth and Beginnings of Jesus' Earthly Ministry
	5–7					Sermonic Discourse: Sermon on the Mount / Entering the Kingdom of Heaven
		8–9				Narrative Discourse: The Authority of Jesus to Heal
			10			Sermonic Discourse: Missiological Sermon to the Community
				11–12		Narrative Discourse: Rejection of Jesus as the Christ by This Generation
					13	Sermonic Discourse: Parabolic Sermon on the Kingdom of Heaven
				14–17		Narrative Discourse: Recognition of Jesus as the Christ by the Disciples
			18			Sermonic Discourse: Ecclesiological Sermon to the Community
		19–22				Narrative Discourse: The Authority of Jesus Challenged
	23–25					Sermonic Discourse: Eschatological Discourse / Coming of the Kingdom of Heaven
26–28						Conclusion: Death and End of Jesus' Earthly Ministry

Table 4.4 enables readers to observe the intentional compositional placement of each of the sermonic discourses as well as each of the narrative discourses throughout the entirety of Matthew's tightly structured Gospel.[33] Therefore, just as there is an observable compositional intentionality in the manifest parallelism between Matthew 27:51–54 and Matthew 28:1–10 evident in the structuring of each resurrection pericope and the placement of the dramatis personae within them, so there is also a compositional intentionality in the placement of individual pericopes throughout the entirety of Matthew's Gospel. Thus, it is not by accident that readers encounter the Matthean pericopal hapax in the passion narrative after Jesus releases the Spirit (Matt. 27:50). Matthew does not begin with an account of Jesus' birth (Matt. 1:18–24) and end with an account of his death and resurrection (Matt. 27:45–28:20) merely because the former are the first events while the latter are the last events chronologically. Jesus' birth is chronologically antecedent to subsequent events in his life, but Matthew's Gospel does more than recount sequential chronological facts. Frank Matera rightly notes

---

[33] Contra Smith, who argues for a five-book, narrative-then-discourse literary structure to Matthew's Gospel. See Christopher R. Smith, "Literary Evidences of a Fivefold Structure in the Gospel of Matthew," *NTS* 43 (1997): 540–51. Following Pennington, this dissertation suggests the teaching blocks (Matt. 5–7, 10, 13, 18, 23–25) begin and end the body of the Matthean narrative. The prologue (Matt. 1–4, birth and beginnings) and the epilogue (Matt. 26–28, death and ending) are placed around the first and fifth sermonic discourses. Similarly, see Philippe Roland, "From Genesis to the End of the World: The Plan of Matthew's Gospel," *BTB* 2 (1972): 155–76. That Matthew's Gospel is highly structured is widely agreed on, though there is significant disagreement in regard to how the Gospel's narrative is structured. Competing structures have been posited. Stanton questions if Matthew intended to provide "a broad overall structure . . . as a way of underlining his main purpose." Graham Stanton, "The Origin and Purpose of Matthew's Gospel: Matthean Scholarship from 1945–1980," *ANRW* 2, 25 (1985): 1905. Yet even Stanton recognizes the five discourses to be "obvious examples" of intentional composition. For a recent treatment of the macro-syntactical structure of Matthew's Gospel, see Weren, *Studies in Matthew's Gospel*, 22–41.

that Matthew's Gospel is more than an accumulation of individual episodes.³⁴ Matthew is telling a theological story in his narrative.³⁵ Readers must be careful to observe *how* Matthew communicates the significance(s) of Jesus' life by the way he narrates the events that constituted Christ's life on earth. Determining "how events are arranged [in Matthew's Gospel] is crucial for interpreting narrative logic."³⁶ Matthew is carefully telling the story of Jesus by means of his compositional intentionality.³⁷ The placement of the discourses as well as individual pericopes throughout the Gospel of Matthew "control" the way Matthew's story is interpreted. As no discourse is

---

[34] Matera analyzes "Matthew's Gospel in terms of plot as understood by literary critics" and contends that close attention to plot yields interpretive insight into the meaning(s) of the biblical data revealed within the Matthean narrative. Matthew's Gospel can be read as a story. Frank J. Matera, "The Plot of Matthew's Gospel," *CBQ* 49 (1987): 233–53. For an adapted version of Matera's thesis, see Warren Carter, "Kernels and Narrative Blocks: The Structure of Matthew's Gospel," *CBQ* 54 (1992): 463–81. Aware that some contend literary analysis is subjective, Carter suggests, "The use of literary theory offers the possibility of an informed consideration of the plot and structure which is marked by some precision and control in the literary analysis." For an example of how literary analysis aids interpretation, see Peter J. Leithart, *Deep Exegesis: The Mystery of Reading Scripture* (Waco, TX: Baylor University Press, 2009), 109–71.

[35] A theological reading of Scripture requires attention to be given to the final form of the Matthean narrative. Observation must be given to *how* the author communicates *what* the point of the text is by means of its structure. See Garland, "Reading Matthew," 5–8.

[36] Matera, "The Plot of Matthew's Gospel," 239.

[37] Failure to observe compositional intentionality inhibits interpretation of the Matthean narrative and leads interpreters like Waters to posit that Matt. 27:51–54 is a "flash forward to the apocalyptic future." Kenneth L. Waters, "Matthew 28:1–6 as Temporally Conflated Text: Temporal-Spatial Collapse in the Gospel of Matthew," *ExpT* 116 (2005): 295–301. Failure to observe the narrative's literary parallelism in Matt. 27:45–28:15 and narrative logic in the death-resurrection scene leads Waters to conclude that "the apocalyptic future is retracted into the literary past and wedged between two events on Good Friday, namely, the earthquake and the centurion's confession." His exegetical conclusions fail to reckon with scriptural data in Matthew's Gospel and are not convincing.

inserted simply because it is "next" chronologically, so also no pericope is inserted merely because it is "next" sequentially.

Therefore, assuming intentionality in pericopal placement, this dissertation suggests that the location of Matthew 27:51–54 bears interpretive weight in our understanding of Jesus' death and resurrection. The very *placement* of Matthew 27:51–54 is intentionally located to help tell the story of Jesus. The structural placement of this passage aids interpretation(s) of the details intricately woven into the fabric of the Gospel's death-resurrection conclusion.

Matthew 27:51–54 as a Hinge Text

Literary analysis encourages recognition of the narrative quality of Matthew's Gospel. Recognizing the narrative quality of the Matthean narrative encourages "recognition of the intricate network of supplemental structural devices" operating within the Gospel's story line to highlight key theological concepts.[38] In the case of Matthew 27:51–54, the narrative parallelism between Matthew 27:51–54 and Matthew 28:1–15 highlights the interconnectedness of the two resurrection pericopes situated at the climax of the Gospel's story line in the death-resurrection scene.[39]

Therefore, this dissertation proposes that Matthew 27:51–54 is functioning as a "hinge text"[40] at the redemptive-historical "turning

---

[38] Carter, "Kernels and Narrative Blocks," 481.

[39] Contra Giblin, who separates the two resurrection pericopes by contending that the scene of Jesus' death (Matt. 27:45–56) is disjointed from the scene of his burial (27:57–66) and resurrection (28:1–10). Giblin argues for a burial-resurrection scene with Matt. 28:1–10 as the central passage rather than a death-resurrection scene with narrative parallelism. See Charles H. Giblin, "Structural and Thematic Correlations in the Matthean Burial-Resurrection Narrative (Matt. XXVII.57–XXVIII.20)," *NTS* 21 (1974–75): 406–20. Similarly, Brown understands Matt. 27:62–28:20 to be a textual unit. See Raymond E. Brown, "The Resurrection in Matthew (27:62–28:20)," *Worship* 64 (March 1990): 157–70.

[40] Weren notes the presence of "hinge texts" in Matthew's Gospel. Hinge

point" of history in the Matthean narrative as the Gospel's story line climaxes.⁴¹ A schematic of the death-resurrection scene matures this proposal.

Table 4.5. Matthew 27:51–54 As a Hinge Text within 27:45–28:20

Death of Jesus	Hinge	Burial of Jesus	Hinge	Resurrection of Jesus	Hinge	Mission of Jesus
27:45–50	27:51–54	27:55–61	27:62–66	28:1–10	28:11–15	28:16–20

Table 4.5 manifests how the significant portents following Jesus' death (Matt. 27:51–54) aid readers by causing them to interpret the significances of Jesus' subsequent resurrection (Matt. 28:1–10) in light of his antecedent death (Matt. 27:45–50).⁴² In Matthew's

---

texts, according to Weren, bring about a "turning point" in the Matthean narrative that is fleshed out in both the preceding *and* subsequent pericopes. Matthean hinge texts weigh more heavily in the determination of the Gospel's plot. See Weren, *Studies in Matthew's Gospel*, 28, 30–31. I am borrowing language from Weren in my treatment of Matt. 27:51–54; 28:1–15. I am not, however, suggesting an amendment to Weren's macro-structural treatment of Matthew's Gospel. Unlike Weren, I am not analyzing the macro-syntactical function of Matt. 27:51–54 in the context of the entirety of the Gospel. Rather, borrowing from Weren, I am suggesting Matt. 27:45–54 functions as a "hinge text" in the finale of the Matthean narrative between 27:45–50 and 28:1–20. This approach will be explained more fully below.

⁴¹ Harrington notes that Jesus' death functions as the turning point on which history pivots. Jesus' death "makes possible the resurrection of other human beings" (cf. Matt. 27:52–53). See Daniel J. Harrington, *The Gospel of Matthew*, Sacra Pagina Series 1 (Collegeville, MN: Liturgical Press, 1991), 401.

⁴² Following Davies and Allison, Weren suggests, "The strange story about the raising of the dead saints functions as a preparation for the story in 28:1–10 about Jesus' resurrection." See Weren, *Studies in Matthew's Gospel*, 81. Cf. W. D. Davies and Dale C. Allison Jr., *A Critical and Exegetical Commentary on the Gospel according to Saint Matthew*, ICC, vol. 3, *Matthew 19–28* (New York: T&T Clark, 2004), 640–41.

Gospel the role of Jesus in salvation history is on display in the death-resurrection scene. The hinge texts in the death-resurrection scene—Matthew 27:51–54; 27:62–66; 28:11–15—carry the story line forward as the Gospel moves toward its missiological conclusion (Matt. 28:16–20). The hinge texts cause readers to interpret the missiological emphasis (Matt. 28:16–20) in light of Jesus' death and resurrection. Jesus' life has cosmic significance(s) for the nations (Matt. 28:16–20) in his death (Matt. 27:51–54) and resurrection (Matt. 28:1–10).[43] Matthew stresses the theological import of Jesus' death by giving attention to the portents surrounding Jesus' crucifixion. This observation manifests the meaning of Jesus' death, not the resurrection of the saints, which is emphasized in the narrative during the death-resurrection scene.

The unity of the death-resurrection scene is observable in Matthew's intentional placement of time adjuncts throughout the death-resurrection conclusion of the Gospel. Four time adjuncts manifest that Matthew 27:45–28:20 is an undivided narrative unit.

Table 4.6. Time Adjuncts in Matthew 27:45–28:20

27:45, 46	ἀπὸ δὲ ἕκτης ὥρας . . . περὶ δὲ τὴν ἐνάτην ὥραν[8]
27:57	ὀψίας δὲ γενομένης
27:62	τῇ δὲ ἐπαύριον
28:1	ὀψὲ δὲ σαββάτων

[43] The portents signal the role of Jesus in the salvation history of Israel. See Brown, "Resurrection in Matthew (27:62–28:20)," 162.
[44] The ἕκτης ὥρας and the ἐνάτην ὥραν are taken together because they refer to the same temporal period of Jesus' death and resurrection.

The noticeable time adjuncts evidence Matthew's intention for the death (Matt. 27:45–54), burial (Matt. 27:55–66), and resurrection (Matt. 28:1–15) scenes to be interpreted together as he prepares his readers for Jesus' proclamatory commission to the nations (Matt. 28:16–20).[45] The christological, missiological, and eschatological theological foci of the Matthean narrative are embedded in the structure of the Gospel's story: the discernable parallelism between Matthew 27:45–54 and Matthew 28:1–15, the apparent structuring of each resurrection pericope (27:51–54; 28:1–10), the intentional placement of the dramatis personae within each resurrection pericope, the death-resurrection hinge texts, and the placement of time adjuncts throughout the conclusion of the Matthean passion narrative.

However, the analysis above does not exhaust the dynamic interconnectedness of the conclusion to the Matthean Gospel. The narrative structure in Matthew 27:45–28:20 comprises four scenes and three hinge texts[46] in the finale of Matthew's Gospel:[47]

---

[45] In his treatment of the Gospel's conclusion, Weren, following Giblin and Brown, takes the burial and resurrection of Jesus as one unit in Matthew's Gospel, though he does analyze Matt. 27:51–54 while discussing corporeal resurrection. See Weren, *Studies in Matthew's Gospel*, 72, 74, 80–83; cf. Giblin, "Structural and Thematic Correlations," 406–20; and Brown, "Resurrection in Matthew (27:62–28:20)," 157–70. Therefore, Weren detects the presence of only three of the four time adjuncts—Matt. 27:57, 62; 28:1.

[46] A possible critique of this proposal is the presence of time adjuncts in only three of the four scenes constituting the Matthean death-resurrection conclusion. Τῇ δὲ ἐπαύριον (27:62) is located in a hinge text; there is no explicit time adjunct in the final scene (28:16–20). However, there is an implied time adjunct in the final scene. Travel time from Jerusalem to Galilee is presupposed in the Gospel's narrative.

[47] Though he does not include 27:45–54 in his analysis, Heil also observes an intimate connection between the death, burial, and resurrection scenes in Matthew's narrative. See John P. Heil, "The Narrative Structure of Matthew 27:55–28:20," *JBL* 110 (1991): 419–38.

Table 4.7. Scene, Hinge Text Structure of Matthew 27:45–28:20

Scene 1	27:45–50	Jesus consciously fulfills Ps. 22 while suspended between heaven and earth on a cross. During his suffering and damnation he cries out to his heavenly Father. He dies on Good Friday after shouting triumphantly and releasing the Spirit.
Hinge	27:51–54	Sensory overload incited by the cosmological imagery and divine portents lead to a positive profession of faith as well as recognition of Jesus' identity as God's Son in the wake of his crucifixion. Jesus' death is interpreted by the portents as the narrative is advanced to his burial.
Scene 2	27:55–61	On Good Friday the Marys witness Jesus' crucifixion as well as his burial by Joseph of Arimathea. After Pilate approves, Jesus' body is wrapped and placed in a new tomb. The tomb is sealed with a great stone.
Hinge	27:62–66	The following day the Pharisees conspire before Pilate, arranging the presence of a guard detail at Jesus' tomb for fear of his body being stolen away. In the wake of his crucifixion, the narrative tension is ratcheted up as Easter morning approaches.
Scene 3	28:1–10	On the third day Jesus is resurrected bodily. The corporeality of Jesus' resurrection on Easter is manifest in the worship of him by the Marys after an angel of the Lord and Jesus appears to them. The Marys are twice commissioned to tell Jesus' disciples to meet him in Galilee.

Hinge	28:11–15	The chief priests and elders will not believe the things they have seen (27:45–54) or heard (28:1–10). A sufficient sum of money procures the silence of the failed temple guards and buys their lie about the reality of Jesus' resurrection from the dead. The denial of his resurrection advances the narrative to his public appearance in Galilee.
Scene 4	28:16–20	The resurrected Jesus meets with the disciples corporeally in Galilee. By means of his authority and because of a promise of immanence, Jesus commissions his disciples to the nations to teach all he has commanded.

The schematic above reveals the interlocking network of literary relationships existing between the resurrection pericopes in the Matthean death-resurrection scene. This representation of Matthew's death-resurrection conclusion is influenced by Wim Weren but with three important modifications. First, this dissertation contends that the conclusion of Matthew's Gospel (Matt. 27:45–28:20) consists of four scenes rather than Weren's suggestion of five.[48] Second, this dissertation argues that the first scene in the narrative's conclusion is Matthew 27:45–50 rather than Weren's suggestion of Matthew 27:55–61.[49] Third, this dissertation proposes that the Gospel's finale begins with the death of Jesus in Matthew 27:45 rather than Weren's suggestion of Jesus' burial in Matthew 27:55.[50] Bifurcating the death of Jesus (Matt. 27:45–50) from his resurrection (Matt. 28:1–10)

---

[48] Weren, *Studies in Matthew's Gospel*, 74. This dissertation consciously moves away from the burial-resurrection analysis of Weren, Giblin, and Brown to a death-resurrection analysis of the Gospel's conclusion.

[49] Ibid.

[50] Weren, *Studies in Matthew's Gospel*, 73.

by beginning the finale with the burial of Jesus (Matt. 27:55–61) disrupts the narrative logic of Matthew's story line. The three textual units—Matthew 27:51–54, 55–61, 62–66—are interconnected and flow together to carry along the death-resurrection plot in Matthew's narrative. Its references to the guards (Matt. 27:51–54, cf. 27:65), the onlookers (Matt. 27:55–56), the undertaker (Matt. 27:57–61), and the clergy (Matt. 27:62–66) carry the story line forward in the wake of the Gospel's (anti)climax—Jesus' death (Matt. 27:45–50). The burial scene (Matt. 27:55–61) is interwoven into the death-resurrection conclusion (Matt. 27:45–28:20) to connect the preceding events (Matt. 27:45–54) to the following events (Matt. 28:1–20) in the Matthean narrative.

The Purpose of Matthew 27:51–54

The logical question is *why* Matthew intentionally placed Matthew 27:51–54 within Matthew 27:45–28:20. First, this dissertation suggests that the narrative's composition is intended to accentuate Jesus' identity: The cosmic portents following Christ's death teach readers something about his identity as the Son of God (Matt. 27:54).[51] Second, Matthew's intentionality in his literary structure is intended to accentuate the mission that Jesus' death necessitates—Jesus' death is life-giving (Matt. 27:52) and ultimately salvific for

---

[51] Schnackenburg acknowledges the symbolism of the Matthean pericope but incorrectly denies its historicity. He contends, "The text is to be understood only as a theological concept portrayed as an event.... The entire passage ... is not to be analyzed historically.... Matthew *imagines* the centurion and his men saw the earthquake and these happenings." Rudolf Schnackenburg, *The Gospel of Matthew*, trans. Robert R. Barr (Grand Rapids: Eerdmans, 2002), 288–91, emphasis added. For a rejection of ahistorical symbolism as well as a defense of the pericope's historicity, see Charles Quarles, "A Roundtable Discussion with Michael Licona on the Resurrection of Jesus: A New Historiographical Approach," *Southeastern Theological Review* 3, 1 (2012): 71–98, esp. 75–76; and Quarles, review of *The Resurrection of Jesus: A New Historiographical Approach*, by Michael R. Licona, *JETS* 54 (2011): 839–44.

persons from every nation who profess faith in his name (Matt. 28:16–20; cf. 2:11; 14:33; 27:54; Rev. 7:9–12). From Jesus' birth (Matt. 1:18–24) through his death (Matt. 27:51–54), Matthew has communicated the soteriological significances of Jesus' life.⁵² Contrary to the belief of the Sadducees and Pharisees (Matt. 27:41–43), Jesus bears much fruit by dying and being buried in a tomb—just as the seed of wheat bears much fruit by falling to the earth (cf. John 12:24).⁵³ Jesus "bears fruit" through the disciples he promises to be with until the end of the age as they are on mission for the renown of the Triune name (Matt. 28:18–20).⁵⁴ Third, Matthew's narrative composition is intended to accentuate the eschatological inbreaking of the kingdom of heaven as the temple cultus is rendered obsolete (Matt. 27:51). The torn veil signified that the temple was no longer sacrosanct. As Quarles puts it, the "temple was now open and vulnerable to desecration."⁵⁵ The cosmological imagery—darkness (Matt. 27:45)—and the earthquake signified God's wrath and judgment (cf. 2 Sam. 22:8; Isa. 13:13; Joel 2:10; Amos 8:9). The new covenant supersedes the old covenant in the death of the Messiah,

---

⁵² Jesus' name connotes the soteriological significance of his life—γὰρ σώσει τὸν λαὸν αὐτοῦ ἀπὸ τῶν ἁμαρτιῶν αὐτῶν (1:21). Matthew reveals that Jesus' lifeblood is poured out for the salvation of others—τοῦτο γάρ ἐστιν τὸ αἷμά μου τῆς διαθήκης τὸ περὶ πολλῶν ἐκχυννόμενον εἰς ἄφεσιν ἁμαρτιῶν (26:28). See also Matt. 9:2; 16:21–23; 17:22–23; 20:17–19.

⁵³ Matthew is clear, though, that it is a life-giving death only for those who love God instead of mammon (Matt. 28:11–15; cf. 6:24), for those who repent at the call of the kingdom (Matt. 3:2; 4:17; 10:7).

⁵⁴ Matthew begins and ends his Gospel with a reference to Jesus' presence with his people. As Immanuel, he is God with us (Matt. 1:23). As the resurrected authority, he is God with us (Matt. 28:16, 20; cf. Gen. 28:15 LXX). He will never leave us. The Gospel's *inclusio* manifests the missiological implications of Jesus' incarnation (cf. Matt. 1:21; John 20:19–23; Acts 1:8) and his death on the cross (cf. Matt. 27:54; 28:18–20).

⁵⁵ Quarles posits the rending of the temple veil may also have "signified the departure of the divine glory from the temple." If correct, this further connects Matt. 27:51–54 with Ezekiel's prophecy (cf. Ezek. 10:18–19). See Quarles, "Matthew 27:51–53 as a Scribal Interpretation," 272.

Jesus. The law will be written on the hearts of those who respond to Jesus in faith (Matt. 27:54; cf. Jer. 31:31–34; Ezek. 36:26–27).

Further, without downplaying the physical or emotional sufferings of Jesus, Matthew stresses the theological import of Jesus' death by means of the minute attention given to the physical pain Jesus experienced during his crucifixion.[56] Prior to the crucifixion Matthew goes to great lengths to describe the mental and physical sufferings of Jesus: he is betrayed (Matt. 26:48), spat on (Matt. 26:67; cf. 27:30), slapped (Matt. 26:67), scourged (Matt. 27:26), stripped (Matt. 27:28), mocked (Matt. 27:29), and beaten with reeds while wearing the crown of thorns (Matt. 27:30; cf. 2:2; 27:11, 37). Prior to the crucifixion scene the gruesome features of Jesus' suffering are described in pronounced detail in the Gospel's narrative. While suspended between heaven and earth on the cross, however, the physical sufferings of Jesus are taken for granted in the Matthean narrative. At Golgotha, Jesus is crucified (Matt. 27:35), derided (Matt. 27:39), and mocked (Matt. 27:41) before he cries aloud into the silent darkness (Matt. 27:46, 50).[57] True to form in the Matthean Gospel, those present with the Crucified One misinterpret the significance of his screams from the cross (Matt. 27:47; cf. 9:3;

---

[56] Hill notes the allusions to the Old Testament, specifically Ps. 22, in the death-resurrection scene of the Matthean narrative. See David Hill, *The Gospel of Matthew*, New Century Bible Commentary (London: Oliphants, 1972), 354.

[57] Harrington notes that some understand Jesus' "cries in the dark" to be his personal "breaking point" in the Matthean narrative. They assume Jesus was no longer in control of his own destiny and could no longer take the torture of the cross. Those advocating the "breaking point" of Jesus conclude the dereliction cries in the dark reveal that Jesus gave up on God. See Harrington, *Gospel of Matthew*, 402. This proposal is highly speculative. The Scripture does not say Jesus gave up on God. Rather, in Matthew's Gospel, it speaks to how Jesus consciously fulfilled Ps. 22 in his death. Jesus endured infinite suffering on the cross because of his infinite love for the elect (Matt. 22:14). In the midst of his pain Jesus held on to the fulfillment of Ps. 22 while enduring infinite suffering and the damnation of God for the elect as a substitute for sinners (cf. Isa. 53:4–6).

12:24; 26:65).⁵⁸ Jesus does not plead for sympathy by acknowledging his suffering ("My pain! My pain!"), nor does he wallow in his abject loneliness by calling for his comrades ("My friends! My friends!"). Rather, he speaks to his Father—ηλι ηλι (Matt. 27:46; cf. Mark 14:36)—fully confident he would not despise the suffering of his Chosen One (Ps. 22:1, 14; cf. Matt. 12:18–21). Jesus' second cry is not a whimper; it is a declaration of triumph—"It is finished" (Matt. 27:50; cf. John 19:30). According to David Scaer, the misunderstanding of those present at the crucifixion manifests

> the failure of the Jews to recognize who Jesus really is, and, more importantly, it reveals a sad inability to grasp what is happening. Confronted with the most sacred of all moments—the Son of Man shedding his blood as atonement for his followers—the crowds faithlessly conclude that Jesus has lapsed into demented fantasy as he asks for deliverance not from God but from a long dead prophet who has become fictionalized in the people's imagination. They cannot see that the crucified one is by this act saving them: "He will save his people from their sins" (1:21).⁵⁹

Those present are unable to interpret his ignominious death (Matt. 27:36–50) until the subsequent Spirit-incited portents testify to his identity as God's Son (Matt. 27:50, 54).

Failure to observe the literary purpose of Matthew 27:51–54 as a hinge text within the death-resurrection conclusion of Matthew's Gospel places unnecessary interpretive stress on each of the passage's five divine portents individually—and in regard to this

---

⁵⁸ ἀνεβόησεν ὁ Ἰησοῦς φωνῇ ... κράξας φωνῇ μεγάλῃ (Matt. 27:46, 50).

⁵⁹ Scaer, *Discourses in Matthew*, 406, cf. 398. Scaer's treatment of the death-resurrection scene has much to commend. He rightly connects the events of Matt. 27 with the events of Matt. 28. Yet, following Waters, his interpretation locates the resurrection of the saints in the apocalyptic future.

dissertation, specifically on the resurrection of the sleeping saints (Matt. 27:52b–53). Consequently, readers are often perplexed by "unanswerable" interpretive questions arising from the pericope. Thus, Scaer states, "Determining a meaning for the final scene of Matthew's sequence of events—the resurrection of the saints—may be the most problematic. It raises questions that may not be answered to the satisfaction of all."[60] In observing Matthew's compositional intentionality, it is manifest that the function of the pericopal hapax is not primarily about the identification of the resurrected dead (Matt. 27:52–53). Rather, the pericope functions as one of the three hinge texts in the death-resurrection scene.[61] Collectively, they accentuate the three theological foci that this dissertation argues form the bedrock of the Matthean Gospel's conclusion.[62]

Table 4.8. Theological Foci Accentuated in the Death-Resurrection Scene

Christology	Eschatology	Missiology
27:45–54	28:1–10	28:16–20

[60] For example, see Scaer, *Discourses in Matthew*, 408. Similarly, outside of a pronouncement of judgment and anticipation of the events in Matt. 28, Chamblin is unable to give a reason for the pericope's inclusion. See Knox Chamblin, *Matthew*, A Mentor Commentary (Fearn, Scotland: Christian Focus Publication, 2010), 2:1427–31. Likewise, following many others, Ridderbos interprets the Matthean pericope in light of Paul's teaching in the Corinthian correspondence. See Herman Ridderbos, *Matthew*, trans. Ray Togtman, Bible Student's Commentary (Grand Rapids: Zondervan, 1987), 536–37.

[61] Observation of textual arrangement and structure has hermeneutical value. It is vital in interpreting narrative logic. Good reading requires interpreters to develop what Leithart calls "a good sense of textual humor" to discern the multiple melodies and complex rhythms of texts. See Leithart, *Deep Exegesis*, 143–53.

[62] These theological themes are not confined to the pericopal breakdowns above. There is significant overlap throughout the death-resurrection scene. However, I argue that each theme is located in the pericope under consideration

The intricate narrative structure emphasizes the theological meaning latent in the text. The apocalyptic signs that accompanied Jesus' death (cf. Matt. 27:51–53) portray Jesus as Messiah (Matt. 27:54) and prepare readers for the in-breaking of the eschatological resurrection on Easter morning (Matt. 28:1–10). Matthew accentuates the death of Jesus as life-giving—the dead rise at the cross of Christ—to make his identity apparent: "This truly was the Son of God!" The mocking of the pharisaic naysayers (Matt. 27:40, 43) is overruled when Jesus' divine sonship (Matt. 27:54) is established by means of the portents (Matt. 27:51–53) accompanying his horrific crucifixion. The "lesser" resurrection of the saints proleptically anticipates the "greater" resurrection of Jesus (Matt. 28:1–10) and visibly manifests his identity as the Son of God (Matt. 27:45). Further, this "lesser" resurrection anticipates the gospel mission to the ends of the earth (Matt. 27:54; 28:16–20).

Conclusion

This chapter has argued that careful attention must be given to the compositional structure(s) of the death-resurrection scene (Matt. 27:45–28:20) and the placement of Matthew 27:51–54 within the Matthean narrative's conclusion. Attention to Matthew's structure manifests a deliberate narrative strategy in his Gospel conclusion and leads to a proper interpretation of the death-resurrection narrative.

Matthew's reader-oriented motivations informed his arrangement of the Gospel material. For Matthew, there is an assumed contract between himself and his readers specifying that interpretive meaning is laden within the very structure(s) and presentation of his narrative, not merely the content contained within a series of randomly placed pericopes throughout his Gospel. Recognizing Matthew's highly structured narrative is essential to ascertaining

---

and is represented uniquely in the divisions above.

the author's meaning(s) of the death-resurrection scene. Awareness of Matthean narrative strategy enables interpreters to successfully receive the meaning embedded in the structural presentation of his Gospel material.

The death-resurrection conclusion to the Matthean narrative is laden with interpretive structural significance because of Matthew's compositional intentionality. Matthew has joined the four scenes (Matt. 27:45–50, 55–61; 28:1–10, 16–20) by employing three hinge texts (Matt. 27:51–54, 62–66; 28:11–15). The hinge texts dispersed throughout the death-resurrection conclusion advance the Gospel narrative to the next respective scene *and* aid readers by leading them to interpret the significances of Jesus' resurrection (Matt. 28:1–10) in light of his antecedent death (Matt. 27:45–50), and vice versa.

Wolfgang Iser was right to contend that "reading is the essential precondition for all processes of literary interpretation."[63] That process includes observing the text's structure, which itself contains some of the text's meaning(s). Careful reading of the Matthean material utilizes "rules of notice" as well as "rules of signification." The former rules refer to details of the Gospel narrative that contain more prominence than others, while the latter rules enable readers to derive significance from the details that the first set of rules have brought to their attention.[64] In relation to this dissertation, the two

---

[63] Iser, *Act of Reading*, 20. Powell is concerned with what real readers are supposed to notice while reading. He argues, "One reason, then, real readers arrive at unexpected interpretations is that they fail to notice or remember information provided within the narrative." See Mark A. Powell, "Expected and Unexpected Readings of Matthew: What the Reader Knows," *ATJ* 48, 2 (1993): 31–51. This dissertation is arguing that failure to observe the compositional intentionality of Matthew's narrative strategy is akin to what Powell would call "under-observance." For a study of what a model reader *does* in the reading/interpretive process, see Leroy A. Huizenga, *The New Isaac: Tradition and Intertextuality in the Gospel of Matthew*, NovTSup 131 (Leiden, Netherlands: Brill, 2009), 21–74.

[64] Rabinowitz actually discusses four general "rules" or conventions: those of notice, signification, configuration, and coherence. See Peter J. Rabinowitz, *Before Reading: Narrative Conventions and the Politics of Interpretation* (Ithaca,

sets of rules work together as readers seek to derive meaning(s) from Matthew 27:51–54. The literary parallels between Matthew 27:51–54 and Matthew 28:1–10 made by the Gospel's author suggests not only intentionality in craft but also parallel meanings.[65] Thus, the resurrection accompanying Jesus' death is one of five portents that Matthew employs to communicate Jesus' identity as the Son of God (Matt. 27:54; cf. 4:3, 6; 8:29; 14:33; 26:63; 27:40, 43; Luke 3:38). The resurrection of Jesus himself (Matt. 28:1–10; cf. John 10:17–18) manifests his divine power as the eternal Son of God (Matt. 24:30; 26:64).[66] He saves his people from their sins (Matt. 1:21; cf. 16:25; 27:40, 42, 49) by his death and resurrection (Matt. 27:45–50; 28:1–10; Rom. 4:25). The literary parallelism between the resurrection pericopes and the structural intentionality of the death-resurrection scene leads readers to interpret these two portions of Matthew's Gospel *together*. Bifurcating the resurrection pericopes places undue interpretive stress on the individual portents. This interpretive stress

---

NY: Cornell University Press, 1987), 47–109.

[65] Ibid., 46. Minear's thesis, primarily, is that Matthew crafted his Gospel in such a way to "teach" his readers about Jesus. See Paul S. Minear, *Matthew: The Teacher's Gospel* (New York: Pilgrim's Press, 1982), 3, 10, 12. Though I disagree with Minear's claim that Matthew primarily had teachers of local churches in mind when composing his Gospel, I agree that Matthew intentionally arranged his material to "teach" about Jesus.

[66] Patte notes, "The power of God is manifested without ambiguity in the striking events surrounding [Jesus'] death-resurrection." Throughout the crucifixion of Jesus, God has been eerily silent, which underscores the absence of God's intervention *until* divine activity dominates the scene after Jesus' death in Matt. 27:51–53. See Daniel Patte, *The Gospel according to Matthew: A Structural Commentary on Matthew's Faith* (Philadelphia: Fortress Press, 1987), 388. Unfortunately, in his treatment of Matt. 27–28, Patte bifurcates the death scene from the burial-resurrection scene. See also John P. Heil, *The Death and Resurrection of Jesus: A Narrative-Critical Reading of Matthew 26–28* (Minneapolis: Fortress Press, 1991), 84–89. Bauer takes the two resurrection pericopes together in his treatment of Matthew's Gospel, but he views the resurrection of the saints as displaced within the Matthean narrative. See David R. Bauer, *The Structure of Matthew's Gospel: A Study in Literary Design*, JSNTSup 31 (Decatur, GA: Almond Press, 1988), 103.

has led either to the separation of the historic act from its theological meaning or to speculation about minor questions related to Matthew 27:52b–53—Who were the resurrected dead? Where did they go as they strolled the streets of the holy city? To whom did they speak in Jerusalem?—rather than the death and resurrection of Jesus. A narrative reading of the death-resurrection scene obviates interpretive stress. What interpreters often take to be the central event (Matt. 27:52b–53) is merely one of five portents in a hinge text within the death-resurrection conclusion of Matthew's Gospel.

This thesis proposes that recognizing the literary parallelism between Matthew 27:51–54 and Matthew 28:1–10 as well as the compositional structural intentionality in the death-resurrection scene (Matt. 27:45–28:20) will yield interpretive clarity in relation to Matthew's *crux interpretum*. A proper understanding of the pericope's translation, the primary Old Testament referent, and the compositional structure and placement enables interpreters to ascertain (1) how Matthew 27:51–54 is functioning in the death-resurrection scene and (2) the three theological foci of the pericope—Christology, missiology, and eschatology.

5

Theological Meaning: The Theological Foci of Matthew 27:51–54—Christology, Missiology, and Eschatology

Theological Import

This dissertation propounds that both Matthean resurrection pericopes (Matt. 27:51–54 and 28:1–10) must be fused and read together in order to understand the theological significance of Matthew 27:51–54. Furthermore, by properly understanding the pericope's translation (see chap. 2), the primary Old Testament referent (see chap. 3), and the compositional structure and placement (see chap. 4), interpreters will be able to ascertain (1) how Matthew 27:51–54 is functioning in the death-resurrection scene and (2) the three theological foci of the pericope—Christology, missiology, and eschatology.

This dissertation has argued that Matthean research has thus far achieved no consensus of opinion on either the broad structure of Matthew's death-resurrection scene (Matt. 27:45–28:20) or on Matthew's intended meaning in relation to the five divine portents included in Matthew 27:51–54. Little attention has been given to the problem of discerning how these two issues relate to each other. This general situation has produced two negative interpretive results. First, only a handful of commentators in recent decades have attempted to ascertain the interpretive significance of Matthew 27:51–54 from the structure of the death-resurrection scene.[1] Second, there have been fewer interpreters who have endeavored to let the structure of the Gospel's death-resurrection scene (Matt. 27:45–28:20) be their guide when interpreting the theological foci accentuated by the portents in the pericope under consideration—Matthew 27:51–54. The objective of this chapter is to delineate the intended theological meaning of Matthew 27:51–54 in such a way that the structure of the Gospel's death-resurrection scene manifests a viable interpretation of the pericopal hapax. This chapter will highlight the significance of three theological foci woven into the fabric of Matthew 27:51–54: Christology, missiology, and eschatology.

The Theological Meaning of Matthew 27:51–54

Three Theological Foci

As discussed above, this Matthean pericope revolves around the themes of Christology, missiology, and eschatology. The extraordinary signs accompanying Jesus' death (cf. Matt. 27:51–53) portray him as the Son of God (Matt. 27:54) and prepare Matthew's readers for the eschatological resurrection on Easter morning (Matt. 28:1–10).[2] Matthew accentuates the death of Jesus as life-giving—the

---

[1] For example, see Wim J. C. Weren, *Studies in Matthew's Gospel: Literary Design, Intertextuality, and Social Setting* (Boston: Brill, 2014), 22–41, 72, 74, 80–83. David R. Bauer, *The Structure of Matthew's Gospel: A Study in Literary Design*, JSNTSup 31 (Decatur, GA: Almond Press, 1988). Daniel Patte, *The Gospel according to Matthew: A Structural Commentary on Matthew's Faith* (Philadelphia: Fortress Press, 1987).

[2] Brown notes similar phenomena were reported at the deaths of Romulus and Julius Caesar. His examples include Plutarch (*Rom. 27.6*; *Caes.* 69:4), Ovid (*Fast.* 2.493), Cicero (*Rep.* 6:22), Virgil (*Georg.* 1.466–88), Josephus (*Ant.* 14.12.3; 309), and Pliny (*Nat.* 2.30; 97). See Raymond E. Brown, *The Death of the Messiah: From Gethsemane to the Grave—A Commentary on the Passion Narratives in the Four Gospels*, ABRL (New York: Doubleday, 1994), 1114,

Theological Meaning

dead rise at the cross of Christ (Matt. 27:52b–53)—to make his divine identity apparent:" "This really was the Son of God!"[3] The mocking of the pharisaic naysayers (Matt. 27:40, 43) and robbers (Matt. 27:44) is invalidated when Jesus' divine sonship (Matt. 27:54) is established by means of the portents (Matt. 27:51–53) accompanying his death. The saints' "lesser" resurrection proleptically anticipates Jesus' "greater" resurrection (Matt. 28:1–10), and the guard's profession of faith anticipates the Great Commission (Matt. 27:54; 28:16–20). In each instance, three critical theological planks serve as interpretive guides that further support a literary reading of the text as definitive for a correct understanding of both the pericope itself and its accompanying theological foci employed by Matthew.

Christology

The crucifixion opens the introductory scene of the Matthean death-resurrection conclusion (Matt. 27:38–54). The significance(s) of Jesus' execution dominates this portion of the Gospel. Thus, Donald Senior notes the uniqueness of Matthew's rendition of the passion narrative. He asserts that a "heightened christological portrait" pervades the conclusion of the Matthean Gospel.[4] The

---

1120–27. Similarly, Licona notes the occurrence of similar phenomena at the death of Claudius, the enslavement of Egypt by Caesar, and the destruction of the temple. His examples come from Dio Cassius (*Roman History* 57.17.4–5; 60.35.1) and Josephus (*Wars* 6.288–309). See Michael Licona, *The Resurrection of Jesus: A New Historiographical Approach* (Downers Grove, IL: InterVarsity Press, 2010), 448–50.

[3] Careful readers will recognize resonances from two Old Testament stories of resurrection found in 1 Kings 17:17–24 and 2 Kings 4:32–37. As the Lord heard the cries of Elijah for the boy, so the Lord heard the cries of Jesus from the cross. As the resurrection of the boy confirmed Elijah's identity as a man of God speaking the words of the Lord, so the resurrection of the sleeping saints—along with the other portents—confirmed Jesus' divine identity as God's Son. Similarly, Elisha's identity as a man of God is confirmed by his raising of the Shunammite's son. Like the centurion cohort, the Shunammite's response to resurrection is worship (2 Kings 4:37; cf. Matt. 27:54).

[4] He argues this is evident by the "use of christological titles such as King

Theological Meaning

location of the series of events taking place on the cross is purposeful to Matthew's understanding of Christology as revealed in the death-resurrection scene. That they occur at the beginning of the narrative in this successive order is the literary vehicle whereby the christological significance(s) become clear.

In this section Matthew attaches importance to Christology, as is evident from the three explicit references to "Son of God" in his narrative (Matt. 27:40, 43, 54). First, Jesus is condemned to death by the religious leaders twice specifically as "the Son of God" (Matt. 27:40, 43).[5] This double earthly condemnation stands in marked contrast to the Father's double heavenly affirmation of Jesus' sonship in Matthew's Gospel. The celestial voice thundered divine approval at his baptism (Matt. 3:17) and at his transfiguration (Matt. 17:5). Second, the centurion and his comrades confess that Jesus is the Son of God (Matt. 27:54). This places the confession of Jesus' sonship on the lips of both Jews and Gentiles in Matthew's Gospel (cf. Matt. 16:16; 27:54). In both instances, the confession of his divine sonship is the product of divine revelation, not human intuition or testimony. Therefore, Jesus said that the heavenly Father—σὰρξ καὶ αἷμα οὐκ—revealed his sonship to Peter (Matt. 16:17). Similarly, the soldiers respond to heavenly portents—τὸν σεισμὸν καὶ τὰ γενόμενα—not the accusations of the religious elite (Matt. 27:54; cf. 27:40, 43). Jesus' sonship becomes the place where Jew and Gentile agree in the Matthean narrative.

Acknowledging the centrality of Christology in the death-resurrection conclusion, Jack Kingsbury suggests that these three "Son of God" references form an outline to this section of Matthew's

---

of the Jews, Christ, Son of God" in the death-resurrection scene. Collectively, these titles enhance the christological portrait found in Matthew's Gospel. Donald Senior, *The Passion Narrative according to Matthew: A Redactional Study*, BETL 39 (Leuven, Belgium: Leuven University Press, 1975), 337.

[5] There are two references on the lips of Jesus' murderers in the pericope. The first is a question, εἰ υἱὸς εἶ τοῦ θεοῦ (27:40), and the second is a statement: θεοῦ εἰμι υἱός (27:43).

Theological Meaning

Gospel.[6] Accordingly, the outline can be devised as follows: First, Matthew 27:38 introduces the scene in which Jesus is blasphemed as the "Son of God" (Matt. 27:39–40). Second, Matthew 27:41–43 introduces the scene in which Jesus is mocked as both the "King of Israel" and the "Son of God."[7] Third, Matthew 27:51–53 introduces the divinely initiated supernatural portents attesting to Jesus' deity as the Son of God.[8] These portents are understood as God the Father's declaration of Jesus' divine sonship following his work on the cross to actualize the forgiveness of sins. This understanding of the portents is subsequently confirmed by the response of the centurion and his companions. Their response to the Matthean epiphany—"the earthquake and what took place" (Matt. 27:54)—emphasizes one of the collective meanings of the portents: christological import. Jesus is blasphemed, mocked, and heralded as the Son of God in the death-resurrection scene in order to accentuate his identity as God's Son.[9] Jesus' divine sonship is on display in the Matthean

---

[6] The observation of this outline is dependent on Kingsbury's contribution. See Jack D. Kingsbury, *Matthew: Structure, Christology, Kingdom* (Philadelphia: Fortress Press, 1975), 74–77.

[7] Though there is not an explicit reference in Matt. 27:44, the narrative notes that Jesus was ridiculed in the same way—τὸ δ' αὐτὸ—by the robbers who were crucified with him. During the crucifixion scene, then, three groups disparage Jesus: the crowds (27:39), the chief priests (27:41), and the robbers (27:44).

[8] Readers will note the uses of the *passivum divinum*—ἐσχίσθη, ἐσείσθη, ἐσχίσθησαν, ἀνεῴχθησαν, ἠγέρθησαν—in this section of the death-resurrection conclusion. God is the obvious agent of action. Their presence indicates God caused these events in response to Jesus' crucifixion. God tore the curtain in two, shook the earth, split the rocks, opened the tombs, and resurrected the sleeping saints who subsequently entered the holy city *after* Jesus' resurrection to testify, along with the Gentile crowd, that Jesus is the Son of God.

[9] Kingsbury proposes that θεέ μου "may be regarded as testimony on the part of Jesus himself that he is the Son of God." He suggests that Matthew's use of θεέ μου is a Matthean idiom derived from passages like Ps. 89:26. Therefore, he states there is a definite observable pattern here in the Matthean narrative: "Three times Jesus is rejected as the Son of God (vss. 38–44), and

Theological Meaning

death-resurrection conclusion.[10] This section of Matthew's narrative pivots on christological import.

Therefore, the logical interpretive question is, Why is Matthew concerned to emphasize the fact that Jesus hangs on the cross and dies specifically as the θεοῦ υἱός in the death-resurrection conclusion of his Gospel? It is evident that Matthew's emphasis is to convey Jesus's divine sonship. It is intended to accentuate Jesus' identity—he *is* the Son of God. The child born of the virgin Mary is the Son of God (Matt. 1:18, 20; cf. 27:54).[11] In the death-resurrection scene, the child become man is the Christ of God lifted up on a Roman cross (John 3:14–15). The dignity of the title "Son of God" would not have been conferred on him at his death unless he truly was the only begotten Son of God. Therefore, John Calvin states, "[He] is believed to be the Son of God because the Word begotten of the Father before all ages took human nature in a hypostatic

---

three times he is attested to as the Son of God (vss. 45–54)." Kingsbury, *Matthew: Structure, Christology, Kingdom*, 75.

[10] Thus, de Jonge notes "Matthew [27:39–54] emphasizes that the essential question is that of Jesus' divine sonship." See M. de Jonge, "The Use of O Cristos in the Passion Narratives," in *Jewish Eschatology, Early Christian Christology and the Testaments of the Twelve Patriarchs: Collected Essays of Marinus De Jonge*, NovTSup 63 (Leiden, Netherlands: Brill, 1991), 77–78.

[11] ἐκ πνεύματος ἁγίου (Matt. 1:18). Luke, in his Gospel, explicitly connects Jesus' sonship to his conception by means of the Holy Spirit, πνεῦμα ἅγιον ἐπελεύσεται ἐπὶ σὲ καὶ δύναμις ὑψίστου ἐπισκιάσει σοι διὸ καὶ τὸ γεννώμενον ἅγιον κληθήσεται υἱὸς θεοῦ (Luke 1:35). Through Mary, the Son of God was begotten of the seed of David—the Son of Man (cf. Matt. 1:1). Reflecting on the wonder of the God-man's hypostatic union, Charnock states, "What a wonder is it, that two natures infinitely distant, should be more intimately united than anything in the world; and yet without any confusion! That the same person should have both a glory and a grief; an infinite joy in the Deity, and an inexpressible sorrow in the humanity! That a God upon a throne should be an infant in a cradle; the thundering Creator be a weeping babe and a suffering man, are such expressions of mighty power, as well as condescending love, that they astonish men upon earth, and angels in heaven." Stephen Charnock, *The Existence and Attributes of God* (Grand Rapids: Baker, 1996), 2:64.

Theological Meaning

union."[12] Jesus is called "Son of God" by virtue of his deity and eternal essence.[13]

Matthew's christological portrait features two specific aspects of Christology designed to emphasize both the person and work of Jesus simultaneously. Interpreters must ascertain the particular aspects of divine sonship that Matthew most wanted to accentuate in his death-resurrection conclusion. In Matthew's Gospel, Jesus is referenced as both "Son of Man" and "Son of God."[14] The former title is attributed to him thirty times in Matthew's Gospel.[15] The latter title, however, is attributed to him only eight times in the Matthean narrative.[16] It is notable that Jesus is referred to only as the "Son of God" in the death-resurrection conclusion—Matthew 27:45–28:20. Clearly, therefore, particular christological aspects are on display in the Matthean narrative.[17]

---

[12] John Calvin, *Institutes* 2.14.5. Similarly, when writing of the centrality of the Son of God's incarnation, Bavinck states, "If . . . Christ is the incarnate Word, then the incarnation is the central fact of the entire history of the world; then, too, it must have been prepared before the ages and have its effects throughout eternity." See Herman Bavinck, *Reformed Dogmatics*, vol. 3, *Sin and Salvation in Christ*, trans. John Vriend (Grand Rapids: Baker, 2006), 274.

[13] Bavinck notes that Scripture repeatedly attributes to Christ's personal eternal preexistence (John 1:1; 8:58; 17:5; Rom. 8:3; 2 Cor. 8:9; Gal. 4:4; Phil. 2:6) *and* divine sonship in a supernatural sense (Matt. 3:17; 11:27; 28:19; John 1:14; 5:18; Rom. 8:32). See Bavinck, *Reformed Dogmatics*, 3:283.

[14] Calvin suggests the two titles distinguish between his two natures—man and God. As the posterity of Adam he is the Son of Man; as the eternal second person of the Trinity he is Son of God. Therefore, Jesus is called Son of Man in reference to his human nature and Son of God in reference to his divine nature. The man Jesus who descended from the Jews according to the flesh is God. Calvin, *Institutes* 2.14.6.

[15] Matt. 8:20; 9:6; 10:23; 11:19; 12:8, 32, 40; 13:37, 41; 16:13, 27, 28; 17:9, 12, 22; 19:28; 20:18, 28; 24:27, 30 (2x), 37, 39, 44; 25:31; 26:2, 24 (2x), 45, 64.

[16] Matt. 4:3, 6; 8:29; 14:33; 26:63; 27:40, 43, 54.

[17] According to Hays, an integral part of what it means for Jesus to be "God with us" in Matthew's narrative is "the story of Jesus' own suffering, culminating in the cross." Richard B. Hays, *Echoes of Scripture in the Gospels* (Waco, TX: Baylor University Press, 2016), 170. Further, concerning christological import in the Matthean Gospel, Hays states, "Christian interpreters lulled

Theological Meaning

First, divine sonship is associated with humble obedience. This is evident by Matthew's use of the clause εἰ υἱὸς εἶ τοῦ θεοῦ in Matthew 27:40. The clause is a direct quotation of Satan's words spoken to Jesus during his wilderness temptation (Matt. 4:3, 6).[18] As Satan did in the temptation scene, so now the religious leaders are tempting Jesus while he hangs on the cross (Matt. 27:40, 42). Yet he does not capitulate to their prodding or meet their demands.[19] Rather, he chooses to do the will of God. The Son of God was obedient to the point of death, even death on a cross (Phil. 2:8; cf. Heb.

---

by familiarity with Matthew's Gospel may not fully appreciate the immense scope of the Christological assertions made at every turn by Matthew. But there can be no doubt that the word spoken by Jesus . . . can be true only if it really is "the word of our God," only if the speaker who says "my words will not pass away" is in fact the God of Israel, God with us." See Richard B. Hays, *Reading Backwards: Figural Christology and the Fourfold Gospel Witness* (Waco, TX: Baylor University Press, 2014), 47.

[18] Kingsbury suggests that the connection to the temptation account explains the reason Jesus did not come down from the cross as the religious leaders and the crowds demanded. As he did in Matthew 4:1–11, so now Jesus resists temptation in order to do the will of God. See Kingsbury, *Matthew: Structure, Christology, Kingdom*, 76. The intratextual connections between the beginning and ending of Matthew's Gospel encourage his readers to exercise their interpretive imagination as those informed by his Gospel, especially its beginning. For more on the intratextual connections between the beginning and ending of Matthew's Gospel, see Jason B. Hood, *The Messiah, His Brothers, and the Nations (Matthew 1:1–17)* (London: T&T Clark, 2011), 137–56. Matthew utilizes literary parallelism between the beginning and ending of his narrative to accentuate theological truth in the death-resurrection scene, in this instance christological import. Thus, as Herod the King (Matt. 2:1) is literarily paralleled with the newborn King of the Jews (Matt. 2:2), as the beginning of Jesus' earthly ministry is literarily paralleled with the beginning of John the Baptist's earthly ministry (Matt. 3:1; 4:1 and 3:2; 4:17), as the scenes surrounding Jesus' birth are literarily paralleled with scenes surrounding Jesus' death (Matt. 2:16; 27:52), so now temptations spoken by Satan are literarily paralleled with those hurled by Jesus' accusers (Matt. 4:3, 6; 27:40) to emphasize Jesus' identity in the death-resurrection scene—he *is* the Son of God (Matt. 27:54).

[19] The silence of Jesus in the face of false accusations by his murderers throughout the end of Matthew's Gospel is deafening (Matt. 26:63; 27:14).

Theological Meaning

5:8). As a true servant, the Son of God chose to obey at the cost his life.[20] According to Kingsbury, throughout the death-resurrection scene, "Jesus declares that even though God should deliver him up to death, he makes no forfeiture of his sonship but remains obedient to the Father's will and continues to rely upon him completely."[21] The immediate impact of the death of the Son of God on those who surrounded his crucifixion is directly connected to the divine portents resulting from his obedience (cf. Matt. 27:54). Thus, Matthew underscores and accentuates christological obedience in the death-resurrection conclusion to his Gospel. Why? Because "only one who relies totally upon God and renders to him perfect obedience can atone for sin, and this person, in turn, can be none other than Jesus Son of God, ideal Israelite" in Matthew's Gospel.[22]

Second, divine sonship is directly associated with the forgiveness of sins. The Son of God took on flesh that he might be the redeemer of God's elect people. Three examples throughout Matthew's Gospel make this obvious. First, Jesus' name has redemptive significance and indicates the salvific implications of his incarnation (Matt. 1:21; cf. Acts 4:12).[23] Second, though God, Jesus took on flesh with the intention of giving his life as a ransom for God's chosen people (Matt. 20:28).[24] Third, the sacrifice of the Son of God

---

[20] None of Jesus' Roman murderers could have been subjected to such a cruel and merciless death. All of his Jewish murderers would have understood his crucifixion as a sign that their victim was cursed by God (Gal. 3:13; cf. Deut. 21:22–23). Richard R. Melick, *Philippians-Colossians-Philemon*, NAC, vol. 32 (Nashville: Broadman Press, 1991), 105.

[21] Kingsbury, *Matthew: Structure, Christology, Kingdom*, 76.

[22] Ibid.

[23] Concerning Jesus' name, Calvin writes, "The name 'Jesus' was bestowed upon him not without reason or by chance, or by the decision of men, but it was brought from heaven by an angel, the proclaimer of the supreme decree. The reason for it is added: he was sent to 'save the people from their sins.'" Calvin, *Institutes* 2.16.1.

[24] Contemplating the significance(s) of Jesus' death requires consideration of his incarnation. Pondering the incarnation forces interpreters to ask, "Why did God send God?" The redemptive mission of the Son of God is foundational

actualized the atonement (Matt. 26:28).²⁵ In Matthew's Gospel, Jesus came to save his people in giving his life as a ransom for their sins. In the Matthean narrative, the cross is the place where the Son of God sheds his blood to actualize the redemption of God's elect (Matt. 27:22–26). The crucifixion of Jesus is the culmination of the sole purpose of Christ's incarnation—redemption.²⁶ The "only reason given in Scripture that the Son of God willed to take our flesh, and accepted this commandment from the Father, is that he would be a sacrifice to appease the Father on our behalf."²⁷

The portents in Matthew 27:51–54 emphasize Matthew's christological portrait in the death-resurrection scene of the Matthean narrative. The portents are God the Father's response to God the Son's substitutionary work on the cross to atone for the sins of his elect people. The accusations leveled by the religious leaders against the Son of God (Matt. 26:61), the blasphemies hurled by the crowds toward him (Matt. 27:40), and the rending of the temple curtain

---

to understanding his name as well as his assumption of humanity. Therefore, Sanders states, "The Son's termination point in divine nature is his eternal deity; his termination point in the human nature is his assumption of humanity in the finite and temporal world of the events of salvation history." Fred Sanders, *The Triune God*, NSD, ed. Michael Allen and Scott Swain (Grand Rapids: Zondervan, 2016), 121–26. The redemptive mission of the Son of God reveals the God willing to suffer on behalf of his elect people. Bates argues the Son of God's work on the cross manifests new layers of depth when interpreting the significance(s) of his mission. See Matthew W. Bates, *The Birth of the Trinity: Jesus, God, and Spirit in the New Testament and Early Christian Interpretations of the Old Testament* (Oxford: Oxford University Press, 2015), 115–35.

²⁵ The cross is an actuality, not an opportunity. Therefore, concerning the question as to whom the benefits of Christ's death and resurrection appertained, Woolsey notes that Ursinus answered unequivocally: "As often as the Gospel extendeth the fruit of Christ's merits and benefits unto all, it must be understood of *the whole number of the faithful and elect.*' . . . Christ died for all who believe." Andrew A. Woolsey, *Unity and Continuity in Covenantal Thought: A Study of the Reformed Tradition to the Westminster Assembly* (Grand Rapids: Reformation Heritage Books, 2012), 420.

²⁶ Calvin, *Institutes* 2.12.4.

²⁷ Ibid.

from top to bottom in the wake of his death (Matt. 27:51) signify that something redemptive-historical in scope occurred that first Good Friday—atonement, actualized by the Son of God himself—Jesus, the Christ of God.[28] These particular aspects of Christology are brought to the fore in the Matthean death-resurrection conclusion. By means of his obedience, Jesus actualized the redemption of God's people through his death on the cross. Reflecting on the redemptive work of the Son of God, Benjamin Warfield states, "We see [the Son of God] everywhere offering to men His life for the salvation of their souls: and when, at last, the forces of evil gathered thick around Him, walking, alike, without display and without dismay, the path of suffering appointed for Him, and giving His life at Calvary that through His death the world might live."[29] Kingsbury adds that Christians are "sons of God because the Son of God has died for their sins and been raised."[30]

Matthew's purposeful narrative strategy that informs the compositional structure of the death-resurrection scene (Matt. 27:45–28:20) and the intentional placement of Matthew 27:51–54 within the scene makes the christological emphasis prominent. Therefore, Senior states, "The natural climax of the Passion is the death of Jesus. This, obviously, is the end toward which each scene of the narrative is directed ... the death scene is charged with christology."[31] The christological portrait of Jesus as the Son of God

---

[28] The three Matthean references manifest the centrality of the destruction of the temple in the crucifixion scene: "This man said, I am able to destroy the temple of God, and to rebuild it in three days ... You who would destroy the temple and rebuild it in three days, save yourself! ... Behold, the curtain of the temple was torn in two from top to bottom." Jesus' work on the cross can only be interpreted, then, "in terms of the destruction of the temple." See Kingsbury, *Matthew: Structure, Christology, Kingdom*, 76.

[29] Benjamin Breckinridge Warfield, *The Person and Work of Christ* (Philadelphia: Presbyterian and Reformed, 1950), 564.

[30] Kingsbury, *Matthew: Structure, Christology, Kingdom*, 77.

[31] Senior notes the significance of Matt. 27:51–54 as a strategic pericope heightening the christological portrait of Jesus in the death-resurrection scene.

is enhanced by the portents surrounding his death recounted in Matthew 27:51–54.

Missiology

The Matthean passion narrative climaxes in Matthew 27:54 when the centurion and those guarding Jesus herald him as the Son of God.[32] The prodigies at his death confirm Jesus' divine sonship and manifest his death as missiological in its scope and significance. This is evidenced by the response of the Gentiles who were eyewitnesses of his crucifixion (Matt. 27:50–54).[33] The guard's confession of

---

Senior, *Passion Narrative according to Matthew*, 337.

[32] Brown describes the conversion of the Roman guards as a "moment of opportunity for the Gentiles." Raymond E. Brown, *A Crucified Christ in Holy Week: Essays on the Four Gospel Passion Narratives* (Collegeville, MN: Liturgical Press, 1986), 44. The Gentile eyewitnesses rightly identify Jesus as God's Son by rightly interpreting the observable phenomena accompanying his death (Matt. 27:54; cf. 4:15–16).

[33] Contra Allison, who contends faulty observation or misinterpretation by "prescientific Christians, more pious than thoughtful" obscures the historicity of what really occurred on the first Good Friday and the first Easter Sunday. The answer to his question—"Are not the fiction-creating capacities of the early Christians on display in Matt. 27:51–53, in the tall tale about the tombs being opened and the bodies of saints exiting to promenade around Jerusalem?"—is no. Dale C. Allison Jr., *Resurrecting Jesus: The Earliest Christian Tradition and Its Interpreters* (New York: T&T Clark, 2005), 201–4, 307. The Gospels belong to a genre of ancient biography (*bios*). See Richard Burridge, *What Are the Gospels? A Comparison with Graeco-Roman Biography* (Grand Rapids: Eerdmans, 2004). Since they were composed within living memory of the events they recount, they draw on eyewitness testimony for their sources. For an argument contending the Gospels contain reliable eyewitness testimony, see Richard Bauckham, *Jesus and the Eyewitnesses: The Gospels as Eyewitness Testimony* (Grand Rapids: Eerdmans, 2006), 43, 62. Regarding the phenomena in Matt. 27:51–53, the eyewitnesses are anonymous (Matt. 27:54). However, anonymity does not negate reliability. For an understanding of the Gospels as oral history and eyewitness testimony, see Samuel Byrskog, *Story as History, History as Story: The Gospels in the Context of Ancient Oral History* (Leiden, Netherlands: Brill, 2002). For a discussion of how the oral Jesus tradition might have been persevered by the early church—that is, how the oral traditions became the written Gospels—see Michael Bird, *The Gospel of*

Theological Meaning

faith is a response to the phenomena accompanying Jesus' crucifixion (Matt. 27:51–53, 54).[34] Jesus died as no other person in history has. His death demanded a response. Their confession comes as a result of something more than christological awareness. The confession reveals a missiological result as both resurrected Jewish saints and Roman Gentiles testify to Jesus' identity as God the Father's Son in the Matthean narrative (Matt. 27:53–54; cf. 3:17; 14:33; 17:5). Thus, Kingsbury states, "In the Matthean reference to both Jewish saints, who come forth from the tombs, and confessing Roman soldiers, one finds a prefigurement of the post-Easter church of people of Jewish and gentile origin (27:52–53, 54)."[35]

The compositional structure of the entire death-resurrection scene (Matt. 27:45–28:20) coupled with the intentional placement of Matthew 27:51–54 within the scene places prominence on the missiological emphasis. It accentuates the mission Jesus' death necessitates—it is life-giving (Matt. 27:54) and ultimately salvific for persons from every nation who profess faith in his name (Matt. 28:16–20). The mission of the Son of God (Matt. 28:16–20) is revealed proleptically on the hillside outside of Jerusalem in the conversion of the soldiers (Matt. 27:54). The central purpose of Jesus' mission is revealed in his passion: the Son of God was crucified to

---

the Lord: How the Early Church Wrote the Story of Jesus (Grand Rapids: Eerdmans, 2014), 1–73.

[34] Reeves notes the resurrection of the saints occurs as a response to the cross. This is true of the other four signs as well. However, Reeves wrongly separates the witness of the resurrected dead from the events of Good Friday when he writes, "The resurrected saints, enter the city to show themselves as evidence of Jesus' resurrection." Contra Reeves, Matthew's death-resurrection presentation appears to indicate that the saints are witnesses of the life-giving nature of Jesus' death that actualized the forgiveness of sins. See Keith Howard Reeves, *The Resurrection Narrative in Matthew: A Literary-Critical Examination* (Lewiston, NY: Mellen Biblical Press, 1993), 10, 63. Brown contends that the signs in Matt. 27:51–54 manifest that God the Father has not forsaken God the Son, Jesus. See Brown, *Crucified Christ in Holy Week*, 44.

[35] Jack D. Kingsbury, *Matthew*, Proclamation Commentaries, 2nd ed. (Philadelphia: Fortress Press, 1986), 57.

Theological Meaning

save his people from their sins (Matt. 1:21; cf. Luke 24:47; Acts 5:31; Rev. 1:5). The Son of God shed his blood for the forgiveness of sins (Matt. 26:28). The people dwelling in darkness (Matt. 27:45) have seen the light of the gospel of the glory of Christ *in* the crucifixion of Jesus, Son of God (Matt. 27:50; 2 Cor. 4:4). The conversion of the Gentiles in Matthew's narrative (Matt. 27:54; cf. 1:5; 2:1) is the fulfillment of Jesus' prophetic proclamation earlier in Matthew's Gospel (Matt. 4:15–16).[36] Light shone in their darkness in the face of the Crucified One (2 Cor. 4:6). When the darkness of death shrouded the heavens (Matt. 27:45), a light dawned on a hill called Calvary.

So how does Jesus' christological identity relate to the missiological implications of his crucifixion? Kingsbury elucidates this relationship when he writes,

> Placed on the cross, Jesus dies as the perfectly obedient and trusting Son of God (27:38–54). By his death, he brings to completion the mission for which he had been born and for which God had chosen and empowered him: he atones for sins, so that through him people have forgiveness (26:28), and thus he accomplishes salvation (1:21; 3:16–17).... The confession of the Roman soldiers to the effect that he truly was the Son of God (27:54) serves at once to call attention to the circumstances that his earthly ministry is now at an end and to vindicate the claim to divine Sonship he had raised at his trial.[37]

---

[36] Hill suggests, "Matthew intended the Roman centurion's words to be a confession of Jesus' divinity." Further, he contends readers of Matthew's Gospel would have intuitively understood the exclamation as a confession of Christian faith on the lips of Gentiles. See David Hill, *The Gospel of Matthew*, New Century Bible Commentary (Grand Rapids: Eerdmans, 1972), 356.

[37] Kingsbury suggests that the disciples see Jesus in a new perspective. The resurrected one bears the marks of the crucified one. Kingsbury, *Matthew*, 56–57.

Theological Meaning

Missiological self-sacrifice brought Jesus into the world (Matt. 1:21; Phil. 2:8; Rev. 1:5).

Therefore, Matthew concludes his Gospel with an *inclusio* that connects the end of his narrative with the beginning (Matt. 28:20; cf. 1:23). The Son of God is "God with us." The One conceived of the Spirit will send his Spirit to remain with the disciples while they are on mission for the renown of the Triune name (Matt. 28:20). For Matthew, the conversion of the guards (Matt. 27:54) is the proleptic fulfillment of the Gospel's concluding pericope—the Great Commission in Matthew 28:16–20.[38] This mission, however, is not only to the lost sheep of the house of Israel (Matt. 10:6). It is to the ends of the earth. His death by crucifixion to actualize the forgiveness of sins (Matt. 1:21; Rev. 1:5) was for all the elect (Matt. 24:31), both Jew and Gentile (Matt. 28:19). His commission to make disciples requires faithful proclamation to all peoples, not silence (Matt. 12:16; 16:20; 17:9). Jesus' commission to the ends of the earth is accompanied by a promise to be with his doubting disciples until the consummation of all things, the end of the age.[39]

In Matthew's Gospel, Jesus' Great Commission (Matt. 28:16–20) is set in the context of the Matthean resurrection stories (Matt. 27:52b–53; 28:1–10) because the scenes of Jesus' death and resurrection manifest his accomplishment of the forgiveness of sins (Matt. 1:21; 9:6; 26:28). This accomplishment requires that "news of it must spread from the One (Jesus) to the many (all humankind), from the center (Jerusalem) to the ends of the earth, and from the middle of

---

[38] The faith-profession of the guards "becomes the place in Matthew's plot where Jesus is, for the first time [in the Matthean narrative], both correctly and publicly affirmed by humans to be the Son of God." According to Kingsbury, the consequence of the soldiers' profession of faith is the way, is in principle, now open for gospel mission to the ends of the earth. See J. D. Kingsbury, *Matthew as Story*, 2nd ed. (Philadelphia: Fortress Press, 1988), 87–90.

[39] Previously Jesus' presence was promised to the church as they practiced his ordinance of church discipline (Matt. 18:20). Now, his presence is promised to the church as they evangelize persons from all nations (Matt. 28:19). Jesus' presence is with the local church. See Hill, *Gospel of Matthew*, 362.

history (in the events of the cross and resurrection) to the consummation of history (at the return of Jesus)."[40] Vested with authority (Matt. 28:18),[41] the One who conquered death (Matt. 27:52b–53; 28:5–6) commissioned his disciples (Matt. 28:19).[42] The disciples are commissioned to make disciples by proclaiming the forgiveness of sins to all nations (Acts 10:43; 13:38; 26:18; Col. 1:14).[43] However, the Great Commission is not merely the process by which the Son

[40] Michael W. Goheen, *A Light to the Nations: The Missional Church and the Biblical Story* (Grand Rapids: Baker Academic, 2011), 173–74. In the New Testament, Acts 1:8 is programmatic for the geographical spread of the gospel recounted in Matthew's Great Commission (Matt. 28:16–20; cf. Luke 24:44–49). News of Jesus' work on the cross and resurrection was not to be confined to Jerusalem (Luke 24:47). Rather, it was to advance to the ends of the earth (Matt. 28:19). In Jesus, a light for the nations has dawned (Matt. 4:15–16; 24:14; 28:19). See also Alan J. Thompson, *The Acts of the Risen Lord Jesus: Luke's Account of God's Unfolding Plan*, NSBT 27 (Downers Grove, IL: InterVarsity Press, 2011), 45, 103–8.

[41] Wright suggests readers should recognize the overthrow of evil in the Matthean narrative's conclusion. Matthew's Gospel tells the story of how the satanic forces that marshaled against Jesus have been decisively defeated through Jesus' death and resurrection. He writes, "Directly linked to this [claim to authority] is the claim of the satan [sic] to possess all authority over the kingdoms of the world, implicit in Matthew 4:9 and explicit in Luke 4:6, and then explicitly reversed in Matthew 28:18, where all authority in heaven and on earth is claimed by Jesus himself. *Something has happened to dethrone the satan* [sic] *and to enthrone Jesus in its place.* The story the gospels [sic] think they are telling is the story of how that happened." According to Wright, the death of Jesus launched a revolution. However, Wright is unclear on *how* the death of Jesus actualized the forgiveness of sins through his mediatorial work on the cross. See N. T. Wright, *The Day the Revolution Began: Reconsidering the Meaning of Jesus' Crucifixion* (San Francisco: HarperOne, 2016), 207, emphasis original; cf. 82, 83, 115.

[42] Commenting on Matt. 28:16–20, Bunyan states, "Jesus Christ by His death and resurrection did not only purchase grace and remission of sins for His elect, with their eternal glory, but He also obtained from the Father to be both Lord and Head over all things, whether they are things in Heaven or things under the earth." John Bunyan, *Resurrection* (n.p.: Sovereign Grace Publishers, n.d.), 40.

[43] Two of the Synoptic Gospels as well as John's Gospel conclude with Jesus' missional commissioning: Matt. 28:16–20; Luke 24:44–49; John 20:19–23.

of God's accomplishment is made known. Rather, *"mission itself is one of God's mighty deeds*, the culminating divine activity whereby all the preceding mighty acts are disclosed and people are incorporated into them."[44] After accomplishing his work of atonement through the crucifixion and resurrection of Jesus, God equips his people with the promised power of the Holy Spirit (Luke 24:49; Acts 1:8; cf. Matt. 10:20; John 20:22–23). Those who respond to Jesus' work on the cross by faith are commissioned as a light for the nations so that news of his salvation may reach the ends of the earth (Isa. 49:6; cf. Isa. 11:9; Hab. 2:14; Matt. 28:19).

Eschatology

Following Delvin Hutton, Keith Reeves contends that the Gospel's author mentioned the prodigies in Matthew 27:51–53 in order to emphasize the eschatological significance(s) of Jesus' death on the cross. The portents surrounding Jesus' crucifixion connote that something eschatologically decisive in salvation history occurred in the death of Jesus.[45] Regarding Matthew 27:51–54, the immediate

---

[44] Goheen, *Light to the Nations*, 174, emphasis original. Following Scobie and Rowley, Goheen describes the ingathering of the nations through gospel-mission as an eschatological event. See Charles Scobie, "Israel and the Nations: An Essay in Biblical Theology," *TynBul* 43, 2 (1992): 291–92; and H. H. Rowley, *The Missionary Message of the Old Testament* (London: Carey Press, 1944), 36–41. This observation further substantiates the claim that Christology, missiology, and eschatology are featured theological foci in the pericope under consideration—Matt. 27:51–54.

[45] Reeves, *Resurrection Narrative in Matthew*, 10. Goheen notes the transformation of God's people from a centripetal to a centrifugal movement indicates that an observable eschatological shift has occurred. See Goheen, *Light to the Nations*, 115. Hurtado illuminates this shift by identifying Christianity as a "bookish" religion that had Jewish origins for its theological commitments, though these commitments no longer identified with Jewish ethnicity. Further, Christianity was a religion that rejected the pagan gods of Rome. Christianity was so different that many Roman-era people accused its adherents of atheism. Hurtado argues that Christianity's religious distinctiveness eventually made appeal to people translocally as a transethnic movement. See Larry W. Hurtado, *Destroyer of the Gods: Early Christian Distinctiveness in the Roman World*

effects of the death of Jesus are most clearly seen in two events that bear eschatological significance. The first event is the rending of the temple veil (*velum scissum*) from top to bottom (Matt. 27:51a).[46] The second event is the bodily resurrection of the dead (Matt. 27:52b–53).[47]

Velum Scissum—Matthew 27:51a

The temple of God was constructed with clear and detailed instructions as to its design for the purpose of the regulated worship of God.[48] The dimensions and furnishings established a visible response and expression predicated on a revealed word from God.[49] Over time, the temple took on greater significance as a nationalistic entity that was ultimately condemned by Jesus as a place of business and commerce (Matt. 21:12–13).

The veil was critical to the temple's construction because it

---

(Waco, TX: Baylor University Press, 2016), 38, 77–104.

[46] καὶ ἰδοὺ τὸ καταπέτασμα τοῦ ναοῦ ἐσχίσθη ἀπ' ἄνωθεν ἕως κάτω εἰς δύο (Matt. 27:51a). The καὶ ἰδοὺ serves as a connector between the death of Jesus in Matt. 27:50 and the phenomena that follow in Matt. 27:51–53. God is inserted into the narrative in response to the death of the Son of God. Matthew's directional emphasis when recounting the *velum scissum* connotes a rending from heaven to earth (cf. Mark 15:38).

[47] καὶ πολλὰ σώματα τῶν κεκοιμημένων ἁγίων ἠγέρθησαν (Matt. 27:52b).

[48] Worship not an invention of man, but a directive of God to man. The lengthy exposition given in Ex. 25:10–31:18 and 35:1–40:33 manifests that God regulates his worship. Worship is prescribed and commanded, and the elements of his worship are revealed (see Col. Eph. 5:19; Col. 3:16).

[49] God has chosen to reveal to man in his Word that which is pleasing to him in worship. Worship is limited by revelation only to what is instituted or prescribed by God himself in the Scriptures. Thus, the WCF and the LBC (1689) state God "may not be worshiped according to the imaginations and devices of men" (WCF 21:1; LBC 22:1). For a treatment of the regulative principle of worship, see Fred A. Malone, *The Baptism of Disciples Alone: A Covenantal Argument for Credobaptism versus Paedobaptism* (Cape Coral, FL: Founders Press, 2007), 35–39.

Theological Meaning

separated priests from the direct presence of God (Ex. 26:31–35).[50] Traditional interpretation of Old Testament passages finds acceptance in the New Testament Gospels as the location of worship and communion with God in accordance with the mediatorial sacrifices required to approach him and be admitted into his holy presence.[51] It was all but impossible for a human being to tear (ἐσχίσθη) the elaborately woven fabric (seventy-two plaits of twenty-four threads each) from the top (a height of more than sixty feet) of the temple to the bottom into two (εἰς δύο).[52] Only God could design the temple,

---

[50] The *velum scissum* recounted in Matt. 27:51a was briefly discussed in chap. 2, nn. 37–39. For helpful surveys, see M. de Jonge, "Matthew 27:51 in Early Christian Exegesis," *HTR* 79 (1986): 67–68; de Jonge, "Two Interesting Interpretations of the Rending of the Temple-Veil in the Testaments of the Twelve Patriarchs," in *Jewish Eschatology, Early Christian Christology and the Testaments of the Twelve Patriarchs: Collected Essays of Marinus De Jonge*, NovTSup 63 (Leiden, Netherlands: Brill, 1991), 220–32. Exodus reveals that the veil separating the Most Holy Place from the Holy Place was made from blue, purple, and scarlet dyed yarns woven with fine twined linen and embroidered with cherubim. It hung on four golden pillars. The innermost veil's design prevented physical and visible accessibility to God. τὸ καταπέτασμα τοῦ ναοῦ refers to the innermost veil separating the Most Holy Place from the rest of the temple. See Donald A. Hagner, *Matthew 14–28*, WBC 33B, vol. 2 (Nashville: Thomas Nelson, 1995), 848–49. In case there be any confusion as to the extent of the damage done to the innermost veil, Matthew notes it was torn in two (εἰς δύο). This irreparable damage manifests the termination of its function. For a detailed examination of the implications of the cessation of the temple's function, see Daniel M. Gurtner, *The Torn Veil: Matthew's Exposition of the Death of Jesus* (Cambridge: Cambridge University Press, 2007), 187–94.

[51] Gurtner elucidates this when he notes physical accessibility was granted only on the Day of Atonement *if* the intruder had high priestly status (cf. Heb. 9:2–7). Otherwise, the intruder would die. Further, he states, "the raising of the saints (27:52–53) and the profession of the solders (27:54) connote *life* in various senses, rather than death." Gurtner, *Torn Veil*, 189.

[52] These are the dimensions of the veil separating the Holy Place from the Most Holy Place (Heb. 6:19; 9:13; 10:20; cf. Ex. 26:31–35; 2 Chron. 3:14), not the curtain over the entrance to the Holy Place (Ex. 26:37; Num. 3:26). See Michael J. Wilkins, *Matthew*, NIV Application Commentary Series (Grand Rapids: Zondervan, 2004), 904–5. Josephus gives a detailed description of the temple curtains in *Ant.* 3.6.4.

and only God could destroy it. In Matthew 27:51a, it pleased God to do this. Therefore, G. K. Beale states, "Irony is neatly woven throughout this passage. Jesus is mocked because he said that he would tear down the temple and rebuild it in three days, and at virtually the same time Matthew tells us that Jesus actually was in the process of destroying the temple when he died."[53] When the καταπέτασμα is torn, the significance of the act symbolized a transition from old covenant requirements to new covenant realities—all of which were contingent on the death of Jesus (Heb. 9:11–10:22). The temple itself, therefore, was no longer sacrosanct.

The tearing of the veil signals the end of the temple as a means of acceptance and communion with God. There would now be a new way: the new covenant established through the flesh of Jesus (Heb. 10:20). The satisfaction of divine justice rendered the old covenant obsolete.[54] The fulfillment of the law's demands whereby it would now be written on the heart (Jer. 31:33; cf. Ezek. 36:26–27; 37:14)[55] became effectual because of the death of Jesus. Communion with

---

[53] The *velum scissum* symbolically represented the destruction of the temple. However, Beale goes further when he states, "When . . . it is remembered from the Old Testament and early Judaism that on the veil was embroidery of the starry heavens, its tearing would be an apt symbol of the beginning destruction, not only of the temple (which itself even as a whole symbolized the cosmos) but of the very cosmos itself." The *velum scissum* (Matt. 27:51a) and the resurrection of the dead (Matt. 27:52b–53), therefore, are signs of the inauguration of the new creation. See G. K. Beale, *The Temple and the Church's Mission: A Biblical Theology of the Dwelling Place of God*, NSBT, vol. 17, ed. D. A. Carson (Downers Grove, IL: InverVarsity Press, 2004), 188–92. However, Beale wrongly displaces the resurrection of the many saints (Matt. 27:52b–53) in the Matthean narrative, incorrectly locating their resurrection on Easter Sunday.

[54] Hence Heb. 8:13: ἐν τῷ λέγειν καινὴν πεπαλαίωκεν τὴν πρώτην· τὸ δὲ παλαιούμενον καὶ γηράσκον ἐγγὺς ἀφανισμοῦ.

[55] Jer. 31 and Ezek. 36–37 reveal the "newness" of the new covenant. What changed? Malone explains when he writes, "New Covenant membership is defined in Jeremiah 31:31–34 and the NT explanation (Hebrews 8–10) as those who receive the law (the Ten Words in historical context) written upon the heart (regeneration), the forgiveness of sins (justification), and the personal knowledge of God (reconciliation). This separates the New Covenant

Theological Meaning

God is now made possible in this life by a new and living way inaugurated through Jesus' flesh.[56] His death, therefore, removed the visible symbol of the old covenant and commenced the beginning of a new age. Thus, Daniel Gurtner states, "The *velum scissum* reveals, in part, the eschatological nature of Jesus' death."[57] The new interim brought about by Jesus' death renders old covenant worship obsolete (Heb. 8:13) and institutes new covenant worship in the interim between now and the second coming of Jesus (Rev. 19:11–16), the result being access to and communion with God, which is contingent on the merits of Jesus applied by the Holy Spirit at the command of the Father for all the people of God (Heb. 10:19, 21–22).

---

fulfillment of the promised Covenant of Grace from the Abrahamic Covenant which included the organic seed of Abraham who mostly were unregenerate . . . this means that each New Covenant member is born again by the Holy Spirit into the New Covenant kingdom of God (John 1:12–13; 3:3, 5), that each New Covenant member is justified by faith alone unto the forgiveness of sins (Romans 5:1–2), and that each New Covenant member is effectually reconciled to God as an adopted child of God forever (Galatians 4:4–6)." Fred A. Malone, "Biblical Hermeneutics & Covenant Theology," in *Covenant Theology: A Baptist Distinctive*, ed. Earl M. Blackburn (Birmingham, AL: Solid Ground Christian Books, 2013), 80–81.

[56] Access to God is gained through the flesh—that is, through the death of Jesus (Matt. 27:50–54). Jesus' death actualized the forgiveness of sins and grants access to God (Matt. 1:21; 5:8; 26:28). This is made explicit in Heb. 10:20. Grammatically, τοῦ καταπετάσματος is in apposition to σαρκὸς αὐτοῦ. Thus, Schreiner states, access to God "is granted through the torn and bloody and dead flesh of Jesus (cf. John 6:50–58). 'Jesus secured access to God's presence 'by means of' his flesh.'" Thomas R. Schreiner, *Commentary on Hebrews*, Biblical Theology for Christian Proclamation (Nashville: B&H Publishing, 2015), 315–17.

[57] Gurtner contends that Matthew's presentation of Jesus' death manifests the inauguration of a salvation-historical turning point as it is depicted in Ezek. 37. See Gurtner, *Torn Veil*, 183. Similarly, Hagner states, "The events themselves are apocalyptic in character and point to the decisive importance of the death of Jesus not only for that generation but for all of subsequent history. There is an air of both judgment and of eschatology in this material." Hagner, *Matthew 14–28*, 848.

Theological Meaning

A Resurrection of Holy Ones—Matthew 27:52b-53

The other event bearing substantial eschatological significance[58] is the bodily resurrection of the dead (Matt. 27:52b–53).[59] The tombs of saints were opened as a result of the death of Jesus, signifying an immediate reversal of the fall (Matt. 27:50, 52; cf. Gen. 2:17).[60] The bodies and souls of these saints were temporarily reunited. Their appearance to people who would recognize them (Matt. 27:53) is an eschatological foreshadowing of when the resurrection of the body would take place (Ezek. 37:12–14; cf. Dan. 12:2; 1 Cor. 15:20–23).[61] The new age has begun in the death and resurrection of Jesus.[62] However, since "this was not

---

[58] Allison suggests the pericope preserves a primitive Christian eschatology. He states, "Properly interpreted within the Matthean passion, the resurrection of the holy ones and the accompanying signs highlight the redactors theology, for Matthew thought of the end of Jesus as an 'eschatological' event." See Dale C. Allison Jr., *The End of the Ages Has Come: An Early Interpretation of the Passion and Resurrection of Jesus* (Philadelphia: Fortress Press, 1985), 41–46.

[59] The secular historian Thallus reports on the darkness recounted in Matt. 27:45. His report supports the historicity of the phenomena recounted in Matt. 27:51–53. See Thallus, "The Extant Fragments of the Five Books of Chronography of Julius Africanus" (18:1), in ANF 6, Logos Libronix ECF 1.6.2.1.3.25. Licona made me aware of this source. See also Licona, *Resurrection of Jesus*, 551.

[60] In Matt. 27:52 the conjunction καί closely connects the two signs in this verse with the three signs in Matt. 27:51 as the immediate effect of Jesus yielding the Spirit (Matt. 27:50). The result of the divine σεισμός is tomb-opening bedrock fissures—τὰ μνημεῖα ἀνεῴχθησαν—exposing the dead buried within (Matt. 27:52).

[61] Matt. 27:52b–53 does not recount the great general resurrection from the dead. The resurrection of τῶν κεκοιμημένων ἁγίων is not glorified resurrection (27:52). Rather, as Wright would say, this "is a strange semi-anticipation of it." The "church is still awaiting the final, complete general resurrection" from the dead. See N. T. Wright, *The Resurrection of the Son of God*, Christian Origins and the Question of God, vol. 3 (Minneapolis: Fortress Press, 2003), 634.

[62] Matera suggests this resurrection marks the beginning of the new age and alludes to Ezek. 37. He states, "God fulfills his ancient promise made through

the consummate end of the world and the final new creation, the saints who did come out of their tombs (vv.52–53) presumably, like Lazarus, died again at some subsequent point, only to be raised again at the very end of history."[63] The question, then, is, *Who* were these saints? On the one hand, the text explicitly states that these were ἁγίων who had fallen asleep or died prior to the death of Jesus himself.[64] "Sleep"—τῶν κεκοιμημένων—is a euphemism for

---

Ezekiel to the covenant people" at the death of the Son of God. This is true, at least in part. See Frank J. Matera, *Passion Narrative and Gospel Theologies: Interpreting the Synoptics through Their Passion Stories*, Studies in Contemporary and Theological Problems, ed. Lawrence Boadt (New York: Paulist Press, 1986), 116–17. Commenting on the development of resurrection thought in the early church, Wright states that the "theme of Jesus raising other – perhaps all the pre-Christians righteous – to new life is developed in several works from the second century onwards: e.g., *Od. Sol.* 42.11; Ign. *Magn.* 9:2; Iren. Frag. 26, making the link with the present passage." See Wright, *Resurrection of the Son of God*, 635.

[63] Beale, *Temple and the Church's Mission*, 190. Contra Calvin, who suggested "it is doubtful if this resurrection took place before [Jesus'] resurrection . . . [it is] more probable that, when Christ died, the graves were opened, and that, when he rose, some of the godly, having received life, went out of their graves, and were seen in the city. *For Christ is called the first-born from the dead.*" See John Calvin, *Commentary on a Harmony of the Evangelists: Matthew, Mark, and Luke*, in *Calvin's Commentaries*, trans. The Calvin Translation Society, (Grand Rapids: Baker, 2005), 324 (emphasis added). Similarly, Bengel argued, "The first who rose from the dead to die no more was Christ . . . [and] after his resurrection, that of the saints also took place." John Albert Bengel, *Bengel's New Testament Commentary*, vol. 1, *Matthew-Acts* (Grand Rapids: Kregel, 1981), 307.

[64] Perhaps these were believers like Simeon (Luke 2:25; see *Acts of Pilate* 17.1); the prophetess Anna (Luke 2:36), and Lazarus (John 11). Though conjecture, believers who had died in recent history would be capable of providing powerful testimony to the legitimacy of Jesus' divine sonship (the focal point of the pericope!). A raising of Old Testament saints like Abraham, Moses, and David would not provide a witness to τὴν ἁγίαν πόλιν filled with Jews who had no idea what these saints look like (Who would believe them?). Therefore, it seems most probable these saints were people others would immediately recognize as they testify to the life-giving power of Jesus' death on the cross (Matt. 27:50–53).

Theological Meaning

death in Matthew 27:52.[65] Further, the text explicitly states that more than one person was raised. The Scripture says many bodies (πολλὰ σώματα) of the ἁγίων were raised. Therefore, this event would have been notable in its impact on and influence of the prevailing thought of the day.[66] On the other hand, the text does not specify their identity or their whereabouts. "Matthew knows perfectly well . . . that the bodies he speaks about were not still walking around, and he makes no attempt to explain what happened to them."[67] Though raised, the text merely says that the πολλὰ σώματα venture into τὴν ἁγίαν πόλιν after the resurrection of Jesus (Matt. 27:53).[68] Their precise identification is left ambiguous. Therefore, their precise identification is not necessary for a correct understanding of the pericope or its accompanying theological foci employed by Matthew.

The compositional structure of the entire death-resurrection scene (Matt. 27:45–28:20) coupled with the intentional placement

---

[65] In Matt. 27:52, τῶν κεκοιμημένων refers to the state of being dead. See BDAG, s.v. "κοιμάω." Similarly, LSJ suggest κοιμάω can refer to "the sleep of death." LSJ, s.v. "κοιμάω."

[66] Ignatius may refer to these saints when he speaks of the prophets raised by Jesus (Ign. *Mag.* 9.1–2). I am thankful for Michael Licona's work for making me aware of this reference. See Licona, *Resurrection of Jesus*, 551.

[67] Wright, *Resurrection of the Son of God*, 635.

[68] Sim notes that the Matthean pericopal hapax is dependent on Ezek. 37. Further, he sees the resurrection of the dead as one of two eschatological end-time events that must take place prior to judgment. According to him, the pericope is an attempt by Matthew to preserve "the Christian tradition of the primacy of Jesus' resurrection." David C. Sim, *Apocalyptic Eschatology in the Gospel of Matthew*, SNTSMS 88 (Cambridge: Cambridge University Press, 1996), 110–11. Similarly, Aus suggests the application of Matt. 27:51b–53 to Jesus' crucifixion is a "Judaic interpretation of 1 Samuel 28 as the Day of Judgment." His death "signified for his followers the real turn of the ages, is such a reality, such a religious truth." However, he wrongly concludes "Matt 27:51b-53 is not 'historical,' it is 'true' in a religious sense." Roger D. Aus, *Samuel, Saul and Jesus: Three Early Palestinian Jewish Christian Gospel Haggadoth*, South Florida Studies in the History of Judaism 105 (Atlanta: Scholars Press, 1994), 115, 120, 124, 130, 132.

Theological Meaning

of Matthew 27:51–54 within the scene emphasizes its eschatological importance.[69] The death of Jesus calls a new people into being (Matt. 27:54; cf. 4:15–16). Yet God does not forsake the saints of his covenant (Matt. 27:52b). Contrary to the taunts of the passersby (Matt. 27:39–40) and the chief priests (Matt. 27:41–42), the Son of God did not come to save himself. Rather, as Francis Watson states, "Jesus dies on behalf of others and as their substitute [in Matthew's Gospel]. . . . Others are saved while he is lost; they are saved, but at his expense."[70] The Son of God's death is neither an end nor an unimaginable disaster. Rather, it is a victory over sin and death and hell. Therefore, Hilary of Poitiers stated,

> The earth shook. . . . Rocks were split, for the Word of God and the power of his eternal goodness rushed in, penetrating every stronghold and principality. Graves were opened, for the gates of death had been unlocked. And a number of the bodies of the saints who had fallen asleep arose. Dispelling the shadows of death illuminating the darkness of hell, Christ destroyed the spoils of hell at the resurrection of the saints.[71]

The Son of God died so that others may live. The resurrection of the dead manifests that his death is actually the cause of life. Hence, when he died others were resurrected to life. The resurrection of the sleeping saints at his death is an eschatological sign testifying to his divine identity as the Son of God.[72] Though the resurrection

---

[69] See Allison, *End of the Ages Has Come*, 41–46; and Sim, *Apocalyptic Eschatology*, 110–28.

[70] Francis Watson, *The Fourfold Gospel: A Theological Reading of the New Testament Portraits of Jesus* (Grand Rapids: Baker Academic, 2016), 152–53.

[71] Manlio Simonetti, *Matthew 14–28*, ACCS, vol. 1b (Downers Grove, IL: InterVarsity Press, 2002), 297.

[72] Hence, Matt. 9:24, ἀναχωρεῖτε, οὐ γὰρ ἀπέθανεν τὸ κοράσιον ἀλλὰ καθεύδει. Jesus raised the sleeping-dead girl in Matt. 9:25 as a testimony to his divine identity. In Matt. 27:52b he raised the saints by his death. Apollinaris

of the sleeping saints is the climactic sign, the crescendo of the series of revelatory signs is the confession of the centurion and his entourage—Jesus *is* the Son of God (Matt. 27:54). The guard's profession of faith manifests that "the ultimate design of the temple was beginning to be fulfilled in Jesus . . . Yahweh's revelatory presence was extending out beyond the boundaries of ethnic Israel to include Gentiles."[73]

Conclusion

Three critical theological planks serve as interpretive guides that support a literary reading of Matthew 27:51–54 as definitive for a correct understanding of both the pericope itself and its accompanying theological foci. The intentional placement of Matthew 27:51–54 within the death-resurrection scene emphasizes the theological meaning latent in this Matthean pericope—Christology, missiology, and eschatology. The extraordinary signs accompanying Jesus' death (cf. Matt. 27:51–53) portray Jesus as the Son of God (Matt. 27:54) and prepare Matthew's readers for the intrusion of the eschatological resurrection on Easter morning (Matt. 28:1–10). The stage is set in Matthew's Gospel for the public vindication of Jesus before his enemies—he is not dead; he rose just as he said he would (Matt. 28:6 cf. 16:21; 17:23; 20:19). Matthew's resurrection narrative in chapter 28 brings his Gospel's plot to its resolution. Jesus' "greater" resurrection is what the religious leaders were afraid of; it proved that they were wrong about him—he *is* the Son of God. His

---

argued, "It is plain that [the saints] have died again, having risen from the dead in order to be a sign." See Simonetti, *Matthew 14–28*, 297. Bauer notes God reveals Jesus' divine sonship through the signs accompanying his death. David R. Bauer, "The Major Characters of Matthew's Story: Their Function and Significance," in *Gospel Interpretation: Narrative-Critical & Social Scientific Approaches*, ed. Jack D. Kingsbury (Harrisburg, PA: Trinity Press International, 1997), 29.

[73] Beale, *Temple and the Church's Mission*, 191; and Gurtner, *Torn Veil*, 188–89.

Theological Meaning

"greater" resurrection proves to his doubting disciples that he is truly alive and does have "all authority in heaven and on earth" (Matt. 28:18). His "greater" resurrection gives hope to all of his followers, for they know that Jesus is the resurrected Son of God. He has conquered sin and death and hell. And now the Son of God is "God with us" (Acts 1:8; 2:4; 1 Cor. 6:19; Eph. 1:13–14) as his people go about proclaiming his gospel of repentance and forgiveness of sins (Matt. 28:20; cf. 1:23).

6

Conclusion

Summary

The grammar of the death-resurrection scene points toward a literary reading based on the compositional structure of the words themselves as well as their exact placement in the pericope. A literary reading of a text incorporates a historical-grammatical exegesis and a presumed theological significance by means of architectonic interpretive keys that both construct and relate different phenomena toward the intended theological meaning.[1] The architectural process of construction and relation (both building *and* connecting) becomes the hermeneutical key to understanding seemingly irreconcilable texts with corresponding theological ideas.

J. W. Wenham's seminal article became the impetus for a shift

---

[1] Anthony Esolen, *Out of the Ashes: Rebuilding American Culture* (Washington, DC: Regnery, 2017), 56–61. Esolen's use of the term "architectonic" incorporates his conception of grammar as a means that both builds and relates one idea to another. It breaks the bounds of language and relates the foundational elements of grammar (organization, observation, and manipulation) to other human sciences viewing them as "grammatical in structure." Grammar, therefore, is never to be understood as disconnected idioms isolated from other academic disciplines. To the contrary, by "thinking grammatically" a more holistic approach toward other academic thought other than language opens new understandings from existing words and ideas toward newfound realizations of intention and meaning.

Conclusion

in interpreting Matthew 27:51–54 by various theologians who separated the first three portents from the latter two, resulting in a displacement of the pericope in the Matthean narrative. Questions emerging from this practice rendered the text all but uninterpretable as to its theological meaning. In the contemporary context, the resulting interpretive dichotomy has obscured the function and meaning of the pericope and established two distinct and opposing readings.

Matthew 27:51–54 is the *crux interpretum* enabling an examination of corresponding resurrection texts (both prophetic and apostolic) that provide interpretive clues toward a resolution between the interpretive polarities. Lexical thought connections compared with Matthew 28:1–15 reveal a parallelism whereby Matthew emphasizes the death-resurrection scene of Jesus as regulative for the resurrection of the saints in Matthew 27:52b–53. Ezekiel 37:1–14 provides the primary prophetic witness for which the resurrection of the saints is foreshadowed and, thereby, partially fulfilled in Matthew 27:52b–53. An examination of each *passivum divinum* is connected by a coordinating conjunction that manifests the entire pericope as one textual hinge in the death-resurrection scene.

Matthew 27:52b–53 is yet another sign bearing theological ramifications at Jesus' crucifixion. As such, it becomes the lens whereby the cumulative theological effect of the pericope is constructed. Each portent, therefore, builds toward a theological crescendo evidenced by the centurion's confession. The events of the text are transposed to broader antinomous theological realities taking place simultaneously. Identification of Jesus as the Son of God by the soldiers attending to the crucifixion bears christological import whereby he becomes the focus for future missiological endeavors as evidenced by the eschatological realities of the *velum scissum* and the resurrection of the sleeping saints in this pericope.

A literary reading of Matthew 27:51–54 encompassing Christology, missiology, and eschatology facilitates a holistic reading of the text whereby historicity and theological meaning are fused to form a complete picture of what is accomplished at the crucifixion event. The bifurcation commonly accepted by many scholars does not fully understand the historical crucifixion as it directly relates to the resurrection as evidence of Jesus' accomplishment. To separate the grammar's syntax from the theological imperative renders the entire event in this text as mythological or legend. In this passage Matthew incorporates the fulfillment of Old Testament prophecy with future effects evidenced by a historical and bodily resurrection of the dead at the time of Jesus' finished work on the cross. While this resurrection was temporal and not reflective of the final state of glorification, it was, nevertheless, representative of the immediate impact of Jesus' death as a reversal of the fall.

Further Study

Areas of research exist in which more work could be done in relation to Matthew 27:51–54. First, the *velum scissum* (Matt. 27:51a) partially fulfilled the beatific vision in the Matthean narrative by making the inaccessible God accessible and visible (2 Cor. 4:4; Col. 1:15).[2] The response of the centurion and those with him to the series of revelatory signs—ἀληθῶς θεοῦ υἱὸς ἦν οὗτος (Matt. 27:54)—harkens the reader to Jesus' words in the Sermon on the Mount, μακάριοι οἱ καθαροὶ τῇ καρδίᾳ ὅτι αὐτοὶ τὸν θεὸν ὄψονται (Matt. 5:8).[3] In Matthew's Gospel the invisible God is *seen* in the face of the Crucified One—Jesus, Son of God (Matt. 27:54; cf. 2 Cor. 4:6). This dissertation did not assert the partial fulfillment of the beatific vision but rather stated that the satisfaction of divine justice rendered the old covenant obsolete (Matt. 27:51a; Heb. 8:13). The fulfillment of the law's demands whereby it would now be written on the heart (Jer. 31:33; cf. Ezek. 36:26–27; 37:14) became effectual because of the death of Jesus (Matt. 27:45–50).

---

[2] Cf. Rom. 5:2; Eph. 2:18; 3:12; Heb. 1:3; 4:16.
[3] This is the highest knowledge of God of which creatures are capable. See also Job 42:5; Ps. 11:7; 1 Cor. 13:12; Heb. 12:14; 1 John 3:2; Rev. 22:4.

Conclusion

Communion with God is now made possible in this life through a new and living way inaugurated by the torn veil of Jesus' flesh (Heb. 10:20).

Jesus' death removed the visible symbol of the old covenant and commenced the beginning of a new age. Therefore, this dissertation did not trace the concept of the beatific vision in the Matthean Gospel and its links to the death-resurrection scene (Matt. 27:45–28:20). Yet the beatific vision is partially realized in the death and resurrection of Jesus (Matt. 1:18–25; cf. John 1:14). Access to and communion with God are actualized through the merits of Jesus on the cross (Matt. 27:45–54). Although other works address the issue of the *velum scissum*, none appear to address its implications for new covenant worship in relation to the beatific vision from this Matthean pericope. A more in-depth study would be useful to both scholars and the church. The *velum scissum* (Matt. 27:51a) rendered old covenant worship obsolete (Heb. 8:13) and instituted new covenant worship in the interim between now and the second coming of Jesus (Rev. 19:11–16).

Second, new covenant worship in communion with the Father, Son, and Holy Spirit is contingent on the accomplishment of Jesus' crucifixion. John Owen notes that the primary benefit of worship under the new covenant is knowing God explicitly in his triune manifestation. Christian worship depends on the Father as the origin of all divine grace, the Son as the One who actualizes the forgiveness of sins through his atonement, and the Spirit as the One who individually applies divine grace. Owen stresses the work of each person in the work of redemption.[4]

Matthew 27:51–54 is a Trinitarian text as it reveals the glory of the triune God in the exclusive work of the three persons in redemption. Public worship, therefore, is a primary means whereby

---

[4] Ryan M. McGraw, "Trinitarian Doxology: Reassessing John Owen's Contribution to Reformed Orthodox Trinitarian Theology," *Studia Historiae Ecclesiasticae* 41, 2 (2015): 38–68.

Conclusion

Christians celebrate the work of each of the three persons—especially the work of the Son of God. Trinitarian thought is embedded in the knowledge of God in divine revelation, but at the moment of the *velum scissum* the innermost veil symbolizes the new reality of unhindered worship between God and humankind. Further research is needed in examining this text as an explicitly Trinitarian text and its implications for new covenant worship.

Third, Matthew 27:51–54 has been appropriated hermeneutically to advocate *descensus Christi ad infernos*—Christ's descent into hell. Trinitarian thought has held a consensus view emanating from the first fifteen centuries of the church that Jesus did, in fact, descend into hell during the interim between his death and resurrection. In this act he preached to and released the righteous dead of the Old Testament.[5]

Further research based on this text as to the extent of this act reaching back to the earliest teaching of the church could build on the literary reading capacities developed in this dissertation. The road map articulated in this study could easily form the basis for future study whereby seemingly conflicting texts could be understood as the basis for a more holistic view of what exactly happened in the interim between the crucifixion and resurrection of Jesus.

A better understanding from this text of Jesus' accomplishment in his atonement could impact the view of the location and activity of Jesus in the interim between his crucifixion and resurrection. This text—with all the resulting phenomena immediately following the death of Jesus—furthers the question as to what took place on the cross and where he was spiritually located immediately upon death. The atonement, therefore, bears critical importance to the events in the wake of Jesus' death.[6] How revealed truth impacts Christian orthodoxy can be further explored by a literary reading of this text.

---

[5] See Bass for a recent treatment of the *Descensus* view. Justin Bass, *The Battle for the Keys: Revelation 1:18 and Christ's Descent into the Underworld* (Eugene, OR: Paternoster, 2014).

[6] For further study on the accomplishment and impact of the atonement,

Conclusion

The intentional placement of Matthew 27:51–54 within the death-resurrection scene (Matt. 27:45–28:20) emphasizes the theological meaning latent in this Matthean pericope—Christology, missiology, and eschatology.

Christological implications are established by the timing of these occurrences in direct relation to the crucifixion event. The proximity of the acts occurring immediately after the physical death of Jesus reveals a distinct christological reality unknown prior to, and subsequent to, the death of Jesus. That human beings were immediately raised from the dead manifests a unique divine power founded on Jesus' identity—he *is* the Son of God (Matt. 27:40, 41, 43, 54). It never happened before, and it will never happen again until the parousia. Matthew's christological portrait simultaneously accentuates the person and work of Jesus. The portents in Matthew 27:51–53 are God the Father's response to God the Son's substitutionary atonement for the sins of his elect people through his crucifixion. Matthew 27:51–54 teaches that, for the sake of his elect people, Jesus paid this one death, which he did not owe, so that death may do his people no harm (Matt. 27:52b–53; 1 Peter 2:24).

The actions of those human beings raised from the dead reveal a certain missiological endeavor as seen by their whereabouts *after* Jesus' resurrection from the dead (Matt. 27:53). Upon their temporal resurrection, they appear bodily in the holy city—Jerusalem—bearing witness to what happened to them and how it happened. These raised saints bear witness to the identity and power of Jesus in the same location where he was mocked, tried, and executed. Their life testified of the victory of Jesus on the cross at the very same moment when it appeared as if Jesus had been defeated—he actualized the redemption of God's chosen people through his death on the cross because his death was the sacrifice for sin. Matthew

---

see John Owen, *The Death of Death in the Death of Christ* (Carlisle, PA: Banner of Truth, 2007), 188–90; Leon Morris, *The Atonement: Its Meaning and Significance* (Downers Grove, IL: InterVarsity Press, 1983), 160–61; and John R. Stott, *The Cross of Christ* (Downers Grove, IL: InterVarsity Press, 2006), 193.

Conclusion

27:51–54 reveals that this accomplishment necessitates that news of it must spread from the One (Jesus) to the many (humankind) from the center (Jerusalem) to the ends of the earth.

A bodily resurrection from the dead is the promised future reality for all who trust in the death of Jesus as their own. His death was, and is, life-giving (Matt. 27:52b–53). This event proleptically foreshadows, in some way, what will take place in the eschaton. They came to death by sin; he came to death by righteousness. They came to resurrection by his voice (Matt. 27:50; John 5:25); he came to resurrection by his own divine power (Matt. 28:1–10; John 10:17). This event discloses, in some way, key realities that will accompany the resurrection of the dead as understood from the words of Jesus in John 5:25–29. Bodies long since dead will leave the domain of death and return to life. Everyone will be recognizable, with an ability to verbally communicate and cognitively perceive reality as they are ushered either to the resurrection of life *or* the resurrection of death (John 5:29).

Christians are called sons of God because the Son of God has died for their sins and has been raised from the dead. By his resurrection from the dead he procured life for his people who were predestined, he justified those who were called before the foundation of the world, and he glorified those who were justified (Rom. 8:29–30). The intentional placement of Matthew 27:51–54 within the death-resurrection scene (Matt. 27:45–28:20) emphasizes the theological meaning latent in this Matthean pericope—Christology, missiology, and eschatology. The theological meaning is obscured by the interpretive dichotomy separating the historicity of the act itself and its placement in the Gospel from its theological meaning.

The extraordinary signs accompanying Jesus' crucifixion (Matt. 27:51–53) portray Jesus as the Son of God (Matt. 27:54), proleptically foreshadow gospel mission to the nations (Matt. 27:54; 28:16–20), and institute new covenant worship in the interim prior to the second coming of Jesus (Matt. 27:51; Rev. 19:11–16).

Bibliography

Albright, W. F., and C. S. Mann. *Matthew: Introduction, Translation, and Notes.* Anchor Bible, vol. 26. New York: Doubleday, 1971.

Allen, Leslie C. "Structure, Tradition and Redaction in Ezekiel's Death Valley Vision." In *Among the Prophets: Language, Image and Structure in the Prophetic Writings,* edited by Philip R. Davis and David J. A. Clines, 127–43. Journal for the Study of the Old Testament Supplement Series 144. Sheffield, England: Journal for the Study of the Old Testament Press, 1993.

Allen, Willoughby C. *The Gospel according to Matthew.* New York: Charles Scribner's Sons, 1907.

Allison, Dale C, Jr. "Anticipating the Passion: The Literary Reach of Matthew 26:47–27:56." *Catholic Biblical Quarterly* 56 (1994): 701–14.

———. *Constructing Jesus: Memory, Imagination, and History.* Grand Rapids: Baker Academic, 2010.

———. *The End of the Ages Has Come: An Early Interpretation of the Passion and Resurrection of Jesus.* Philadelphia: Fortress Press, 1985.

———. *The Historical Christ and the Theological Jesus.* Grand Rapids: Eerdmans, 2009.

———. *Resurrecting Jesus: The Earliest Christian Tradition and Its Interpretation.* New York: T&T Clark, 2005.

Bibliography

———. *Studies in Matthew: Interpretation Past and Present*. Grand Rapids: Baker, 2005.

Alter, Robert. *The Art of Biblical Narrative*. New York: Basic Books, 1981.

Anderson, Douglas. "The Origin and Purpose of Matthew 27:51b–53." PhD diss., University of Otago, 2014.

Aus, Roger D. *Samuel, Saul and Jesus: Three Early Palestinian Jewish Christian Gospel Haggadoth*. South Florida Studies in the History of Judaism 105. Edited by Jacob Neusner. Atlanta: Scholars Press, 1994.

Barr, David. "The Drama of Matthew's Gospel: A Reconsideration of Its Structure and Purpose." *Theology Digest* 24, 4 (1976): 349–59.

Bass, Justin. *The Battle for the Keys: Revelation 1:18 and Christ's Descent into the Underworld*. Eugene, OR: Paternoster, 2014.

Bates, Matthew W. *The Birth of the Trinity: Jesus, God, and Spirit in the New Testament and Early Christian Interpretations of the Old Testament*. Oxford: Oxford University Press, 2015.

Bauckham, Richard. "The Eschatological Earthquake in the Apocalypse of John." *Novum Testamentum* 19 (1977): 224–33.

———. *Jesus and the Eyewitnesses: The Gospels as Eyewitness Testimony*. Grand Rapids: Eerdmans, 2006.

Bauer, David R. "The Major Characters of Matthew's Story: Their Function and Significance." In *Gospel Interpretation: Narrative-Critical & Social Scientific Approaches*, edited by Jack D. Kingsbury, 27–37. Harrisburg, PA: Trinity Press International, 1997.

———. *The Structure of Matthew's Gospel: A Study in Literary Design*. Journal for the Study of New Testament Supplement 31, Biblical and Literature Series 15. Edited by David Hill. Decatur, GA: Almond Press, 1988.

Bavinck, Herman. *Reformed Dogmatics*. Vol. 3, Sin and Salvation in Christ. Translated by John Vriend. Grand Rapids: Baker, 2006.

Beale, G. K. *The Temple and the Church's Mission: A Biblical Theology*

of the Dwelling Place of God. New Studies in Biblical Theology 17. Downers Grove, IL: InterVarsity Press, 2004.
Beale, G. K., and D. A. Carson, eds. *Commentary on the New Testament Use of the Old Testament*. Grand Rapids: Baker, 2007.
Bengel, John A. *Bengel's New Testament Commentary*. Vol. 1, *Matthew–Acts*. Translated by Charlton T. Lewis and Marvin R. Vincent. Grand Rapids: Kregel, 1981.
Bieringer, R., V. Koperski, and B. Lataire, eds. *Resurrection in the New Testament*. Bibliotheca Ephemeridum Theologicarum Lovaniensium 165. Leuven, Belgium: Leuven University Press, 2002.
Bird, Michael. *The Gospel of the Lord: How the Early Church Wrote the Story of Jesus*. Grand Rapids: Eerdmans, 2014.
Blass, F., and A. Debrunner. *A Greek Grammar of the New Testament and Other Early Christian Literature*. Translated by Robert W. Funk. Chicago: University of Chicago Press, 1961.
Block, Daniel I. *The Book of Ezekiel: Chapters 25–48*. New International Commentary on the Old Testament. Grand Rapids: Eerdmans, 1998.
Blomberg, Craig L. *Matthew*. New American Commentary, vol. 22. Nashville: Broadman Press, 1992.
Brown, Raymond E. *A Crucified Christ in Holy Week: Essays on the Four Gospel Passion Narratives*. Collegeville, MN: Liturgical Press, 1984.
———. *The Death of the Messiah: From Gethsemane to the Grave—A Commentary on the Passion Narratives in the Four Gospels*. Anchor Bible Reference Library. New York: Doubleday, 1994.
———. "The Resurrection in Matthew (27:62–28:20)." *Worship* 64 (March 1990): 157–70.
Bruce, F. F. *The Epistle to the Hebrews*. New International Commentary on the New Testament. Grand Rapids: Eerdmans, 1964.
Bruner, Frederick D. *The Churchbook: Matthew 13–28*. Vol. 2. Grand Rapids: Eerdmans, 2004.
Bunyan, John. *Resurrection*. N.p.: Sovereign Grace Publishers, n.d.

Burridge, Richard. *What Are the Gospels? A Comparison with Graeco-Roman Biography*. Grand Rapids: Eerdmans, 2004.

Byrskog, Samuel. *Story as History, History as Story: The Gospels in the Context of Ancient Oral History*. Leiden, Netherlands: Brill, 2002.

Calvin, John. *Commentary on a Harmony of the Evangelists, Matthew, Mark, and Luke*. Calvin's Commentaries, vol. 16. Translated by William Pringle. Grand Rapids: Baker, 2005.

———. *Institutes of the Christian Religion*. Edited by John T. McNeil. Translated by Ford Lewis Battles. 2 vols. Louisville, KY: Westminster John Knox Press, 2011.

Carson, D. A. *The Expositor's Bible Commentary*. Vol. 2, *Matthew 13–28*, edited by Frank E. Gaebelein, 1–272. Grand Rapids: Zondervan, 1995.

Carter, Warren. "Kernels and Narrative Blocks: The Structure of Matthew's Gospel." *Catholic Biblical Quarterly* 54 (1992): 463–81.

———. *Matthew: Storyteller, Interpreter, Evangelist*. Peabody, MA: Hendrickson, 2004.

———. *Matthew and the Margins: A Socio-Political and Religious Reading*. Journal for the Study of New Testament Supplement 204. Sheffield, England: Sheffield Academic Press, 2000.

Chamblin, Knox. *Matthew*. Vol. 2, *Chapters 14–28*. A Mentor Commentary. Fearn, Scotland: Christian Focus Publication, 2010.

Charette, Blaine. "'Never Has Anything like This Been Seen in Israel': The Spirit as Eschatological Sign in Matthew's Gospel." *Journal of Pentecostal Theology* 8 (1996): 31–51.

———. *Restoring Presence: The Spirit in Matthew's Gospel*. Journal of Pentecostal Theology Supplement Series 18. Edited by John Christopher Thomas. Sheffield, England: Sheffield Academic Press, 2000.

Charnock, Stephen. *The Existence and Attributes of God*. Vol. 2. Grand Rapids: Baker, 1996.

Chase, Mitchell Lloyd. "Resurrection Hope in Daniel 12:2: An

Exercise in Biblical Theology." PhD diss., Southern Baptist Theological Seminary, 2013.

Chatman, Seymour. *Story and Discourse: Narrative Structure in Fiction and Film.* Ithaca, NY: Cornell University Press, 1978.

Childs, Brevard S. *Biblical Theology of the Old and New Testaments: Theological Reflection on the Christian Bible.* Minneapolis: Fortress Press, 1993.

———. *The New Testament as Canon: An Introduction.* Philadelphia: Fortress Press, 1984.

Chronis, Harry L. "The Torn Veil: Cultus and Christology in Mark 15:37–39." *Journal of Biblical Literature* 101, 1 (1982): 97–114.

Clarke, Howard. *The Gospel of Matthew and Its Readers: A Historical Introduction to the First Gospel.* Bloomington: Indiana University Press, 2003.

Combrink, H. J. Bernard. "The Structure of the Gospel of Matthew as Narrative." *Tyndale Bulletin* 34 (1983): 61–90.

Cotterell, Peter. "Hermeneutics: Some Linguistic Considerations." *Evangel* 13, 3 (Autumn 1995): 78–83.

Dahl, Nils A. *The Crucified Messiah and Other Essays.* Minneapolis: Augsburg Publishing House, 1974.

Davies, W. D., and Dale C. Allison Jr. *A Critical and Exegetical Commentary on the Gospel according to Saint Matthew.* International Critical Commentary on the Holy Scriptures of the Old and New Testaments, vol. 3. New York: T&T Clark, 2004.

de Jonge, M. "Matthew 27:51 in Early Christian Exegesis." *Harvard Theological Review* 79, 1–3 (1986): 67–79.

———. "Two Interesting Interpretations of the Rending of the Temple-Veil in the Testaments of the Twelve Patriarchs." In *Jewish Eschatology, Early Christian Christology and the Testaments of the Twelve Patriarchs: Collected Essays of Marinus De Jonge*, 220–32. Supplements to Novum Testamentum 63. Leiden, Netherlands: Brill, 1991.

———. "The Use of O Cristos in the Passion Narratives." In *Jewish Eschatology, Early Christian Christology and the Testaments of the*

Twelve Patriarchs: Collected Essays of Marinus De Jonge, 64–86. Supplements to Novum Testamentum 63. Leiden, Netherlands: Brill, 1991.

Dempster, Stephen G. *Dominion and Dynasty: A Biblical Theology of the Hebrew Bible*. New Studies in Biblical Theology 15. Edited by D. A. Carson. Downers Grove, IL: InterVarsity Press, 2003.

———. "From Slight Peg to Corner Stone to Capstone: The Resurrection of Christ on 'the Third Day' according to the Scriptures." *Westminster Theological Journal* 76, 2 (2014): 371–409.

Denault, Pascal. *The Distinctiveness of Baptist Covenant Theology: A Comparison between Seventeenth-Century Particular Baptist and Paedobaptist Federalism*. Birmingham, AL: Solid Ground Christian Books, 2013.

Denaux, Adelbert. "Matthew's Story of Jesus' Burial and Resurrection (Mt 27, 57–28, 20)." In *Resurrection in the New Testament*, edited by R. Bieringer, V. Koperski, and B. Lataire, 123–45. Leuven, Belgium: Leuven University Press, 2002.

Doole, J. Andrew. *What Was Mark for Matthew? An Examination of Matthew's Relationship and Attitude to His Primary Source*. Tübingen: Mohr Siebeck, 2013.

Dunn, James D. G. "How Did Matthew Go about Composing His Gospel?." In *Jesus, Matthew's Gospel and Early Christianity: Studies in Memory of Graham N. Stanton*. Library of New Testament Studies. Edited by Daniel Gurtner, Joel Willitts, and Richard A. Burridge. New York: T&T Clark, 2011.

Eco, Umberto, and Stefan Collini, eds. *Interpretation and Overinterpretation*. Cambridge: Cambridge University Press, 1992.

Ehrman, Bart D., and Zlatko Plese. *The Other Gospels: Accounts of Jesus from Outside the New Testament*. Oxford: Oxford University Press, 2014.

Esolen, Anthony. Out of the Ashes: *Rebuilding American Culture*. Washington, DC: Regnery Publishing, 2017.

Evans, Craig. *Matthew*. New Cambridge Bible Commentary. Cambridge: Cambridge University Press, 2012.

Fensham, F. C. "The Curse of the Dry Bones in Ezekiel 37:1–14: Changed to a Blessing of Resurrection." *Journal of Northwest Semitic Language* 13 (1987): 59–60.

Fenton, J. C. "Inclusio and Chiasmus in Matthew." In *Studia Evangelica: Papers Presented to the International Congress on "The Four Gospels in 1957,"* edited by Kurt Aland and F. L. Cross, 174–79. Berlin: Akademie Verlag, 1959.

Fishbane, Michael. *Biblical Interpretation in Ancient Israel*. Oxford: Clarendon Press, 1988.

Fox, Michael V. "The Rhetoric of Ezekiel's Vision of the Valley of Dry Bones." *Hebrew Union College Annual* 51 (1980): 1–15.

France, R. T. "The Formula-Quotations of Matthew 2 and the Problem of Communication." *New Testament Studies: An International Journal* 27 (1981): 233–51.

———. *The Gospel of Matthew*. New International Commentary on the New Testament. Grand Rapids: Eerdmans, 2007.

———. *The Gospel of Mark*. New International Greek Testament Commentary. Downers Grove, IL: InterVarsity Press, 1989.

———. *Jesus and the Old Testament: His Application of Old Testament Passages to Himself and His Mission*. Vancouver: Regent College Publishing, 1998.

———. *Matthew: Evangelist and Teacher*. Eugene, OR: Wipf & Stock, 1989.

Fuller, R. H. "The Bodies of the Saints, Mt 27:52–3." *Scripture* 3 (1948): 86–87.

Garland, David. *Reading Matthew: A Literary and Theological Commentary*. Macon, GA: Smyth & Helwys, 2001.

Geisler, Norman L. "Licona Controversy Articles." *NormanGeisler.net*. Accessed February 11, 2014. http://normangeisler.com/licona-articles/.

Gentry, Peter J., and Stephen J. Wellum. *Kingdom through Covenant: A Biblical-Theological Understanding of the Covenants*. Wheaton, IL: Crossway, 2012.

Giblin, Charles H. "Structural and Thematic Correlations in the

Matthean Burial-Resurrection Narrative (Matt. XXVII.57–XXVIII.20)." *New Testament Studies* 21 (1974–75): 406–20.

Gnilka, Joachim. *Das Matthäusevangelium. Zweiter Teil: Kommentar zu Kapitel 14,1–28,20 und Einleitungsfragen.* Herders theologischer Kommentar zum Neuen Testament 1, no. 2. Freiburg: Herder, 1988.

Goheen, Michael W. *A Light to the Nations: The Missional Church and the Biblical Story.* Grand Rapids: Baker Academic, 2011.

Goldsworthy, Graeme. Gospel-Centered Hermeneutics: Foundations and Principles of Evangelical Biblical Interpretation. Downers Grove, IL: InterVarsity Press, 2006.

Grassi, J. A. "Ezekiel 37, 1–14 and the New Testament." *New Testament Studies* 11 (1964–1965): 162–64.

Green, Benedict H. *The Gospel according to Matthew in the Revised Standard Version: Introduction and Commentary.* Oxford: Oxford University Press, 1975.

Gundry, Robert H. Matthew: *A Commentary on His Handbook for a Mixed Church under Persecution.* 2nd ed. Grand Rapids: Eerdmans, 1994.

———. *The Use of the Old Testament in St. Matthew's Gospel: With Special Reference to the Messianic Hope.* Leiden, Netherlands: Brill, 1967.

Gurtner, Daniel M. "Interpreting Apocalyptic Symbolism in the Gospel of Matthew." Paper presented at the Evangelical Theological Society National Conference, New Orleans, November 2009.

———. *The Torn Veil: Matthew's Exposition of the Death of Jesus.* Cambridge: Cambridge University Press, 2007.

Gurtner, Daniel, and John Nolland, eds. *Built upon the Rock: Studies in the Gospel of Matthew.* Grand Rapids: Eerdmans, 2008.

Hagner, Donald A. *Hebrews.* New International Biblical Commentary. Peabody, MA: Hendrickson, 1990.

———. *Matthew 14–28.* Word Biblical Commentary, vol. 33b. Nashville: Thomas Nelson, 1995.

BIBLIOGRAPHY

Hahn, Scott W. *The Kingdom of God as Liturgical Empire: A Theological Commentary on 1–2 Chronicles.* Grand Rapids: Baker, 2012.

Hamilton, James M., Jr. *God's Glory in Salvation through Judgment: A Biblical Theology.* Wheaton, IL: Crossway, 2010.

———. *With the Clouds of Heaven: The Book of Daniel in Biblical Theology.* New Studies in Biblical Theology 32. Downers Grove, IL: InterVarsity Press, 2014.

Harrington, Daniel J. *The Gospel of Matthew.* Sacra Pagina 1. Collegeville, MN: Liturgical Press, 1991.

Hauerwas, Stanley. *Matthew.* Brazos Theological Commentary on the Bible. Grand Rapids: Brazos Press, 2006.

Hays, Richard B. *Echoes of Scripture in the Gospels.* Waco, TX: Baylor University Press, 2016.

———. *Reading Backwards: Figural Christology and the Fourfold Gospel Witness.* Waco, TX: Baylor University Press, 2014.

Heil, John P. *The Death and Resurrection of Jesus: A Narrative-Critical Reading of Matthew 26–28.* Minneapolis: Fortress Press, 1991.

———. "The Narrative Structure of Matthew 27:55–28:20." *Journal of Biblical Literature* 110 (1991): 419–38.

Henry, Matthew. *Matthew Henry's Commentary on the Whole Bible.* Vol. 5, *Matthew to John.* New York: Fleming & Revel, 1950.

Herzer, Jens. "The Riddle of the Holy Ones in Matthew 27:51b–53: A New Proposal for a *Crux Interpretum.*" In *"What Does the Scripture Say?" Studies in the Function of Scripture in Early Judaism and Christianity.* Library of New Testament Studies, edited by Craig Evans and H. Daniel Zacharias, 1:142–57. New York: T&T Clark, 2012.

Hill, David. *The Gospel of Matthew.* New Century Bible Commentary. Grand Rapids: Eerdmans, 1972.

———. "Matthew 27:51–53 in the Theology of the Evangelist." *Irish Biblical Studies* 7 (1985): 76–87.

Hood, Jason B. "The Beginning and Ending of Matthew." In *The Messiah, His Brothers, and the Nations (Matthew 1:1–17),* 139–51. London: T&T Clark, 2011.

———. "Matthew 23–25: The Extent of Jesus' Fifth Discourse." *Journal of Biblical Literature* 3 (2009): 527–43.

———. *The Messiah, His Brothers, and the Nations (Matthew 1:1–17)*. London: T&T Clark, 2011.

House, Paul R. *Old Testament Theology*. Downers Grove, IL: InterVarsity Press, 1998.

Huizenga, Leroy A. *The New Isaac: Tradition and Intertextuality in the Gospel of Matthew*. Supplements to Novum Testamentum 131. Leiden, Netherlands: Brill, 2009.

Hurtado, Larry W. *Destroyer of the Gods: Early Christian Distinctiveness in the Roman World*. Waco, TX: Baylor University Press, 2016.

Hutton, Delvin D. "The Resurrection of the Holy Ones (Matt 27:51b–53): A Study of the Theology of the Matthean Passion Narrative." Th.D. diss., Harvard University, 1970.

———. Review of *The Passion Narrative according to Matthew: A Redactional Study*, by Donald P. Senior, Journal of Biblical Literature 96 (1977): 308–9.

Iser, Wolfgang. *The Act of Reading: A Theory of Aesthetic Response*. Baltimore: Johns Hopkins University Press, 1978.

Johnson, Raymond. "The Church's Mission: John 20:19–23 Reconsidered." *Currents in Theology and Mission* 43, 4 (October 2016): 22–28.

———. "Matthew 27:51–54 Revisited: A Narratological Reappropriation." *Southern Baptist Journal of Theology* 18, 4 (2014): 31–50.

Kingsbury, Jack Dean, ed. *Gospel Interpretation: Narrative-Critical & Social Scientific Approaches*. Harrisburg, PA: Trinity Press International, 1997.

———. *Matthew*. Proclamation Commentaries. 2nd ed. Philadelphia: Fortress Press, 1986.

———. *Matthew: Structure, Christology, Kingdom*. Philadelphia: Fortress Press, 1975.

———. *Matthew as Story*. 2nd ed. Philadelphia: Fortress Press, 1988.

Bibliography

Leithart, Peter J. *Deep Exegesis: The Mystery of Reading Scripture.* Waco, TX: Baylor University Press, 2009.

———. *The Four: A Survey of the Gospels.* Moscow, ID: Canon Press, 2010.

———. *A House for My Name: A Survey of the Old Testament.* Moscow, ID: Canon Press, 2000.

———. "Jesus as Israel: The Typological Structure of Matthew's Gospel." *Leithart.com.* Accessed February 10, 2013. https://theopolisinstitute.com/wp-content/uploads/edd/2015/09/jesus-as-israel-the-typological-structure-of-matthew-s-gospel.pdf.

———. "Structure of Matthew 27–28." *First Things*, March 15, 2010. Accessed January 23, 2014. http://www.leithart.com/2010/03/15/structure-of-matthew-27-28/ (no longer posted).

Licona, Michael. *The Resurrection of Jesus: A New Historiographical Approach.* Downers Grove, IL: InterVarsity Press, 2010.

Liddell, Henry George, and Robert Scott. *Lexicon: Abridged from Liddell and Scott's Greek-English Lexicon.* Oxford: Clarendon Press, 1896.

Lohr, Charles H. "Oral Techniques in the Gospel of Matthew." *Catholic Biblical Quarterly* 23 (1961): 403–35.

———. "Major Divergences between LXX and MT in Ezekiel." In *Messianisms and the Septuagint: Collected Essays.* Edited by K. Hauspie. Leuven, Belgium: Leuven University Press, 2004.

Luz, Ulrich. *Matthew 21–28.* Hermeneia. Edited by Helmut Koester. Translated by James E. Crouch. Minneapolis: Fortress Press, 2005.

———. *Studies in Matthew.* Translated by Rosemary Selle. Grand Rapids: Eerdmans, 2005.

Malone, Fred A. *The Baptism of Disciples Alone: A Covenantal Argument for Credobaptism versus Paedobaptism.* Cape Coral, FL: Founders Press, 2007.

———. "Biblical Hermeneutics & Covenant Theology." In *Covenant Theology: A Baptist Distinctive*, edited by Earl M. Blackburn,

63–87. Birmingham, AL: Solid Ground Christian Books, 2013.

Martin-Archard, Robert. *From Death to Life: A Study of the Doctrine of the Resurrection in the Old Testament*. Edinburgh: Oliver and Boyd, 1960.

Matera, Frank J. *Passion Narrative and Gospel Theologies: Interpreting the Synoptics through Their Passion Stories*. Studies in Contemporary and Theological Problems. Edited by Lawrence Boadt. New York: Paulist Press, 1986.

———. "The Plot of Matthew's Gospel." *Catholic Biblical Quarterly* 49 (1987): 233–53.

McCasland, S. V. "Portents in Josephus and in the Gospels." *Journal of Biblical Literature* 51, 4 (1932): 323–35.

McGraw, Ryan M. "Trinitarian Doxology: Reassessing John Owen's Contribution to Reformed Orthodox Trinitarian Theology." *Studia Historiae Ecclesiasticae* 41, 2 (2015): 38–68.

Melick, Richard R. *Philippians-Colossians-Philemon*. New American Commentary, vol. 32. Nashville: Broadman Press, 1991.

Menken, Maarten J. J. *Matthew's Bible: The Old Testament Text of the Evangelist*. Bibliotheca Ephemeridum Theologicarum Lovaniensium 173. Leuven, Belgium: Leuven University Press, 2004.

Merx, *Adalbert. Die vier kanonischen Evangelien nach ihrem ältesten bekannten Texte: Übersetzung und Erläuterung der syrischen im Sinaikloster gefundenen Palimpsesthandschrift; Zweiter Teil, erste Hälfte, Erläuterung. Matthaeus*. Berlin: Reimer, 1902.

Metzger, Bruce M. *A Textual Commentary on the Greek New Testament*. 2nd ed. New York: United Bible Societies, 1994.

Minear, Paul S. *Matthew: The Teacher's Gospel*. New York: Pilgrim's Press, 1982.

Mitch, Curtis, and Edward Sri. *The Gospel of Matthew*. Catholic Commentary on Sacred Scripture. Grand Rapids: Baker, 2010.

Mohler, R. Albert, Jr. "The Devil Is in the Details: Biblical Inerrancy and the Licona Controversy." *AlbertMohler.com*, September 14, 2011.

http://www.albertmohler.com/2011/09/14/the-devil-is-in-the-details-biblical-inerrancy-and-the-licona-controversy/.

Monasterio, Rafael. "Cross and Kingdom in Matthew's Theology." *Theology Digest* 29, 2 (1981): 149.

———. *Exegesis de Mateo, 27, 51b–53: Para una teologia de la muerte de Jesus en el Evangelio de Mateo*. Vitoria, Brazil: Eset, 1980.

Morris, Leon. *The Atonement: Its Meaning and Significance*. Downers Grove, IL: InterVarsity Press, 1983.

Motyer, S. "The Rending of the Veil: A Markan Pentecost?" *New Testament Studies* 33 (1987): 155–57.

Murphy-O'Connor, Jerome. "The Structure of Matthew XIV–XVII." *Revue Biblique* 82 (1975): 360–84.

Nickelsburg, George W. E. *Resurrection, Immortality, and Eternal Life in Intertestamental Judaism and Early Christianity*. Harvard Theological Studies 56. Cambridge, MA: Harvard University Press, 1972.

Nickelsburg, George W. E., and James C. VanderKam. *1 Enoch: A New Translation Based on the Hermeneia Commentary*. Minneapolis: Fortress Press, 2004.

Nolland, John. *The Gospel of Matthew: A Commentary on the Greek Text*. New International Greek Testament Commentary. Grand Rapids: Eerdmans, 2005.

Olley, John W. *Ezekiel: A Commentary Based on Iezekiēl in Codex Vaticanus*. Septuagint Commentary Series. Boston: Brill, 2009.

Osborne, Grant R. *Matthew*. Zondervan Exegetical Commentary on the New Testament. Grand Rapids: Zondervan, 2010.

Owen, John. *The Death of Death in the Death of Christ*. Carlisle, PA: Banner of Truth, 2007.

Patte, Daniel. *The Gospel according to Matthew: A Structural Commentary on Matthew's Faith*. Philadelphia: Fortress Press, 1987.

Pearson, Brook. "New Testament Literary Criticism." In *Handbook to Exegesis of the New Testament*, edited by Stanley E. Porter, 131–166. Leiden, Netherlands: Brill, 1997.

Pelikan, Jaroslav. *Divine Rhetoric: The Sermon on the Mount as Message and Model in Augustine, Chrysostom, and Luther.* Crestwood, NY: St. Vladimir's Seminary Press, 2000.

Pennington, Jonathan T. *Heaven and Earth in the Gospel of Matthew.* Grand Rapids: Baker Academic, 2009.

———. *Reading the Gospels Wisely: A Narrative and Theological Introduction.* Grand Rapids: Baker, 2012.

———. *The Sermon on the Mount and Human Flourishing: A Theological Commentary.* Grand Rapids: Baker, 2017.

Perry, Menakhem. "Literary Dynamics: How the Order of a Text Creates Its Meaning [With an Analysis of Faulkner's 'A Rose for Emily']." *Poetics Today* 1, 1–2 (1979): 35–64, 311–61.

Petersen, William L. "Romanos and the Diatessaron." *New Testament Studies* 29 (1983): 500.

Porter, Stanley E. *Idioms of the Greek New Testament.* London: Sheffield Academic Press, 2005.

Powell, Mark A. "Expected and Unexpected Readings of Matthew: What the Reader Knows." *Asbury Theological Journal* 48, 2 (1993): 31–51.

———. *Methods for Matthew.* In Methods in Biblical Interpretation. Cambridge: Cambridge University Press, 2009.

Prabhu, G. M. Soares. *The Formula Quotations in the Infancy Narrative of Matthew.* Rome: Biblical Institute Press, 1976.

Quarles, Charles. "Cei ce și-au părăsit mormintele după învierea lui Isus în Mat. 27:51–53" [Those coming out of the tombs after Jesus' resurrection in Matthew 27:51–53]. In *Lucruri greu de inteles: Interpretarea unor pasaje dificile din Noul Testament* [*Some things hard to understand: Interpreting difficult passages in the New Testament*], edited by Sorin Sabou and Amiel Drimbe, 1–15. Bucharest: Editura Universitara, 2015.

———. "Matthew 27:51–53: Meaning Genre, Intertextuality, Theology, and Reception History." *Journal of the Evangelical Theological Society* 59, 2 (2016): 271–86.

———. "Matthew 27:52–53 as a Scribal Interpolation: Testing a Recent Proposal." Paper presented at the Evangelical

Theological Society National Conference, San Diego, California, November 2014.

———. "ΜΕΤΑ ΤΗΝ ΕΓΕΡΣΙΝ ΑΥΤΟΥ: A Scribal Interpolation in Matthew 27:53?" *A Journal of Biblical Textual Criticism* 20 (2015): 1–15.

———. Review of *The Resurrection of Jesus: A New Historiographical Approach*, by Michael R. Licona. *Journal of the Evangelical Theological Society* 54 (2011): 839–44.

———. "A Roundtable Discussion with Michael Licona on the Resurrection of Jesus: A New Historiographical Approach." *Southeastern Theological Review* 3, 1 (2012).

———. *A Theology of Matthew: Jesus Revealed as Deliverer, King, and Incarnate Creator*. Explorations in Biblical Theology. Edited by Robert Patterson. Phillipsburg, NJ: P&R Publishing, 2013.

Rabbi Eliezer. *Pirke de Rabbi Êlizer*. Translated by G. Friedlander. New York: Hermon Press, 1970.

Rabinowitz, Peter J. *Before Reading: Narrative Conventions and the Politics of Interpretation*. Ithaca, NY: Cornell University Press, 1987.

Reeves, Keith Howard. *The Resurrection Narrative in Matthew: A Literary-Critical Examination*. Lewiston, NY: Mellen Biblical Press, 1993.

Ridderbos, Herman. *Matthew*. Bible Student's Commentary. Grand Rapids: Zondervan, 1987.

Riebel, Maria. *Auferstehung Jesu in der Stunde seines Todes? Zur Botschaft von Mt 27, 51b–53*. Stuttgart: Katholisches Bibelwerk, 1978.

Riesenfeld, Harald. *The Resurrection in Ezekiel XXXVII and in the Dura-Europos Paintings*. Leipzig: Otto Harrassowitz, 1948.

Robertson, A. T. Word Pictures in the New Testament. Vol. 1, *The Gospel according to Matthew, the Gospel according to Mark*. Grand Rapids: Baker, 1930.

Rochais, Gérard. *Les récits de résurrection des morts dans le Nouveau Testament*. Cambridge: Cambridge University Press, 1981.

Roland, Philippe. "From Genesis to the End of the World: The Plan of Matthew's Gospel." *Biblical Theology Bulletin* 2 (1972): 155–76.

Rossé, Gérard. *The Cry of Jesus on the Cross: A Biblical and Theological Study.* Translated by Stephen W. Arndt. New York: Paulist Press, 1987.

Rowley, H. H. *The Missionary Message of the Old Testament.* London: Carey Press, 1944.

Runge, Steven E. *Discourse Grammar of the Greek New Testament: A Practical Introduction for Teaching and Exegesis.* Peabody, MA: Hendrickson, 2010.

Sanders, Fred. *The Triune God.* New Studies in Dogmatics. Edited by Michael Allen and Scott Swain. Grand Rapids: Zondervan, 2016.

Scaer, David P. *Discourses in Matthew: Jesus Teaches the Church.* St. Louis: Concordia Publishing House, 2004.

Schnackenburg, Rudolf. *The Gospel of Matthew.* Grand Rapids: Eerdmans, 2002.

Schreiner, Thomas R. *Commentary on Hebrews.* Biblical Theology for Christian Proclamation. Edited by T. Desmond Alexander, Andreas J. Kostenberger, and Thomas R. Schreiner. Nashville: B&H Publishing, 2015.

Schweizer, Eduard. *The Good News according to Matthew.* Translated by David E. Green. Atlanta: John Knox Press, 1975.

Scobie, Charles. "Israel and the Nations: An Essay in Biblical Theology." *Tyndale Bulletin* 43, 2 (1992): 283–305.

Senior, Donald. "The Death of God's Son and the Beginning of the New Age (Matthew 27:51–54)." In *The Language of the Cross*, edited by Aelred Lacomara, 29–51. Chicago: Franciscan Herald Press, 1977.

———. "The Death of Jesus and the Resurrection of the Holy Ones (Mt 27:51–53)." *Catholic Biblical Quarterly* 38 (1976): 312–29.

———. *Matthew.* Abingdon New Testament Commentaries. Nashville: Abingdon Press, 1998.

———. "Matthew's Special Material in the Passion Story: Implications for the Evangelist's Redactional Technique and Theological Perspective." *Ephemerides Theological Lovanienses* 63 (1987): 273.

———. *The Passion according to Matthew: A Redactional Study.* Bibliotheca Ephemeridum Theologicarum Lovaniensium 39. Leuven, Belgium: Leuven University Press, 1975.

———. *The Passion of Jesus in the Gospel of Mark.* Wilmington, DE: Michael Glazier, 1984.

Silva, Moises. "Are Translators Traitors? Some Personal Reflections." In *The Challenge of Bible Translation: Communicating God's Word to the World* (Essays in Honor of Ronald F. Youngblood), edited by Glen G. Scorgie, Mark L. Strauss, and Steven M. Voth, 37–50. Grand Rapids: Zondervan, 2002.

Sim, David C. *Apocalyptic Eschatology in the Gospel of Matthew.* Society for New Testament Studies 88. Cambridge: Cambridge University Press, 1996.

———. "The 'Confession' of the Soldiers in Matthew 27:54." *Heythrop Journal* 34 (1993): 416.

Simonetti, Manlio, ed. *Matthew 14–28.* Ancient Christian Commentary on Scripture: New Testament, vol. 1b. Downers Grove, IL: InterVarsity Press, 2002.

Smith, Christopher R. "Literary Evidences of a Fivefold Structure in the Gospel of Matthew." *New Testament Studies* 43 (1997): 540–51.

Smyth, Herbert W. *Greek Grammar.* Cambridge, MA: Harvard University Press, 1984.

Spurgeon, Charles H. *Spurgeon's Popular Exposition of Matthew.* Grand Rapids: Baker, 1979.

———. *12 Sermons on the Resurrection.* Grand Rapids: Baker, 1968.

Stanton, Graham N. *A Gospel of a New People: Studies in Matthew.* Edinburgh: T&T Clark, 1992.

———. "The Origin and Purpose of Matthew's Gospel: Matthean Scholarship from 1945–1980." *Aufstieg und Niedergang der römischen Welt* II.25.3 (1985): 1905.

Sternberg, Meir. *The Poetics of Biblical Narrative: Ideological Literature and the Drama of Reading*. Bloomington: Indiana University Press, 1985.

Stewart, Robert, ed. *The Resurrection of Jesus: John Dominic Crossan and N. T. Wright in Dialogue*. Minneapolis: Fortress Press, 2006.

Stone, Michael E. *Fourth Ezra: A Commentary on the Book of Fourth Ezra*. A Critical and Historical Commentary on the Bible. Minneapolis: Fortress Press, 1990.

Stott, John R. *The Cross of Christ*. Downers Grove, IL: InterVarsity Press, 2006.

Strauss, Mark L. *Four Portraits, One Jesus: An Introduction to Jesus and the Gospels*. Grand Rapids: Zondervan, 2007.

Stuart, Douglas. *Ezekiel*. Communicator's Commentary, vol. 18. Dallas: Word, 1989.

Thallus. "The Extant Fragments of the Five Books of Chronography of Julius Africanus." In Ante-Nicene Fathers 6, Logos Libronix ECF, 1.6.2.1.3.25.

Thomas, Heath, ed. "A Roundtable Discussion with Michael Licona on the Resurrection of Jesus: A New Historiographical Approach." *Southeastern Theological Review* 3, 1 (2012): 71–98.

Thompson, Alan J. *The Acts of the Risen Lord Jesus: Luke's Account of God's Unfolding Plan*. New Studies in Biblical Theology 27. Downers Grove, IL: InterVarsity Press, 2011.

Troxel, Ronald L. "Matt 27.51–4 Reconsidered: Its Role in the Passion Narrative, Meaning and Origin." *New Testament Studies* 48 (2002): 30–47.

Turner, David. *Matthew*. Baker Exegetical Commentary on the New Testament. Grand Rapids: Baker, 2008.

Van Aarde, Andries. "Matthew 27:45–53 and the Turning of the Tide in Israel's History." *Biblical Theology Bulletin* 28, 1 (1998): 16–26.

Verseput, Donald J. "The Role and Meaning of the 'Son of God' Title in Matthew's Gospel." *New Testament Studies* 33 (1987): 532–56.

Bibliography

Wallace, Daniel B. *Greek Grammar beyond the Basics: An Exegetical Syntax of the New Testament*. Grand Rapids: Zondervan, 1996.

Warfield, Benjamin Breckenridge. *The Person and Work of Christ*. Philadelphia: Presbyterian and Reformed, 1950.

Waters, Kenneth L. "Matthew 27:52–53 as Apocalyptic Apostrophe: Temporal-Spatial Collapse in the Gospel of Matthew." *Journal of Biblical Literature* 122, 3 (2003): 489–515.

———. "Matthew 28:1–6 as Temporally Conflated Text: Temporal-Spatial Collapse in the Gospel of Matthew." *Expository Times* 116 (2005): 295–301.

Watson, Francis. *The Fourfold Gospel: A Theological Reading of the New Testament Portraits of Jesus*. Grand Rapids: Baker Academic, 2016.

Wenham, David. "The Resurrection Narratives in Matthew's Gospel." *Tyndale Bulletin* 24 (1973): 21–54.

Wenham, J. W. "When Were the Saints Raised?" *Journal of Theological Studies* 32, 1 (1981): 150–52.

Weren, Wim J. C. *Studies in Matthew's Gospel: Literary Design, Intertextuality, and Social Setting*. Leiden, Netherlands: Brill, 2014.

Wiarda, Timothy. *Interpreting Gospel Narratives: Scenes, People, and Theology*. Nashville: B&H Publishing, 2010.

Wiersbe, Warren W. *The Bible Exposition Commentary: New Testament*. Vol. 1, *Matthew–Galatians*. Colorado Springs: Victor, 2001.

Wilkins, Michael J. *Matthew*. NIV Application Commentary Series. Grand Rapids: Zondervan, 2004.

Witherington, Ben. "The Cross of Jesus: A Literary-Critical Study of Matthew 27." Ph.D. diss., Union Theological Seminary, 1985.

———. *Matthew*. Smyth & Helwys Bible Commentary. Macon, GA: Smyth & Helwys Publishing, 2006.

Witherup, Ronald D. "The Cross of Jesus: A Literary-Critical Study of Matthew 27." PhD diss., Union Theological Seminary, 1985.

———. "The Death of Jesus and the Raising of the Saints: Matthew

27:51–54 in Context." *Society of Biblical Literature Seminar Papers* 26 (1987): 578–79.

Woolsey, Andrew A. *Unity and Continuity in Covenantal Thought: A Study of the Reformed Tradition to the Westminster Assembly*. Grand Rapids: Reformation Heritage Books, 2012.

Wright, Christopher J. H. *The Message of Ezekiel: A New Heart and a New Spirit*. The Bible Speaks Today. Downers Grove, IL: InterVarsity Press, 2001.

Wright, N. T. *The Day the Revolution Began: Reconsidering the Meaning of Jesus' Crucifixion*. San Francisco: HarperOne, 2016.

———. *The Resurrection of the Son of God*. Christian Origins and the Question of God, vol. 3. Minneapolis: Fortress Press, 2003.

Wüthrich, Serge. "Naître de mourir: la mort de Jésus dans l'Évangile de Matthieu (Matt 27.51– 56)." *New Testament Studies* 56 (2010): 313–25.

Index of Scripture

Genesis
1:1—69n3
2—76n16
2:7—76n16, 90n53
2:17—154
3:6—31
3:15—74n13
5:25—3
8:20–22—1n2
28:15—125n54

Exodus
10:22—70n6
19:16–20—59n41, 78
20:18–21—59n41, 78
25:10–31:18—150n48
26:31–35—70n6, 151
26:37—151n52
35:1–40:33—150n48

Leviticus
21:1—83n32

Numbers
3:26—151n52
20:10–13—31

Deuteronomy
18:15–22—30
21:22–23—141n20
32:39—84n34

1 Samuel
28—156n68

2 Samuel
22:8—37n3, 125

1 Kings
12—95
17:17–24—61n45, 135n3

2 Kings
4:32–37—135n3
4:37—135n3
13:21—61n45

2 Chronicles
3:14—151n52

Ezra
7:32—71

Job
42:5—162n3

Psalms
11:7—162n3
22—126n56
22:1—127
22:14—14
69:21—70n6
77:19—70
89:26—137
104:30—70

Isaiah
11:9—149
13:13—60n42
24:18–20—60n42

25:7—58n37
26—70n4
26:19—70, 72n8, 89
42:18—84
49:6—149
52:13-15—74n12
53:4-6—126
53:5—74n12

Jeremiah
8:1-3—37n3
15:9—37n3, 70
17:13—74n12
23:1-8—76
31—152n55
31:31-34—75n14, 100n3, 126, 152n55
31:33—152, 162
34:23—76
34:23-31—76
36:35—76
51:29—60n42

Ezekiel
1:3—77n18, 83
2:3—95
3:12—89n49, 90
3:13—89n49, 90
3:14—83
3:16—77n18
3:22—83
3:22-23—83
4:6—96
6:1—77n18

6:3—77n18
6:4-7—95
6:7—82n29
6:13—82n29
6:14—77n17
7:1—77n18
8-11—83
8:1—83
8:4—83
9:9—95
10:18-19—57n37, 125n55
11:10—82n29
11:12—82n29
11:14—77n18
11:17—73
11:19—78n21
11:19-20—75
12:1—77n18
12:8—77n18
12:17—77n18
12:20—82n29
12:21—77n18
12:26—77n18
13:1—77n18
13:1-14:11—95
13:9—82n29
13:14—82n29
13:21—82n29
13:23—82n29
14:2—77n18
14:8—82n29
14:12—77n18
15:1—77n18

16:1—77n18
16:35—77n18
16:62—82n29
17:1—77n18
17:11—77n18
17:21—82n29
17:22-24—75
17:24—76
18:1—77n18
18:31—75, 78n21
20:2—77n18
20:42—73, 82n29
20:44—82n29
21:1—77n18
21:3—77n18
21:6—77n18
21:13—77n18
21:23—77n18
22:1—77n18
22:16—82n29
22:17—77n18
22:22—82n29
22:23—77n18
23:1—77n18
23:49—82n29
24:1—77n18
24:15—77n18
24:20—77n18
24:27—77n17
25-32—78n19
25:1—77n18
25:3—77n18
25:11—77n17
25:17—77n17

Index of Scripture

26:1—77n18
26:6—77n17
27:1—77n18
27:51—151n50
27:53—103
28:1—77n18
28:11—77n18
28:20—77n18
28:23—77n17
28:26—77n17
29:1—77n18
29:9—77n17
29:16—77n17
29:17—77n18
29:21—77n17
30:1—77n18
30:8—77n17
30:19—77n17
30:20—77n18
30:26—77n17
31:1—77n18
32:1—77n18
32:15—77n17
32:17—77n18
33:1—77n18
33:21—83
33:23—77n18
33:29—77n17
34:1—77n18
34:1-10—75, 95
34:7—77n18
34:23—76, 78n21
34:23-24—75
35:1—77n18

35:4—82n29
35:12—82n29
35:15—77n17
36—75n15, 81n26
36-37—74n13, 96, 152
36:1—77n18
36:4—77n18
36:16—77n18
36:16-38—95n60
36:16-37:14—73
36:16-37:28—95-96
36:17-20—73
36:21-23—77
36:23—77
36:24—73, 78n19
36:24-29—78n19
36:24-32—74n13
36:25—74
36:26—74-75, 78n21
36:26-27—75n15, 81, 100n3, 126, 152, 162
36:27—81n26
36:27-30—91
36:32—76
36:36—82n29
36:38—77, 77n17
37—7, 9, 37, 69n4, 70n4, 76n16, 78n19, 80n23, 86n39, 89-92, 93n59, 94, 98, 100, 103, 153-54, 156n68
37-48—78n19
37:1—75n15, 81-83, 88

37:1-2—83, 99
37:1-3—79n22
37:1-10—79, 82-83, 90
37:1-14—8, 67, 68n1, 69n3, 72, 75, 78n19, 79-80, 81n26, 82, 84n34, 85n36, 86-87, 89, 91-92, 94-95, 98, 100, 103, 161-62
37:2—83, 85, 88
37:3—79, 81, 84, 85n36
37:4—77n18, 78, 85n36
37:4-6—84
37:4-8—79n22
37:4-10—75n15, 81, 84
37:5—81, 91, 92n56
37:6—81-82, 82n29, 88, 91, 92n56
37:7—84, 88-89, 89n49
37:7-8—84, 89
37:7-10—76n16, 90n53
37:8—81, 85
37:8-10—79n22
37:9—76n16, 81, 85, 91, 92n56
37:10—81, 85, 90-91, 92n56
37:11—79, 82, 85-86
37:11-14—68n1,

Index of Scripture

75n15, 79n22, 81
37:12—9, 70n6, 73, 79, 85–86, 88–89, 91
37:12-14—37n3, 63n53, 72n10, 73n11, 78–79, 82, 85, 91, 92n58, 98, 154
37:13—82, 82n29, 86, 89n48, 103
37:14—81–82, 85n36, 86, 88, 91, 92n56, 152
37:15— 77n18
37:15-23—75n15, 81
37:15-28—95
37:21—73
37:24—74n13, 78n20, 96n24
37:24-25—75
37:24-28—75n14
38-39—86n39
38:1—77n18
38:1-4—77n20
38:8—78n20
38:11—78n20
38:16-39:24—78n19
38:19—89n49
38:20—60n42
38:23—77n17
39:29—78n21
40-48—78n20
40:1—83n31
44:25—83n32

Daniel
12:1-3—70n5, 89
12:2—37n3, 70, 154
12:3—72n8

Joel
2:10—60n42, 70, 125

Amos
8:9—37n3, 70, 125

Nahum
1:5—60n42
1:5-6—70

Habakkuk
2:14—149

Haggai
2:6—70

Zechariah
14—70n4
14:4-5—37n3, 57n35, 70, 72n10, 89
14:15—103

Matthew
1-4—32, 114n31, 115, 116n33
1:1—69n3, 96n63, 100, 138n11
1:1-17—52, 59n41, 140n18
1:5—37n4
1:16—100n2

1:17—95
1:18—100n2, 138
1:18-24—116, 125
1:18-25—105n15, 163
1:18-2:23—52
1:20—59n40, 138
1:21—52, 61n45, 127, 125n52, 131, 141, 146–47, 153n56
1:22—69n3
1:23-24, 16n41, 125, 147, 159
2—69n3
2:1—30, 140n18
2:1-12—52–53
2:1-23—105n2
2:2—30, 126, 140n18
2:5—12, 69n3
2:6—16n41, 111n24
2:11—125
2:15—69n3
2:16—31, 114n30, 140n18
2:17—69n3
2:18—16n41
2:20—111n24
2:21—111n24
3:1—16n41, 30, 140n18
3:2—6, 30, 37, 65, 125, 140n18
3:7—16n40
3:15—29
3:16—29, 36n2, 59n40, 69n3

190

3:16–17—146
3:17—29, 37, 136, 139n13, 145
4:1—30
4:1–11—140n18
4:3—15, 131, 139n16, 140
4:5—29, 36n2
4:6—15, 131, 139n16, 140
4:6–7—29
4:9—148n41
4:14—16n41, 69n3
4:15–16—144n32, 148, 157
4:17—6, 30, 37, 65, 95, 125, 140n18
5—31n88
5–7—31n88, 32, 115, 116n33
5:8—153n56, 162
5:17—33n88, 95
5:17–20—101n5
6:24—33, 125
7:29—33n88
8–9—32, 114n31, 115
8:17—69n3
8:20—139n15
8:24—89n49
8:25–27—89n49
8:29—131, 139n16
9—60n44
9:2—95, 125n52
9:3—126

9:6—60n44, 139n15, 147
9:12–13—60n44
9:15—60n44
9:18–19—111n24
9:23–26—111n24
9:24—60n43, 157n72
9:24–25—14, 44
9:25—60, 61n45, 157n72
9:26—14, 44, 111n24
9:30—60n44
9:33—60n44
10—32, 115, 116n33, 149
10:6—147
10:7—6, 37, 65, 125
10:8—111n24
10:20—149
10:23—139n15
11–12—32, 114n31, 115
11:2—100n2
11:5—111n24
11:19—139n15
11:27—139n13
12:8—139n15
12:16—147
12:17—69n3
12:18–21—16n41, 127
12:23—95
12:24—127
12:32—139n15
12:40—139n15

13—31n88, 32, 115, 116n33
13–28—3n3, 42
13:14–15—16n41
13:35—16n41, 69n3
13:37—139n15
13:41—139n15
14–17—32, 114n31, 115
14–28—153n57, 157n71, 158
14:33—52, 125, 131, 139n16, 145
15:8–9—16n41
15:22—95
15:38—150
16:13—139n15
16:16—37, 69n3, 100n2, 136
16:17—136
16:20—100n2, 147
16:21—3, 158
16:21–23—125n52
16:25—131
16:27—139n15
16:28—139n15
17:1–8—109n20
17:5—37, 69n3, 136, 145
17:9—139n15, 147
17:12—139n15
17:22—139n15
17:22–23—125n52
17:23—3, 158
18—32, 115, 116n33

191

19–22—31n88, 32, 114n31, 115
19–28—4, 53n28
19:28—139n15
20:17–19—125n52
20:18—139n15
20:19—3
20:28—139n15, 141
20:30—95
21–28—19n49, 54n30
21:4—69n3
21:5—16n41
21:12–13—150
21:15—96
21:16—16n41
21:19—95, 158
21:42—16n41
22:14—126
22:41–45—96
23—31n88
23–25—32, 115, 116n33
23:29— 112n27, 113n27
23:35—111n24
23:38—57n37
23:39—113n27
24–25—32
24:2—101n5
24:7—89n49
24:14—148n40
24:27—139n15
24:30—111n24, 131, 139n15

24:37—139n15
24:39—139n15
24:44—139n15
24:44–49—148n40
24:47—148n40
25:31—139n15
25:51—9
26–28—7, 17, 101n3, 106, 114n31, 115–16, 131n66
26:1–5—1
26:2—139n15
26:24—139n15
26:28—125n52, 142, 146–47, 153n56
26:45—139n15
26:47–27:56—109n21
26:48—126
26:52–54—1
26:56—16n41, 69n3
26:62–66—1, 8n15
26:63—37n4, 100n2, 131, 139n16, 140n19
26:64—131, 139n15
26:65—127
26:67—126
26:68—100n2
27—7, 17–18, 68n2, 80n24, 90, 96, 98n70, 109n19, 110, 112, 127
27–28—29, 41, 111, 131n66

27:3–10—1, 7
27:9—69n3
27:11—126
27:14— 140n19
27:14–15—20
27:17—100n2
27:19—1, 7
27:20—28
27:21–43—125
27:22—100n2
27:22–26—142
27:24–25—1, 7
27:26–44—59n41
27:30—126
27:32–50—3, 56
27:35—126
27:36–50—127
27:37—126
27:38—137
27:38–44—137
27:38–54—135, 146
27:39—126, 137
27:39–40—137, 157
27:39–54—138n10
27:40—64, 129, 131, 134–36, 139n16, 140, 142, 165
27:41—126, 137, 165
27:41–42—157
27:41–43—137
27:42—131, 140
27:43—28, 64, 129, 131, 135–36, 139n16, 165

Index of Scripture

27:44—135, 137
27:45—9, 22, 29, 33, 52, 105n16, 107–8, 112n26, 120, 123, 125, 129, 146
27:45–50—119, 122–24, 130–31, 162
27:45–53—59n41
27:45–54—24, 70n6, 75n15, 119n40, 121, 128, 163
27:45–56—118n39
27:45–66—29, 59, 107–8, 110, 112
27:45–28:15—117n37
27:45–28:20—6, 9, 27, 53, 105n16, 116, 120–24, 129, 132–34, 139, 143, 145, 156, 163, 165–66
27:46—29, 109, 120, 126–27
27:47—126
27:49—131
27:50—1, 6, 12, 29, 36, 38, 41, 48, 52, 54, 59n40, 66, 88, 90, 92n56, 106, 109, 111–12, 116, 126–27, 146, 150n46, 154, 166
27:50ff—91
27:50–51—55, 56n34
27:50–53—155n64
27:50–54—36n2, 59n40, 144, 153n56
27:51—2, 5–7, 9, 13, 22, 26, 29, 33, 36, 41–42, 45–48, 50–55, 57–61, 63–64, 88, 89n49, 94, 97, 101n5, 107–8, 109n19, 110, 112, 125, 143, 150, 152, 154n60, 162–63, 166
27:51–52—51, 54n30, 61, 89
27:51–53—1, 7, 7n12, 10–13, 18, 20, 24–26, 35n1, 37, 39, 44, 48n22, 52, 54, 55n31, 57n37, 58n39, 63n51, 66, 69n4, 70n4, 72, 88n45, 91–92, 95, 109n19, 112n26, 113n27, 114n29, 125n55, 129, 131n66, 134, 144n33, 145, 149–50, 154, 156n68, 158, 166
27:51–54—1, 2n2, 3, 5–6, 8–10, 15–18, 21, 23, 26–28, 34–37, 40–41, 44, 46–49, 50n24, 53–54, 55n31, 56n35, 57, 59n40, 61n46, 62, 64, 66–67, 68n2, 69–70, 71n8, 72n8, 73, 80, 87–91, 94, 96, 98–100, 102, 106, 109n20, 110n22, 111n25, 112n26, 113, 116, 117n37, 118–22, 124–25, 129–34, 142–45, 149, 157–58, 161–66
27:51–56—110n22
27:52—1, 5–6, 12, 29, 31, 36, 38, 42, 45–48, 50–51, 53, 55, 59–60, 63, 88, 107–8, 112–13, 114n30, 124, 140n18, 150n47, 154, 156–57
27:52–53—5, 8n14, 9, 13–14, 18, 20, 22, 26, 28–29, 34–35, 43–44, 52, 53n27, 65, 89, 91–92, 107, 119n40, 128, 132, 135, 145, 147–49, 151, 154n60, 155, 161, 165–66
27:53—18, 29, 36n2, 43, 45, 47, 50–51, 53, 54n28, 57n35, 61, 63, 89, 91, 103,

Index of Scripture

107, 110, 112n27, 113, 154–56
27:53–54—145
27:54—2n3, 7, 16–17, 25, 28–30, 33, 37, 44, 47, 51–52, 54n30, 55, 59n41, 61, 63–65, 69n3, 78, 88, 89n49, 90, 92, 96–97, 101n4, 107–10, 112, 124–27, 129, 131, 134–38, 139n16, 140n18, 141, 144–47, 151, 157–58, 162, 165–66
27:55—111n24, 123
27:55–56—57n35, 122, 124
27:55–61—119, 122–24, 130
27:55–66—121
27:55–28:20—3
27:56—30, 108, 110
27:57—30, 108, 120, 121n45
27:60—30, 108
27:61—142
27:62—30, 108, 120, 121n45
27:62–66—30, 108, 119–20, 122, 124, 130
27:62–28:15—29, 107
27:62–28:20—118n39, 120n43, 121
27:67—126
28—10, 42, 105n16, 110, 127, 158
28:1—29–30, 89n48, 107–8, 110, 120, 121n45
28:1–6—26, 117n37
28:1–10—1n2, 2n2, 9, 13, 17–18, 27, 35, 38, 41–42, 87n42, 89, 96n66, 116, 118n39, 119–23, 128–34, 147, 158, 166
28:1–15—66, 102, 108, 110, 112, 118, 119n40, 121–22, 161
28:1–20—119n40, 124
28:2—29–30, 89n49, 107–12
28:2–4—11
28:4—29–30, 107–8, 110, 112
28:5—30, 107, 112
28:5–6—148
28:6—3, 13, 29, 43, 107, 109, 158
28:8—30, 107
28:9—110
28:10—30, 107
28:11—29, 107
28:11–15—33, 110, 119–20, 125, 130
28:12—29, 107
28:12–15—4
28:13–15—30, 108
28:16—125n54
28:16–20—2n2, 7, 14, 16, 28, 33, 37, 44, 52–53, 65, 101n4, 119–22, 124–25, 128–30, 135, 145, 147–48, 166
28:18—4, 33, 52, 95, 148, 158
28:18–20—52, 96–97, 125
28:19—96, 139, 147–49
28:20—4, 125n54, 147, 159

Mark
1:10—58n40, 59n40
14:36—127
15:37–39—59n40
15:38—58n40, 59n40
15:39—61n46
16:9–20—53n27

Luke
1:35—138
2:25—155n64
2:36—155n64
3:8—131
4:6—148n41
22:43–44—53n27
24:44—69
24:44–49—148n40

Index of Scripture

24:47—146, 148n40
24:49—149

John
1:1—59n41, 69n3, 78, 139n13
1:12–13—153n55
1:14—139n13, 163
3:3—153n55
3:5—153n55
3:14–15—138
5:3–4—53n27
5:18—139n13
5:25—52, 166
5:25–29—166
5:28—52
5:29—166
6:14—30
6:50–58—153n56
7:38—74n12
8:1—11n27
8:58—139n13
10:11—26
10:17–18—131, 166
11—155n64
11:14–15—61n45
11:42—61n45
11:43–44—61n45
12:10–11—61n45
12:24—33, 125
17–18—26
17:5—139n13
19:30—127
20—76n16

20:19–23—4, 76n16, 90n53, 125n54, 148n43
20:22—76n16, 90n53
20:22–23—149

Acts
1:8—4, 125n54, 148–49, 158
2:4—4, 158
4:12—141
5:31—146
10:43—148
13:38—148
26:18—148

Romans
4:25—131
5:1–2—153n55
5:2—162n2
8:3—139n13
8:29–30—166
8:32—139n13
10:17—78
11:11–24—37n4

1 Corinthians
6:19—4, 158
13:12—162n3
15—3
15:20—3, 5, 13, 14, 41, 43–44, 44n20, 60n45, 89
15:20–22—43
25:20–23—154

2 Corinthians
4:4—146, 162
4:6—162
8:9—139n13

Galatians
3:13—141n20
4:4—139n13
4:4–6—153n55

Ephesians
1:13–14—4, 158
2:13–16—58n37
2:18—162n2
3:12—162
5:19—150n48

Philippians
2:6—139n13
2:8—140, 147

Colossians
1:13–14—108
1:14—148
1:15—162
1:18—3, 5, 13, 41, 60n45, 89
2:15—108
3:16—150

Hebrews
1:3—162
4:16—162
5:8—140
6:9—56n34
6:19—57, 151n52

7:22–28—26
8–10—152n55
8:1–13—26
8:6—26
8:8–12—101n3
8:13—152n54, 153, 162–63
9:2–7—151n51
9:11–28—26
9:11–10:22—152
9:12–13—56n34, 57
9:13—151n52
10:1–18—26
10:19—153
10:19–20—56n34, 57
10:20—151n52, 152, 163

10:21–22—153
12:14—162n3

1 Peter
2:24—165

1 John
3:2—162n3

Revelation
1:5—3, 5, 13, 41, 60n45, 89, 146–47
1:18—164n5
7:9–12—125
19:11–16—153, 163, 166
20–22—78n20

20:4–6—78n20
20:7–8—78n20
20:9–10—78n20
21–22—78n20
22:4—162n3

Old Testament Apocrypha and Pseudepigrapha

4 Ezra
4:35–43—72

1 Enoch
1:3–8

T. Levi
3:9

Index of Subjects and Names

ahistorical, 3, 9, 21–23, 27, 102, 124, 162
Albright, W. F., 102, 167
Allen, Leslie C., 79, 81, 142, 167, 182
Allen, Willoughby C., 54
Allison, Dale, 4, 53–54, 56, 62, 70, 72, 102, 109, 119, 144, 154, 157, 167, 171
Alter, Robert, 97, 168
Anderson, Douglas W., xvi, 24–26, 111–13, 168
Apollinaris, 157
apologetics, xi
Aus, Roger D., 156, 168

Barr, David, 114, 124, 168
Bass, Justin, 164, 168
Bates, Matthew W., 142, 168
Bauckham, Richard, 59–60, 144, 168
Bauer, David R., 131, 134, 158, 168
Bavinck, Herman, 139, 168
Beale, G. K., 70, 152, 155, 158, 168–69
Bengel, John A., 155, 169

Bieringer, R., 4, 172
Bird, Michael, 144
Blass, F., 53
Block, Daniel I., 91, 169
Blomberg, Craig L., 5, 12, 42–43, 50, 169
Briggs, C., 81
Brown, F., 81
Brown, Raymond E., 52, 62, 70, 72, 118, 120–21, 123, 134, 144–45, 169
Bruce, F. F., 53, 56, 169, 178
Bruner, Frederick D., 56–57, 64, 169
Bunyan, John, 148, 169
Burridge, Richard, 144
Byrskog, Samuel, 144

Calvin, John, 138–39, 141–42, 155, 170
Carson, D. A., 3, 5, 12, 41–43, 70, 76, 152, 169–70, 172
Carter, Warren, 103–5, 111, 117–18, 170

Index of Subjects and Names

centurion, 2, 6, 16–17, 19, 29, 37, 48, 55, 61, 64, 66, 90, 92, 100–101, 107, 109, 117, 124, 135–37, 144, 146, 158, 161–62
Chamblin, Knox, 128, 170
Charette, Blaine, 36–37, 170
Charnock, Stephen, 138, 170
Chase, Mitchell L., 70
Chatman, Seymour, 14, 171
Childs, Brevard S., 67–68, 78, 171
Christology, xvi, 6, 9, 13, 15, 27, 34, 37, 39, 58–59, 64, 66, 93–94, 98–100, 128, 132–41, 143, 149, 151, 158, 161, 165–66, 171, 175–76
Chronis, Harry L., 59
Cicero, 134
Clarke, Howard, 171
Collini, Stefan, 87, 172
conversion, xvi, 101, 109, 144–45, 147
Cotterell, Peter, 68, 171
covenant
    New Covenant, 152
Crossan, John Dominic, 21, 184
cross-death, xvi, 1–2, 6, 12, 15–17, 23, 25–26, 36–38, 41–42, 52, 55, 61–62, 66, 80, 90, 92, 97, 103, 110, 114, 122, 125–26, 129, 135–40, 142–43, 145–46, 148–49, 155, 162–65, 173, 179, 182, 184–85
crucifixion, 9–10, 21–22, 36, 38–39, 48, 62–63, 65, 90, 92–94, 96–97, 102, 108, 112, 120, 122, 126, 129, 131, 135, 137, 141–44, 146–49, 156, 161, 163–66, 186
crux interpretum, 62, 132, 161

Davidson, Ivor, 24
Davies, W. D., 4, 53–54, 56, 62, 119, 171
death, xv–xvii, 1–2, 4–6, 8, 11–23, 25–26, 28–29, 31–33, 35–37, 41–42, 44, 51–52, 54–56, 58–66, 69–72, 74, 78–80, 83–84, 86–87, 89–92, 94, 97–98, 101, 103, 106, 108–10, 112–16, 118–31, 134–38, 140–58, 161–67, 169, 174–75, 178–79, 182, 185
Debrunner, A., 53, 169
de Jonge, M., 57–58, 138, 151, 171–72
Dempster, Stephen G., 41, 75–76, 172
Denault, Pascal, 74, 172
descencus
    the harrowing of hell, 23
Dio Cassius, 108, 135
discourse, 31
Doole, J. Andrew, 59
dramatis personae, 112, 116, 121
Driver, S., 81

earthquake, 2, 5–6, 9, 13, 22, 29, 41–42, 48, 55, 58–61, 64, 66, 72, 88–89, 93–94, 100, 107, 109, 112, 117, 124–25, 137, 154, 168

198

Index of Subjects and Names

Easter Sunday, xvi, 38, 42, 44, 46–47, 50–51, 63, 66, 102, 112–13, 122, 129, 134, 144, 152, 158
Eco, Umberto, 87, 172
Edwards, Jonathan, 197
Ehrman, Bart, 21, 112
eschatology, xv–xvi, 4, 6, 9–11, 13, 18, 22, 26–28, 31–34, 36–37, 43, 55, 58–60, 65–66, 69–71, 74, 78, 86, 90, 92–94, 97–99, 114–15, 121, 125, 128–29, 132–34, 149, 151, 153–54, 156–58, 161, 165–66, 168, 170–71, 183
Esolen, Anthony, 160
Evans, Craig, 4, 35, 53, 62, 113, 172, 175

Fensham, F. C., 86, 173
Fishbane, Michael, 82, 173
Fox, Michael V., 80, 173
France, R. T., 20, 36, 54, 62, 69, 72, 173
Fuller, R. H., 44, 173

Garland, David, 108–9, 117, 173
Geisler, Norman L., 23, 173
Gentry, Peter J., 74, 173
Giblin, Charles H., 118, 121, 123, 173
Gnilka, Joachim, 112, 174
Goheen, Michael W., 148–49, 174
Goldsworthy, Graeme, 68
Good Friday, 6, 12–13, 37–39, 42, 44, 46–47, 50–51, 54, 63–64, 66, 102, 113, 117, 122, 143–45

Grassi, J. A., 8, 98, 174
Green, H. Benedict, 56, 62–63, 174, 182
Gundry, Robert H., 61, 73, 174
Gurtner, Daniel M., 2, 56, 151

Hagner, Donald, 50, 56, 62, 151, 153, 174
Hahn, Scott W., 97, 175
Hamilton, James M., 74, 78, 175
hapax, 8, 70, 94, 98, 116, 128, 134, 156
Harrington, Daniel J., 119, 126, 175
Hays, Richard B., 39, 139, 175
Heil, John P., 121, 131, 175
hermeneutical, 3, 9–10, 27–28, 69, 87, 113, 128, 160, 164
Herzer, Jens, 112, 175
Hilary of Poitiers, 157
Hill, David, 7, 55, 126, 146–47, 168, 175
hinge text, 118–23, 127, 130, 132, 161
Hodge, Charles, 197
holy city, 6, 13, 19, 21–22, 29, 39, 43, 45, 48, 50, 56, 59, 62–64, 66, 72, 78, 83, 89, 91, 93, 100, 102, 107, 110–11, 113, 121, 132, 137, 144–45, 147–48, 165
Hood, Jason, 31, 52, 140, 175
House, Paul R., 75, 78, 96, 104, 171, 176–77, 182
Huizenga, Leroy A., 130
Hurtado, Larry W., 149, 176
Hutton, Delvin, xvi, 8, 10–12, 149, 176

199

Index of Subjects and Names

Ignatius, 22, 35, 156
interpolation, 35, 53–54, 62, 88, 180–81
Iser, Wolfgang, 104, 130, 176

Jesus, xiii–xvii, 1–6, 8–9, 11–13, 15–26, 28–33, 36–39, 41–48, 50–71, 73–74, 76, 78, 80, 84, 87, 89–98, 100–102, 105, 108–9, 111–16, 118–27, 129–31, 134–58, 161–69, 172–77, 179–86
Johnson, Raymond, xv–xvii, 90, 111
Josephus, 108, 134, 151, 178

kingdom, xiv, xvii, 15, 22, 30–32, 37, 74–75, 92, 97, 114–15, 125, 137–38, 140–41, 143, 153, 173, 175–76, 179
Kingsbury, Jack D., xvi, 14–17, 136–37, 140–41, 143, 145–47, 158, 168, 176
Koperski, V., 4, 169, 172

Lataire, B., 4, 169, 172
Leithart, Peter J., 39, 69, 78, 117, 128, 177
Licona, Michael, xvi, 3, 11, 21–23, 124, 135, 154, 156, 173, 177–78, 181, 184
literary parallelism, 4, 9, 17, 27–29, 31, 33, 53, 80, 87–89, 96, 107, 111, 113–14, 116–18, 121, 131–32, 140, 161

literary reading, xix, 3, 27–28, 34, 87, 102, 113, 135, 158, 160–61, 164
Lohr, Charles H., 31, 177
Lust, J., 86
Luz, Ulrich, xvi, 18–19, 54, 61, 177

Malone, Fred A., 150, 152, 177
Mann, C. S., 102, 167
Matera, Frank J., 116–17, 154, 178
McGraw, Ryan M., 163
Melick, Richard R., 141
Menken, Maarten J. J., 109, 178
Merx, Adalbert, 54
Metzger, Bruce M., 53, 178
Minear, Paul S., 131, 178
misplacement, 5, 9, 99, 101
missiology, xvi, 4, 6, 9–10, 13, 17, 26–28, 32–34, 37, 43, 63, 65–66, 93–94, 98–99, 115, 120–21, 125, 128, 132–34, 144–47, 149, 158, 161, 165–66
mistranslation, 5, 99
Mohler, R. Albert, 23, 178
Monasterio, Rafael A., 91–92, 179
Morris, Leon, 165
Motyer, S., 58, 179
Murphy-O'Conner, Jerome, 31

narrative strategy, 9–10, 27, 97, 101–4, 106, 111, 129–30, 143
compositional structure, 9, 27, 39, 79, 87, 97, 101–2, 111, 113–14, 116–17, 128–30, 132–33, 143, 145, 156, 160

Index of Subjects and Names

Nickelsburg, George W. E., 70–71, 179

Olley, John W., 81, 85–86, 90, 179
Osborne, Grant R., 50, 55–56, 179
Ovid, 134
Owen, John, 163, 165, 178–79

passion narrative, 1, 5, 7, 18, 28, 56, 87, 101–2, 106–8, 112–13, 116, 121, 135, 144
passivum divinum, 53, 55–56, 60, 137, 161
Patte, Daniel, 131, 134, 179
Paul, 3, 21, 24, 43–44, 75, 96, 104, 128, 131, 176, 178
Pearson, Brook W. R., 54, 179
Pelikan, Jaroslav, 33, 179
Pennington, Jonathan, xx, 15, 31, 39, 104, 116, 180
Perry, Menakhem, 104–6, 180
Petersen, William L., 80, 180
Philo, 108
Plese, Zatko, 112, 172
Pliny, 134
Plummer, Rob, 51
Plutarch, 134
pneumatology, xiii, 1–2, 4, 29, 36, 41, 55, 58, 60, 66, 75–76, 78, 81, 83, 85, 88, 90–91, 95, 100, 103, 109, 116, 122, 138, 142, 147, 149, 153–54, 163, 168, 170, 186
portents, 2, 11–12, 14–18, 20, 23–24, 26–28, 34–35, 44, 48, 55, 65, 92–93, 106, 108–9, 112, 119–20, 122, 124, 127, 129, 131, 133, 135–37, 141–42, 144, 149, 161, 165, 178
Porter, Stanley E., 54, 56, 179–80
Powell, Mark A., 130, 180
Prabhu, G. M. Soares, 73

Quarles, Charles, 35, 37, 48, 57–58, 62–63, 68, 88, 111, 124–25, 180

Rabbi Eliezer, 88, 181
Rabinowitz, Peter J., 130, 181
redemption, xvi, 12, 16, 24, 26, 37, 55–56, 74, 77, 79, 92, 120, 125, 127, 139, 142–43, 146, 149, 151, 153, 163–65, 168, 175, 179
Reeves, Keith H., 145, 149, 181
Reformed, xi
resurrection, xiv–xvii, xix, 1–6, 8–13, 15, 17–23, 26–28, 34–36, 38–39, 41–48, 50–51, 55, 59–60, 62–66, 68–72, 75–76, 78, 80, 84, 86, 89–96, 98, 100–2, 109–14, 116, 118–24, 127–31, 133–35, 137, 142, 145, 147–50, 152, 154–58, 161–67, 169–70, 172–73, 175–86
Ridderbos, Herman, 128, 181
Riebl, Maria, 113
Riesenfeld, Harald, 70, 93, 181
Robertson, A. T., 6, 181
Roland, Philippe, 116

Index of Subjects and Names

Rowley, H. H., 149, 182
Runge, Steven E., 53

saints, xv–xvi, 1–6, 10, 12–14, 17–22, 25, 28, 35–39, 41, 43–48, 50–51, 55, 59–66, 71, 89–91, 93–94, 100, 102, 111–12, 119–20, 127–29, 131, 135, 137, 144–45, 151–52, 154–57, 161, 165, 173, 175–76, 182, 185
Sanders, Fred, 142, 182
Scaer, David P., 114, 127–28, 182
Schnackenburg, Rudolf, 124, 182
Schreiner, Thomas R., 153, 182
Schweizer, Eduard, 62, 182
Scobie, Charles, 149, 182
Senior, Donald, 1, 7–8, 55, 61, 65, 69, 135–36, 143, 176, 182
signs, xv–xvi, 1–2, 6, 8, 19, 28, 36, 41–42, 46, 50–52, 54–56, 58–64, 66–67, 69, 81, 84, 90, 93, 98, 101–2, 109, 129, 134, 141, 145, 152–54, 157–58, 161–63, 166, 170
Silva, Moises, 46
Sim, David C., 2, 55, 156–57, 183
Simonetti, Manlio, 157–58, 183
Smith, Christopher R., 76, 116, 183
Smyth, Herbert W., 53
Spurgeon, C. H., 58, 183
Stanton, Graham N., 8, 100, 116, 172, 183
Sternberg, Meir, 96, 184
Stone, Michael E., 71

Stott, John R., 165
Strange, Alan D., 197
Strauss, Mark L., 2, 47, 183–84
Stuart, Douglas, 95–96, 184

temple, xv, 2, 6, 9, 16, 19, 22–23, 28, 33, 39, 45, 47–48, 50–51, 53, 56–58, 64, 66, 78, 83, 91, 93, 97, 100–101, 123, 125, 135, 142–43, 150–52, 155, 158, 168
Thallus, 22, 154, 184
Thomas, Heath, 24
Thompson, Alan J., 148
tomb, 6, 29–30, 33, 36, 38, 41–43, 45, 48, 52, 62–63, 70, 86, 88–89, 107–8, 122, 125, 134, 155, 157, 169
Trebilco, Paul, 24
Turner, David, 4, 50, 101–3, 184

VanderKam, James C., 71, 179
velum scissum, xv, 2, 6–7, 16, 22, 33, 39, 41, 45–48, 50, 55–58, 64, 66, 91, 93, 100–102, 125, 137, 142–43, 150–52, 161–64
Verseput, Donald J., 109, 184
Virgil, 134

Wallace, Daniel B., 53, 56, 185
Warfield, B. B., 143, 185
Waters, Kenneth L., 117, 127, 185
Watson, Francis, 157
Wellum, Stephen J., 74, 173
Wenham, David, 63, 109

Index of Subjects and Names

Wenham, J. W., xvi, 5, 12–13, 20, 36–39, 41–44, 50–51, 55, 62–63, 109–10, 160, 185

Weren, Wim J. C., 71, 114, 116, 118–19, 121, 123, 134, 185

Wiarda, Timothy, 28, 39

Wilkins, Michael J., 151

Witherup, Ronald D., xvi, 17–18, 61, 185

Woolsey, Andrew A., 142, 186

Wright, Christopher J. H., 5, 83–84, 148, 154–56, 184, 186

Raymond M. Johnson (MDiv, ThM, PhD, The Southern Baptist Theological Seminary) is senior pastor at Christ Church West Chester (SBC) in West Chester, Pennsylvania. He has published with *The Southern Baptist Journal of Theology* as well as *Currents in Theology in Mission*. He was a recipient of the Clyde T. Francisco Preaching Award & Scholarship through SBTS in 2011, as well as the John Stott Award for Pastoral Engagement through TEDS in 2017. He serves on the board of directors for Harvest USA. He resides in West Chester with his wife, Meghan, and their five children.

Available in the Reformed Academic Dissertation Series

◆

It Has Not Yet Appeared What We Shall Be: A Reconsideration of the Imago Dei *in Light of Those with Severe Cognitive Disabilities,* by George C. Hammond

How Should We Treat Detainees? An Examination of "Enhanced Interrogation Techniques" under the Light of Scripture and the Just War Tradition, by J. Porter Harlow

Marks of Saving Grace: Theological Method and the Doctrine of Assurance in Jonathan Edwards's A Treatise Concerning Religious Affections, by Eric J. Lehner

The Doctrine of the Spirituality of the Church in the Ecclesiology of Charles Hodge, by Alan D. Strange

From Inscrutability to Concursus: Benjamin B. Warfield's Theological Construction of Revelation's Mode from 1880 to 1915, by Jeffrey A. Stivason

Preaching with Biblical Motivation: How to Incorporate the Motivation Found in the Inspired Preaching of the Apostles into Your Sermons, by Ray E. Heiple Jr.

The Triune God of Unity in Diversity: An Analysis of Perspectivalism, the Trinitarian Theological Method of John Frame and Vern Poythress, by Timothy E. Miller

*A Development, Not a Departure: The Lacunae in the
Debate of the Doctrine of the Trinity and Gender Roles*,
by Hongyi Yang

*"King of Israel" and "Do Not Fear, Daughter of Zion":
The Use of Zephaniah 3 in John 12*,
by Christopher S. Tachick

Free to Be Sons of God
by Geoffrey M. Ziegler

*The Trinity, Language, and Human Behavior:
A Reformed Exposition of the Language Theory of Kenneth L. Pike*,
by Pierce Taylor Hibbs

*I See Dead People: The Function of the
Resurrection of the Saints in Matthew 27:51–54*,
by Raymond Michael Johnson

FORTHCOMING

*Do Good to All People as You Have the Opportunity: A Biblical Theology
of the Good Deeds Mission of the New Covenenat Community*,
by John A. Wind

*A Strategy for Incorporating Biblical Counseling
in North American Church Plants*,
by Rush Witt

*Early Reformation Covenant Theology:
English Reception of Swiss Reformed Thought, 1520–1555*,
by Robert J. D. Wainwright

www.ingramcontent.com/pod-product-compliance
Lightning Source LLC
Chambersburg PA
CBHW020118010526
44115CB00008B/872